Water in the Roman World

Water in the Roman World

Engineering, Trade, Religion and Daily Life

Edited by

Martin Henig and Jason Lundock

ARCHAEOPRESS ROMAN ARCHAEOLOGY 91

ARCHAEOPRESS PUBLISHING LTD
Summertown Pavilion
18-24 Middle Way
Summertown
Oxford OX2 7LG
www.archaeopress.com

ISBN 978-1-80327-300-6
ISBN 978-1-80327-301-3 (e-Pdf)

Front cover image designed by Jon Fort.
Back cover image: The Pont du Gard near Nimes, oblique view (Photo: Tony King).
See p.184, Fig.3 for direct view.

This book is available direct from Archaeopress or from our website www.archaeopress.com

Contents

Preface

This volume surveys a range of themes concerned with the Roman engagement with water, embracing theoretical, religious and practical aspects. Topics covered include trade and harbours, canals and wells, as well as swimming pools and bathing establishments. The papers draw on archaeological, art-historical, literary and epigraphic evidence. Some aspects are covered in some detail, though others such as sea-power and merchant shipping and indeed aqueducts which have indeed been well studied in the past receive less detailed treatment here. The place of the Sea as well as rivers in Roman thought and literature is a vast topic in itself. In any case there will always be more to say about the relationship of Greeks and Romans to their watery environment. As far as we know this is the first selection of papers to survey this theme as a whole and it is our fervent hope it will stimulate further research in future.

Martin Henig

Jason Lundock

Water and Why Materiality Matters in Roman Studies

Jason Lundock

Introduction: motivation and purpose of this volume

This volume is the result of a conundrum I experienced during my doctoral research into copper alloy vessels in Roman Britain some years ago. During this time, I developed the theory that copper alloy as a material (and, by extension, copper alloy vessels) had a cultural association with cleanliness and purification;[1] particularly in their use for ritual hand washing and ablutions.[2] This line of thought caused me to wonder about the cultural and psychological aspects associated with ritual ablutions and water more widely in the Roman world. Unfortunately, at the time I was unable to find a collection of material focused on theories regarding water in the Roman world; thus, the inception of this volume. Little did I know, at the time, quite how large of a rabbit hole I was diving into (or, perhaps, a ritual spring or a cenote would be a better metaphor).

To put into context why I am of the opinion that such a volume will be of value to the wider community of archaeological and cultural theorists, perhaps it would be of use to make a short case for the value of materiality studies within the field of ancient research. Materiality is, in short, the study of how particular materials (silk, silver, plastic, cheese; what have you) are grouped together and valued within a particular culture system. Value may include many things from practical utility to economic exchange, gender association, class orientation, ritual significance and beyond; it is the association which is networked within a societal system to a particular material. For example, among the Netsilik Inuit of North America, materials are grouped into four broad categories: snow, skin, stone and bone. These materials are utilised for specific practical applications, but are also gendered as the tasks associated with each material is seen to be within the realm of a particular gender group within the society; for instance, stone is seen as a cooking material and feminine, whereas bone (being gendered masculine) is used for spears and harpoon points.[3]

This observation of the relation between materiality and value assignment stayed with me throughout my collegiate studies and formed a foundation for my doctoral and continuing research into the use and perception of copper alloys in the ancient world. As my research has developed, I have become interested in how these common symbols and associations are related to the basic mechanics of our brain networks and if research in this avenue could lead to predictive models we could develop to help interpret ancient data.[4] I have also been inspired by the theories of Carl Jung regarding the collective subconscious, which proposes

---

[1] Douglas 2002
[2] Lundock 2015
[3] Balikci 1970, 3-19
[4] Hawrylycz *et al.* 2015, 3-16; Sporns 2015, 90-99

that our brains are likely to develop similar interpretations of our world based on our collective experience as a species with shared ancestry and evolutionary development.[5]

Water as material and symbol

The relation between water and human societies is often complex and nuanced, as it is both a bringer of life and health as well as a perilous danger. One aspect of water which is often visualised across cultures is its liminal value, a place of transition from one state to another. This may be seen in its aspects as a purifying agent as well as its place in separating the living world from the underworld or spirit world; the River Styx being perhaps the most famous example of such from Classical antiquity, but the danger of water and its value of liminality is arguably also at the core of the *Odyssey*, as Odysseus seeks his way home through the mysterious travails of the unknown seas.[6] This perception of water as a liminal space is also a factor in Mayan ritual belief, with cenotes being places of ritual devotion and aquatic depositions of offerings.[7] This perception of water as a liminal space between flesh and spirit extends to materials which appear like water, such as jade,[8] as well as to animals that move between land and water such as jaguars.[9] This aspect of liminality with water is approached from a Gallo-Roman perspective in Aaron Irvin's article and in a northern Romano-British context in Phillipa Walton's contribution to this volume.

This liminal value of water is as much a connection as a division. In a postindustrial world with trains and automobiles, it is easy for us to view land as the great connector and water as a more challenging terrain. However, water transport was by far the most cost effective and safest means of transportation in the ancient world; comparisons with known shipping prices in pre-Industrial England suggest that land travel was nearly five times as expensive as river travel and between twenty two and twenty eight times as expensive as sea travel.[10] In fact, when lecturing on ancient geography, I like to invite the students to shift their perspectives on the maps in order to see the blue areas as areas of connection and green areas as vast areas of separation.

Across human cultures, water is both a connector and separator; a source of life and fertility as well as a danger of unknown depths. It is both a purifier and a putrefying agent. It is a source of wonder, comfort and fear. Most of all, it is an unescapable necessity for all human civilisations and by attempting to understand how a given culture conceptualised this material we can begin to have insight into a large part of the lived experience of those who are so remote and yet so very similar to ourselves. Papers which address some of these aspects specifically in this volume include the contributions of James Gerrard, Blanka Misic and Eleri Cousins.

[5] Jung 1933
[6] Beaulieu 2016, 21-89
[7] Miller and Taube 2020, 58
[8] Miller and Taube 2020, 101-102
[9] Evans 2013, 167; Miller and Taube 2020, 103-104
[10] Greene 1990, 40

Some personal observations on water

As I type this, it is an early morning near Ocala, Florida and a light rain is falling outside of the window; few more fitting moments or places could be wished for to inspire some personal reflections on water and its impact on the human psyche (central Florida is popularly called 'the swamp' for a reason). I grew up in Florida, with water ever present; in fact, as a slightly embarrassing sidenote, as I child I would sit on my parents' porch and watch the rain for hours, crying when it ended.

The ocean, in particular, is often regarded with inspiration. Few, indeed, are those who can watch a sunrise or sunset over a calm sea and not have an emotional response. It is a place of inspiration and fear; one needs only to watch its waves, swim in its currents or dive in its depths to feel its size and wonder. The importance of the oceans to our symbolic thought is so evident as to be beyond the need of footnoting; I will simply advise the reader to look up any number of songs or films in which the seas play a fundamental role.

Waters may often have a sense of primordial wonder and reality, as being the beginning of all things. Particular myths of the origin of the world from primordial waters which come immediately to mind include those told by Ovid in the *Metamorphoses,* the origin myth of the Yoruba people of western Africa and any one of several myths of ancient Egypt.

Rain also is a source of wonder, comfort and fear. Living and growing up on a farm in the Caribbean, it is evident for me the necessity and also danger of waters from the sky; a year with too much rain and storms is only matched for its destructiveness by a year with too few rains and storms. The dependence we have on water and the rains makes one humbled to their efforts to harness the natural world and reminds one of how much they depend on that which is outside of themselves and their control.

As I am completing some final edits, I have just returned from Tulum in Quintana Roo, Mexico; the location of a Mayan ritual site on the coast of the Caribbean Sea as well as uncounted cenotes of practical and ritual significance for millennia of peoples.[11] This has been another experience which has both humbled me and inspired me by the common wonder and symbolic meaning that humans across time and geographic regions connect with water.

I am hoping these personal reflections offer perspective on why, as a human, I find this to be a self-reflective investigation worth examining and why I hope that the work of the researchers contributing to this volume will be of value and inspiration to the minds of its readers.

Suggestions for future research

It is hoped that this volume will be of consequence beyond only its own material, but will help to inspire future research in the area of focused materiality studies. Psychologically and sociologically, materials are grouped, valued and utilised based upon the elemental or

---

[11] Martos 2006

composite material by which we, as humans, perceive them. It could be argued that this is at the base of our value judgements by which individual humans and wider societies organise themselves. Indeed, this line of research may be useful far beyond the realms of academic theory, but could be of practical application in cross-cultural studies and anthropological efforts to establish common grounds between peoples.

Materials themselves form ideas which may be compared with the concept of Jungian archetypes, the basic structures upon which we construct our understandings of the world. I realised this while undertaking research on copper alloys which led me to ideas of purification which, in turn, caused interest in the relation of dogs to purification rituals in the Near East and Europe.[12] By thinking about objects and material in their simplest, or symbolic, forms; one is encouraged to look for patterns within their use and perception through a society. It then becomes possible to discover systems of thought and patterns of behavior which can lead to the development of theories offering potential illumination to both the conscious and subconscious structuring of societies through their ritual and mundane practices.

It is my hope that more research will be conducted in our field on materials themselves and the symbolic networks they form within the construction of societies and their value systems.

Acknowledgements and appreciation

The researchers whose contributions compose this volume I became aware of principally through two different conference series: the Theoretical Roman Archaeology Conference (TRAC) series and The Imperialism and Identities on the Edges of the Roman World series. The organisers of conferences like these do a wonderful service to our research and build spaces for the exchange and development of ideas. I am hoping that these series, and small to medium conferences in general, recover after the Covid shut down and continue to be a place of growth and exchange of research into the ancient world and materiality. It goes without saying that I would like to thank each of the contributors to this volume, especially for indulging me and offering me patience during the publication process. I would like to thank Jonathan Fort for his beautiful cover illustration and for working with me to make it into what I had envisioned. I have had many colleagues, friends and mentors who have helped my thoughts develop during the formation of this volume and some of them include: Andrew Birley, Kaja Stemberger Flegar, Matthew Mandich, Sam Moorhead, Brad Owens, John Pearce, David Reutter, Justin Richardson, Darrell Rohl, Michelle Sivilich Damien, Jessica Socorro, Jay Thompson, David Walsh, Will Wooton and Justin Yoo. I would like to thank my parents, Margaret and Rodney Lundock, for their constant support and being indulgent when I will go on tangents about my research. Most of all, I would like to thank Martin Henig, whose help and guidance has not only been an inspiration to me but was also instrumental in the completion of this volume and made it into something much better than it would have been without his efforts.

---

12 Irvin and Lundock 2021

Bibliography

Balikci 1970, A. Balikci, *The Netsilik Eskimo.* Waveland Press. Long Grove, Illinois.

Beaulieu 2016, M. Beaulieu, *The Sea in the Greek Imagination.* University of Pennsylvania Press. Philadelphia, Pennsylvania.

Douglas 2002, M. Douglas, *Purity and Danger.* Routledge Classics. New York, New York.

Evans 2013, S. Evans, *Ancient Mexico & Central America: Archaeology and Culture History.* Thames & Hudson. New York, New York.

Greene 1990, K. Greene, *The Archaeology of the Roman Economy.* University of California Press. Berkley, California.

Hawrylycz, M. *et al.* 2015, M. Hawrylycz *et al*, Building Atlases of the Brain. In G. Marcus and J. Freeman (eds) *The Future of the Brain.* Princeton University Press. Princeton, New Jersey.

Irvin and Lundock 2021, A. Irvin and J. Lundock, Purification through Puppies: Dog Symbolism and Sacrifice in the Mediterranean. In A. Irvin (ed) *Community and Identity at the Edges of the Classical World.* Wiley Blackwell. Hoboken, New Jersey.

Jung 1933, C. Jung, *Modern Man in Search of a Soul.* Kegan Paul, Trench, Trubner and Company. London, United Kingdom.

Lundock 2015, J. Lundock, *A Study of the Deposition and Distribution of Copper Alloy Vessels in Roman Britain.* Archaeopress Roman Archaeology 9. Archaeopress Publishing. Oxford, United Kingdom.

Martos 2006, L. Martos, *Tulum: Histoire, Art et Monuments.* Monclem Ediciones. Mexico City, Mexico.

Miller and Taube 2020, M. Miller and K. Taube, *An Illustrated Dictionary of The Gods and Symbols of Ancient Mexico and the Maya.* Thames & Hudson, New York.

Sporns 2015, O. Sporns, Network Neuroscience. In G. Marcus and J. Freeman (eds) *The Future of the Brain.* Princeton University Press. Princeton, New Jersey.

Iconography of the Lighthouse in Roman Antiquity: Symbolism, Identity and Power Across the Mediterranean

Federico Ugolini

Abstract

Sailors and mariners in antiquity have often perceived night sailing as risky, full of dangers and particularly threats. The construction of permanent harbours across the Mediterranean in the Imperial period has gradually shifted the negative perceptions on the connections between waters and darkness. Lighthouses in this sense played a significant role in enlightening waters. However, rich iconographic and archaeological evidence from the Imperial period inform us not only about the canonic functions of these buildings but also about diverse perspectives. This evidence show how these buildings reflected hidden details about symbolism and identity as metaphoric expressions of power across the Mediterranean waters and beyond. Controlling and enlightening waters, as expressed in the valuable iconographic evidence, suggest Roman supremacy over waters and territories, commerces and trades. This new view on the relationships between waters and lighthouses therefore explores the symbolic function of these monumental buildings and their role in showing unrevealed and original aspects of Romans in controlling waters.

Premise

The Roman Mediterranean hosted man-made, permanent harbour structures, dating to the early and mid-Imperial periods. From the 1st to the 3rd century AD Roman hegemony dominated the pan-Mediterranean world and, during this period, representations of ports (marine cityscapes and harbour scenes) became a popular subject in works of art, including black-and-white and polychrome mosaics, coins, wall-paintings, frescos, graffiti, reliefs and sarcophagi.[1] These motifs, via which the development and sophistication of Roman Imperial art can be noted, also convey messages related to Roman control and supremacy over Mediterranean waters. In fact, the visual repertoire of port images highlights the level of military and economic control exerted over the entire Mediterranean region and further emphasises the significance of architectonical elements such as harbour structures and lighthouses in early and mid-Imperial artistic productions. Of these architectonical elements, the lighthouse seems to be the principal subject in most of these artworks and is rendered frequently in Roman art.

Recent scholarly works have not contributed greatly to our knowledge of the overall iconographic programme of the lighthouse and marine motifs in Roman art, which these works continue to associate with specific contexts and settings. Only short introductory works by Reddé (1979) and more recently by Tuck (2008) and Cuyler (2014) have focused on the imagery and symbolic meaning of some of these representations, but the latter two

---

[1] Belz 1978; Clarke 1979; Dall'Olio 1995; Ugolini 2020.

concentrates on the harbour scene in all its complexity, rather than on lighthouses specifically. Only Delacroix (2013) has examined the meaning of this structure, and he explores certain aspects of lighthouse archaeology and iconography, but this work discusses structures from the Channel and Atlantic Ocean coasts only. Lastly, the monograph on ancient lighthouses of the Mediterranean by Giardina (2010), which is complex and sometimes problematic in its approach, focuses on the theme of iconography but without further exploring the alternative messages and related meanings of these images of lighthouses. Beyond the above-mentioned works, which constitute the most valid publications on lighthouses in antiquity, there has been little debate on the themes of harbour iconography and little interest in proposing alternative interpretations; therefore, in many cases, studies based on the topographic identification of the structures depicted are still considered the principal scholarly reference.[2] Thus, it is clear that the metaphorical messages on identity and supremacy over Mediterranean waters, as conveyed by such artworks, have been left behind by the modern scholarly tradition.

The lighthouse representations I am discussing here come from a polychrome mosaic of the Torlonia relief at Portus, the polychrome mosaic from the *domus* of the Antiquarium Comunale at Rome, the black-and-white mosaics of the House of the Harbour and the House of the Lighthouse of the Baths at Ostia, and finally the frieze of the sarcophagus with harbour scene from Portus (now at the Ny Carlsberg Glyptotek at Copenhagen). All these images depict harbour scenes and marine cityscapes related to Portus (and Alexandria?) and all include monumental lighthouses; these buildings have drawn the attention of scholars who have sought to understand the portrayed topographic disposition and iconographic messages. As most scholars have not focused their research on aspects such as the relationships between the representations of these monumental structures and Roman domination of seas and waters (and beyond),[3] lighthouses have been left behind in this regard and are treated mostly as architectural elements alone.[4] In ancient iconography lighthouses may have been bearers of a multivalent message, and we should take into account symbolism, identity and power when studying these architectural features. In fact, these representations may have served as a reminder of Imperial achievements in taking control over water within the Mediterranean context and of improved infrastructures.

In light of this scenario, a preliminary but detailed analysis of the iconographic representations and meanings behind these representations of lighthouses is undertaken here, as a means to elucidate their significance in Roman waters and the role they played in controlling the sea. This study involves an iconographic analysis of selected images and representations, taking into account archaeological evidence, which then allows for an examination of the layout of Roman lighthouses and ancient depictions of such structures. This work re-evaluates this motif using 5 case studies mentioned above and stresses the value of artworks that depict lighthouses; finally, the specific messages behind these depictions lighthouses are briefly mentioned. The visual media discussed here include both fixed and portable objects such as mosaics, reliefs and sarcophagi, on which are depictions of complex scenes of lighthouses (these have often been identified as those at Alexandria, Portus and Ostia). This paper is divided into four sections: firstly, the textual and historical sources for ancient lighthouses

---

[2] Picard 1952, 94; Becatti 1961, 86; Fraser 1972; Clarke 1979; Settis *et al.* 1988; Salvetti 1995, 384.

[3] Reddé 1979, 845; Zanker 1997, 181.

[4] Tuck 2008; Giardina 2010.

are presented, with focus on the cases of Alexandria and Portus; secondly, the depictions of Portus' lighthouse are investigated and their iconographic aspects analysed; thirdly, a new reading of such representations is suggested; fourthly, conclusions on the multivalent messages of lighthouses in Roman art are proposed to discuss power narratives and express liminal boundaries as well as the negotiation of maritime identities.

An insight into the textual and historical sources for Roman lighthouses

Textual sources provide plenty of information on the perils of the maritime world, from the danger of the sea to the risks of navigation and the perils of adverse winds.[5] However, few detailed accounts report on harbour structures and facilities, and only a few short sources allude more directly to lighthouses. However, all those available detail the monumentality of these structures and their function, which was to make navigation secure and the Mediterranean a safer place. Of these accounts, those by Diodorus of Sicily, Strabo, Pliny the Elder and Pliny the Younger stand out for their descriptions of aspects of the layout of these buildings; they emphasise the role of these buildings and the benefits derived from them. Two of these buildings, from Alexandria in Egypt and Portus in Rome, are key monumental structures. These are reported in textual accounts and likely influenced the visual representations of lighthouses.[6] Textual sources also provide information on smaller but nonetheless important lighthouses, such as those at Ostia, Puteoli, Ravenna, Dover and Boulogne-sur-Mer.[7]

The *pharos* at Alexandria has historically been interpreted as a monumental lighthouse in textual sources. In the words of Caesar, this lighthouse is a symbol of power: he described Alexandria's lighthouse, reporting that the *pharos* is a very tall tower which is located on an island and which is built with extraordinary workmanship; he also underlined that it takes its name from that of the island which is located in front of Alexandria and which shapes the layout of the harbour.[8] The historian Diodorus of Sicily also provides us with an account of this lighthouse. He states that the sea voyage along the Mediterranean coast is extremely long and that landing operations are particularly challenging; he also provides some geographical references by reporting that the sea voyage (undertaken via cabotage) from Paraetonium (Libya) to Iopê (Syria) was some 5,000 *stades* long (equal to ca 500 nautical miles), and that along this route there are no safe harbours apart from that at Alexandria.[9] This seems a clear exaggeration; but by naming this harbour Pharos, the author marks it as the only one with signalling structures – structures which made it probably the safest port of the Levantine and Libyan Seas. Diodorus of Sicily emphasises the presence of a sandbank that runs the length of the Egyptian coasts and states that this feature is not discernible to unexperienced sailors who approach these waters. He also specifies that this area represented a threat to those who, upon nearing the harbour, thought they had escaped the perils of the sea: because of the sands, sailors approaching the coast could not see land in time and often encountered a shipwreck. This description underlines the purpose of the lighthouse: it served to guide the sailors and shed light over the waters of the Alexandrian harbour.

[5] Casson 1971; Beresford 2012.
[6] Picard 1952; Reddé 1979; Kolendo 1982.
[7] Delacroix 2013.
[8] Caes. *BCiv*, 3.111-112.
[9] Diod. Sic. *HL*, 1.31.2-5.

Strabo, who probably visited Alexandria in 24 BC, refers to this building in his description of landing at the eastern harbour of the city. He provides reference to an island, at the centre of which is a 'rock'. He also reports that this is equipped with a tower (*pharos*), which has the same name as the island;[10] it is built with white marble and equipped with many storeys. Strabo also mentions that this lighthouse was planned by Sostratus of Cnidus and was constructed to ensure the safety of sailors, as the shore had reefs and shallows and the sailors arriving from the open sea needed signals in order to identify the entrance of the harbour and to maintain their course towards it. In their descriptions of the function of pharos at Alexandria, both Pliny the Elder and Lucan indicate that the lighthouse was used for signalling during the night.[11]

On the lighthouse of Portus, which was ordered and built by Claudius, Suetonius says that in order to provide a strong foundation for the mole, the emperor (Claudius) sank the ship used to carry the obelisk brought from Egypt, and after securing it with piles he ordered men to construct upon this foundation a very high tower, mirroring the pattern of the Pharos at Alexandria.[12] It was to be lit during the night and used to guide the ships towards the entrance of the port. Suetonius also reports that a statue stood on top of the lighthouse, as is also the case on the Pharos at Alexandria. Indeed, in Suetonius the attention is on a feature that suggests imitation of Alexandrian style and similar building techniques: he reports that the lighthouse was built upon piles, in imitation of the Pharos at Alexandria.

During the early Imperial period, coastal centres, including Portus, Ostia, Puteoli and Ravenna, grew and became maritime centres of the Mediterranean, although most of these centres needed further harbour facilities. During the mid-1st and early 2nd century AD, emperors such as Claudius, Nero and Trajan undertook work, such as the construction of quays, moles and warehouses as well as lighthouses, in order to improve visibility and nocturnal navigation and to direct sailors approaching the harbours.[13] This huge effort was crucial for the success of Roman maritime facilities and for Rome itself; this effort is also visible in the account of Suetonius, in which he relates the Romans' attempts to replicate the Alexandrian model and the emperors' sponsorship (above all the sponsorship of Claudius), in the construction of such facilities, e.g. at Portus.[14]

At Portus the planning and the construction of the lighthouse affected the area where the moles terminated, which enclosed the harbour basin. The lighthouse was perfectly suited to this location, as it was sufficient to spread light to the entrance of the harbour basin and signal the right direction during nocturnal navigation to large ships and cargo vessels. Here, the lighthouse of Claudius, however, did not completely overcome the problems involved in sailing and docking at port during night sailing. The shipwrecks occurred as a result of inclement weather conditions, and trouble with navigation prompted the emperor to order the construction of the lighthouse. Subsequently, Trajan later constructed a hexagonal harbour, which would have provided additional protection and security for ships, and also for

---

[10] Strab. *Geo.*, 17.1.6.

[11] Pliny, *NH*, 5.129, i.e. 'it guides the course of the ships at night'; Lucan *Pharsalia*, 9.1004-1005; 'The west wind never slackned the cordage of the ships until the seventh night revealed the coast of Egypt by the flame of the Pharos'.

[12] Suet. *Claud.*, 20.

[13] Tuck 2008; Cuyler 2014.

[14] Keay *et al.* 2005, 23.

the harbour communities. The success of the facilities built at Portus, Ostia, but also across the Mediterranean, was widely known.[15]

Pliny's accounts also focus on the monumentality and role of Roman lighthouses in the Mediterranean. Pliny's background would suggest it is likely that he saw first-hand several harbour sites, from Alexandria to Portus and from Misenum to Ravenna, as prefect of the fleet of Misenum. In his accounts, he describes the *pharos* of Alexandria as the template which was used for the main monumental lighthouses scattered across the Mediterranean.[16] He mirrors the previous accounts from Diodorus and Suetonius, who mention that this tower stands on the island of Pharos, situated at the entrance of the harbour at Alexandria, and serves to guide the movements of the vessels at night and to highlight the entrance of the harbour. He states that similar signalling structures are located in several other places, such as at Ostia and Ravenna. Pliny also states that, burning uninterruptedly, the danger lies in mistakenly interpreting its flame as a star, which would be a reasonable mistake to make if one was approaching from a considerable distance.[17]

Pliny the Younger does not refer directly to the lighthouse of Portus, or to other towering structures, but he does provide a detailed report of the process of construction of another of these monumental structures, observing the similar structure of the lighthouse of Centumcellae (45 km away).[18] Pliny is reported to have been appointed by Trajan as advisor at Centumcellae, in which capacity he would have witnessed first-hand the harbour facilities. He states that the left arm of the harbour was reinforced by a solid mole and at its entrance there was an island which served as a breakwater, providing safe passage to ships entering from both sides. He specifies that its construction was well worth seeing, as big stones were brought by large ships and piled on top of one another, gradually forming a pile that rose into a sort of rampart. He reports that a pier was to be built soon after on the stone foundation, and that this building would shape the layout and function of this natural island. The completion of this harbour structure, according to Pliny, would make Centumcellae a safe place and he also suggests that this facility would save countless lives by providing a secure landing point on this long shore, which had hitherto not been provided with a harbour.

Later, the textual sources on these gigantic structures become scant. In the *Historia Augustae*, it is reported that the lighthouse of Portus was restored by Antoninus Pius (*Phari restitutio*); it is also mentioned in a list of restoration work that took place across Italy.[19] In approximately the AD 330-340, Lucius Crepereius Madalianus is cited in an inscription as *consul(aris) molium phari at(que) purgaturae* – that is as being responsible for the maintenance of the mole and the lighthouse, and for dredging the harbour.[20]

In all the textual sources from the early and mid-Imperial periods, we can identify awareness of how both Alexandria's and Portus' models radically changed perceptions of the 'monument' as a key element within the port complex, though the size and dimensions appear to have

[15] Hohlfelder 2008; Keay 2012.
[16] Plin. *NH*, 36.18.83.
[17] Plin. *NH*, 36.18.83.
[18] Plin. the Young. *Epist.*, 7.31.
[19] Suet. *HA*, 8.2-3.
[20] Thylander 1952, B336; Keay *et al.* 2005.

remained underrated by ancient authors.[21] The functions of the lighthouse in both Alexandria and Portus are, however, clearly expressed: they are key architectonical elements that were built to guarantee safety and security for the sailors, ships and related cargos. Certainly, the fortune of major ports from the Imperial period depended on their layout and scale, but much of their fame derived from this towering structure and from the capacity for docking. Spacious ports such as Portus, Ostia and Alexandria would have permitted hundreds of cargo ships to moor safely, but the landing operation would largely have depended on successfully approaching and entering the basin.[22] Landing (especially at night or during adverse weather conditions) would have been possible by a functional lighthouse. In a major harbour, the presence of a lighthouse would have meant that the harbour was lauded as a safe landing point but also that it would be reputed as a port city. In this context, the relations between lighthouses and the expression of supremacy and identity across the Roman (pan-) Mediterranean world are also relevant aspects to note.

Further parallels for the iconography of the Roman lighthouse

Lighthouses in Roman harbours were a major architectural feature, and their construction emphasises the Romans' ability to plan monumental marine structures in the main port cities of the Mediterranean. After the completion of the lighthouse at Portus, a few decades after the devastating storm that hit the port of Rome (AD 62), artworks such as mosaics, reliefs and friezes depicting lighthouses and other harbour facilities became popular and port scenes including lighthouses became a privileged subject.[23] These infrastructural works also became sources of inspiration for artists and allowed them to develop a vast maritime repertoire when depicting port buildings, and also to render lighthouses in a very detailed manner.

By 'lighthouse scene', we mean a visual representation of a lighthouse and/or its related elements; such representations could include depictions of storeys, steps and fires, sometimes even details of quays, docks and platforms, but also instances of daily life such as signalling to boats, and the landing and anchoring ships, the movement of goods, the loading or unloading of materials or animals and the presence of votive elements. Most extant representations depicted the lighthouse of Portus, and took inspiration mostly from Alexandria's model, thus aiming to celebrate the security and prosperity provided by the improvements undertaken by Claudius, Nero and Trajan; these representations likely served as a reminder of Imperial endeavours and achievements in expanding control over water and also of sea hegemony within the Mediterranean context and of improved trade and infrastructures. The lighthouse is the central focus of a wide panorama of visual scenes involving the port of Claudius, but it is also often accompanied by elaborate pictures of other harbour structures and also deities, emperors, ships, sailors, harbour workers doing their duties, sea creatures and commemorated guests. This elaborates on how the imagery of the lighthouse relates to the wider images in the overall impact of displaying imperial power and the control of water. Rome's lighthouse made its first appearance on a Roman sestertius, dating from the Neronian period, and this

---

[21] Tabarroni 1976, 191-198.

[22] Testaguzza 1970; Keay 2012.

[23] In Roman art there are some ca 50 artworks, dating from the 2nd century BC to the 3rd century AD, that have lighthouses as privileged subjects, see Pensa 1997; 1999.

depiction marked the beginning of depictions of lighthouses spreading to broader artistic media.[24]

The lighthouse is employed as a key element of depictions on both fixed and portable objects, becoming the main architectural structure depicting harbour cities and marine cityscapes.[25] It is evidence of the interest in recording the features of these coastal centres and also provides details on identity, conquest, achievement and control. Of course, the lighthouse is principally related to the enlightenment of waters, and would also have signalled landing places to sailors, but in the representations emphasis was not necessarily on the architectonic features, and adhering strictly to accurate topographic reconstruction was pointless.[26] Rather, emphasis was on the symbols of prosperity: e.g. prosperity would have been clearly conveyed in an image of a structure which was portrayed as having been sponsored and built by the Roman Imperial authority. These representations conveyed a story with propagandistic resonance by expressing the strength of the Roman authority and by displaying control over the dangerous element of water.

After Alexandria, major ports including Portus and Ostia, but also Ravenna, Leptis Magna, and Dover, received improvement works, including the construction of lighthouses; other supplementary port facilities such as quays and moles then became inspirational subjects and were rendered in visual media.[27] As we will explore in the following section, Portus' lighthouse in particular, after its first appearance on the Neronian sestertius coin,[28] was an important artwork from the Severan period onwards, and was portrayed in Torlonia's relief (Portus), the polychrome mosaic of the domus of the Antiquarium Comunale (Rome), the bi-chrome mosaics from the House of the Lighthouse and the House of the Harbour (Ostia), as well as the frieze of the sarcophagus Collezione Borghese (inv. 1299) with harbour scene which is held in the Ny Glyptotek (Copenhagen).

Torlonia relief

The Torlonia relief, made of Greek marble and measuring ca 1.22 x 0.75 metres, is a unique artefact and was found at Portus, between the harbours of Claudius and Trajan (Fig. 1). It can be identified as a votive offering portraying personified deities, dockworkers, ships and harbour structures. The scene focuses on a group of traders on the left-hand side, who make sacrifices on their ship while entering the port, to thank the gods for a safe journey. On the sails of the ships approaching the landing points we find depicted the letters V L, which perhaps indicate *V(otum) L(ibero)* or *V(otum) L(ibens) S(olvit)*. Based on the style of the work and of the figures portrayed, this artefact can be dated to the Severan period (AD 190-210).[29]

---

[24] Tabarroni 1976; Bailey 1984; Cuyler 2014.

[25] Reddé 1979, 845.

[26] Pensa 1988; 1997.

[27] Giardina 2010; Delacroix 2013.

[28] Cuyler 2014, 133.

[29] Calza 1940; Testaguzza 1970; Ugolini 2020.

Figure 1. Torlonia relief. Torlonia Collection, Rome.

On the lower right side of the relief, a ship anchoring to a mooring block is represented. Evidence of similar blocks come from remains of Trajan's port basin as well as of major port sites, including Anzio, Terracina, Aquileia and Leptis.[30] The harbour worker unloading a wine amphora to the quay suggests the identification of the relief's dedicator with a wine merchant. The large eye above the ship is an apotropaic element, which serves the purpose of averting evil. The god Neptune stands between the two ships holding a trident. In the background, the monumental lighthouse of Claudius, with a flame on top of it, can be observed while on its right there is a statue either of Claudius or of Nero.[31] Another undefined statue of person (or deity) holding a wreath and a horn of plenty can be observed on the left side of the lighthouse. On the upper left corner, there is a female figure with a lighthouse on top of her head, a signaling element perhaps evoking Portus itself. Portus' lighthouse, with a burning fire, is visible in the background, on the left side. The person who drives the chariot pulled by elephants in the upper right corner can be identified with the emperor Domitian, as this figure holds a sceptre terminating in a human head, similarly as on several Domitian's coins.[32]

Portus' lighthouse, standing at the centre of the scene, can be identified as the key architectural element of its harbour context. It is a five-storey structure with five openings, in *opus quadratum*, placed at the entrance of the harbour similarly to the Alexandrian lighthouse.[33] Thanks to the presence of the lighthouse, together with other elements animating the scene

---

[30] Ugolini 2017.

[31] Becatti 1961; Ojeda 2017; Ugolini 2020.

[32] Becatti 1961; Testaguzza 1970; Tuck 2008.

[33] Reddé 1979; Salvetti 1995; Cuyler 2014.

such as the cargoes, maritime workers, as well as the imperial and divine figures evoked, the relief suggests the liveliness and monumentality. More specifically the lighthouse, which is a source of light (e.g. the divine light, or the light provided by the deified imperial figures), conveys a message of safety and security not only in the Mediterranean sea, but also in the main port of the Roman Empire, therefore standing as a symbol of imperial power.

Mosaic of the Antiquarium Comunale, Rome

The level of architectural detail of the scene depicted in the polychrome mosaic of the Antiquarium Comunale in Rome is unparalleled among Roman artworks from the mid-Imperial period (mid-2nd century - early 3rd century AD) (Fig. 2).[34] The scene represents a ship and a sailor approaching the quay, which are illuminated and guided by a lighthouse with a burning flame on its top. Such a monumental lighthouse may be compared with similar structures at Ostia and Rome.[35] Attempting to identify the lighthouse as a specific structure,

Figure 2. Mosaic of the Antiquarium Comunale. Capitoline Museums, Rome.

---

[34] Salvetti 1995, 383; Ojeda 2017, 85.
[35] Gentili 1979; Salvetti 1995; Ugolini 2015; Ojeda 2017.

and to situate it for instance at Alexandria and Portus, is not a fruitful avenue of research. Nevertheless, we can assume that the structure draws on an Alexandrian mode,[36] although it shows striking formal similarities with the Roman models.

More importantly, the structure of the scene with figures of sailors and mariners in the background, overshadowed by the image of the lighthouse. suggests that the mosaic was intended to represent a harbour scene in its entirety, whose monumentality is conveyed by the lighthouse, which ensures safety at sea. The architectural complexity of the scene is conveyed by specific elements, such as the peculiar vaulted structures acting as breakwaters, the quays and the platforms. The lighthouse in the mosaic of the Antiquarium Comunale is a towering structure that seems to be built over a platform; such placement parallels that of the lighthouses at Portus, Cosa and Terracina and suggests a dating for its construction in the early or mid-Imperial period. In this the lighthouse differs slightly from similar structures in Alexandria and Portus that, as suggested by textual sources, were vertical structures erected on a small island, and therefore not immediately surrounded by port structures. Finally, representations of port deities are not present in this mosaic scene from the Antiquarium Comunale, which therefore differs also from similar scenes from Torlonia and Ostia.

A closer examination of the iconography of the Antiquarium Comunale suggests that mosaic makers were inspired by the Alexandrian lighthouse, which three centuries after its construction it had still represented the main model for monumental lighthouses in the Mediterranean; the mosaic's images of towering structures and night sailing convey a message of advancement, as well as sea power and control.

Mosaic of the Baths of the Lighthouse; Mosaic of the House of the Harbour, Ostia

The Baths of the Lighthouse (IV, II, 1) date to the late Trajanic or early Hadrianic period (AD 115-125) and take the name from a mosaic scene depicting a monumental lighthouse. The Baths were later modified under Antoninus Pius and Marcus Aurelius (AD 140-180), and many rooms were rebuilt under Caracalla (AD 211-217), during which reign several mosaic floors and wall paintings were created.[37] These structures could be accessed from the vestibule, beyond which there were two dressing-rooms (*apodyteria*); on the floor of one of these rooms (south-east), there is a large black-and-white mosaic representing a maritime scene that featured sea animals, including marine monsters, and the lighthouse of Portus.[38]

In the Ostia mosaics, Portus' lighthouse is portrayed as a four-storey structure (i.e. as in the example from Piazzale delle Corporazioni), while in the Mosaic of the Baths this lighthouse is also provided with a fifth and sixth storey (Fig. 3).[39] Huge blocks of stone were used for the lower storeys, which were provided with arched openings. The storeys and openings become smaller as we move towards the top of the lighthouse, except for the fourth storey. Deities and sea creatures surround the lighthouse: Venus is depicted on the left side inside a shell, which is carried by Tritons and a Nereid; Europa is on the right side, and is depicted while she is

---

[36] Reddé 1979.

[37] Calza 1940; Becatti 1961, 64.

[38] Pavolini 1983.

[39] Becatti 1961; Dunbabin 1999.

Figure 3. Mosaic of the Baths of the Lighthouse (IV, II, 1). Ostia.

Figure 4. Mosaic of the House of the Harbour (I, XIV, 2). Ostia.

carried to Crete by Jupiter disguised as a bull. Similar marine motifs occur also in other spaces of the baths, e.g. in room 9, where marine monsters, Nereids, and an *amorino* on a dolphin are depicted in a black-and-white mosaic.[40]

The towering building in the Mosaic of the Baths of the Lighthouse is very similar to the lighthouse of the House of the Harbour Mosaic (I, XIV, 2) (Fig. 4),[41] which probably dates to the principate of Commodus (end of the 2nd century AD) and has also six storeys.[42] Large blocks of stone were used for the lowest storey, which is also provided with an arched opening. The lower storeys are of different heights and the three highest storeys are the same height.

A further parallel in our analysis of the lighthouse in visual media as a symbol of power and control over the sea is provided by the bichrome mosaic of the *domus* of the Harbour Mosaic at Ostia, dated to the mid-3rd century AD; this depicts harbour structures together with ships, deities, sea monsters and a gigantic lighthouse as its key element.[43] This structure is made of block steps on six levels, surmounted by a statue of Neptune, who firmly grasps the trident while offering a fish to a sailor.[44] The port structures are the same as those depicted in the Mosaic of the Antiquarium Comunale and on Nero's sestertius;[45] similarly, the pedestal and the lighthouse might have been inspired by the earlier example from the Antiquarium Comunale.

Depictions of the lighthouse in these mosaic scenes conveyed a message pertaining to improved infrastructures and imperial success at sea. The columns and stairs extending from the bottom, which represent the quay line and moles (as reported in Pliny and Suetonius), attest to the technological achievement of the time and to the successful conquest of and control over the liminal space between land and water. More specifically, the lighthouse represents supremacy and dominion over the sea, to which message the representation of the deified emperor, in the form of the god Neptune, also contributes. In portraying the lighthouse, the artists may have been inspired by the similar lighthouses of Pharos at Alexandria and Portus, thus following a universal iconographic pattern for port scenes in Roman art.[46] In this context, in order to underline the importance symbolic value of the lighthouse, this structure is always situated in the foreground, at the entrance of the harbour, and it occupies a large part in the centre of the scene.

The two mosaics from the House of the Harbour and from the Baths of the Lighthouse provide the only examples available of lighthouses with six storeys: all the others mosaics (especially at Ostia and Piazza delle Corporazioni) represent three- or four-storey structures.[47] Textual sources do not provide information on the size and heights of Portus' lighthouse; this suggests that discussing its symbolic value was more important for ancient authors than providing details about its actual setting and the topography of its location. Nevertheless, the representations of Portus' lighthouse in the Ostia mosaics suggest clearly that this was

[40] Becatti 1961.
[41] Becatti 1961; Pavolini 1983.
[42] Dunbabin 1999.
[43] Bailey 1984; Dunbabin 1999.
[44] Becatti 1961.
[45] Abaecherli Boyce 1966.
[46] Reddè 1979.
[47] Becatti 1961; Belz 1978.

a monumental building, following the example of the lighthouse at Alexandria. Suetonius establishes a clear relationship between the two towers in saying that the lighthouse of Portus was an *altissimam turrem in exemplum Alexandrini Phari*.[48] The lighthouse of Alexandria was renowned across the Mediterranean as one of the highest buildings in the ancient world; therefore, it is likely that Claudius, by commissioning a lighthouse, attempted to imitate such monumentality in order to emphasise the supremacy of Rome both at lands and sea.[49] The lighthouse of Portus, the main signalling structure of the biggest port of the ancient world, would have been by no means smaller than the lighthouse of Alexandria, nor less relevant in literary sources.

Ny Carlsberg Glyptotek sarcophagus, Copenhagen

A relief depicting three ships entering a port, likely Portus or Ostia, is carved on a white marble Roman sarcophagus dating to the Severan period (early 3rd century AD). This artefact is held in the 'Collezione Borghese' at the Ny Carlsberg Glyptotek (inv. 1299, Copenhagen, Fig. 5) and measures approximately 1.78 x 0.54 x 0.52 metres. The level of detail of the relief, which still features traces of the original coloration,[50] is remarkable: the ships depicted are *corbitae* (cargo boats), similar to those in the Torlonia relief and in the mosaic of Altiburous, Tunisia.[51] The central ship has a spritsail with a mast which is situated far forward, in the hull. The spirit is hidden behind the sail but is visible when the relief is viewed from the left. The other two vessels have square sails with *artemon* foresails, and the artist has employed variation in the depiction of their sails: the left vessel has a conventional outward-curved bow, while the right vessel has a concave bow forming a cutwater. On the margins of the scene monumental signalling structures are depicted, which recall those at Alexandria and Portus. A three-storey lighthouse, erected on a rock and with a burning flame on top, is depicted on the right side. The first two floors are built using *opus quadratum*, the second and fourth floor have openings on two different sides, and the upper floor has a circular tower with two open windows, aligned with the openings on the lower storeys.[52]

The lighthouse on the sarcophagus' frieze is very similar to that on the Torlonia relief, although both the Alexandrian and Portus' models seem also to be evoked by the representation on the sarcophagus. Another scene carved on this artefact depicts a rocky shore, overlooking the sea, with two attendants on it surveying the arrival of the ships.[53] Three mariners sail the ship on the left, and they are portrayed while they unload a *scapha* (small ship) and guide the helm. On the ship on the far right, two men are dealing with the rigging of the sail and direct the vessel; animal heads decorate the bow and the stern, probably of a goose or a swan. The central ship slightly differs from the other two vessels, as it is bigger and similar to the large cargo ship depicted in the Torlonia relief. Three mariners guide the vessel, whose sail is anchored to a mast close to the bow, and which has a helm and a cabin. Close to the helm, there is the representation of a young man who perhaps fell into the water during the navigation. The scene is not worrisome, though, as the port is at a short distance and the man is surrounded

---

[48] Suet. *Claud.*, 20.
[49] Tuck 2008; Cuyler 2014.
[50] Poulsen 1951.
[51] Dunbabin 1978.
[52] Ugolini 2020.
[53] Testaguzza 1970.

Figure 5. Sarcophagus, Ostia-Rome. Ny Carlsberg Glyptotek n. 1299, Copenhagen.

by dolphins, which may also represent the safety of the port. It could be assumed that the man is seeking help from his fellow mariners, while swimming towards the *scapha*.

The architectural structure of the lighthouse is key to most of the Imperial representations of harbours.[54] The Antiquarian Comunale and Carlsberg Glyptotek representations have further elements in common, such as the absence of deities and votive offerings. The Antiquarium Comunale mosaic is unique because of its polychromy, which adds further emphasis to the monumentality of the lighthouse. The sarcophagus in the Ny Carlsberg Glyptotek was probably commissioned by a private individual, and the carving may have depicted a generic location; it is likely that the main aim of the individual commissioning it was to emphasise the centrality of themes such as the perils of life, the importance of safe navigation and the safety of the port, which is guaranteed by improved infrastructures and the lighthouse. The sarcophagus and its relief were created by and for the commissioner, specifically to fulfill a funerary function, and thus it is reasonable to assume that they were meant to convey messages of good fortune and safe journeys for shipping activities. The scene may also contain further symbolic meanings, such as the association between sea travels and the deceased's journey from the land of the living to the underworld.

The Ny Carlsberg Glyptotek sarcophagus differs from the Ostia mosaics, and from the Torlonia and Antiquarium Comunale reliefs; in all these artworks the focus is on the impressive lighthouse, its blocky stone steps and burning fires. The chronology of the sarcophagus is similar to that of the polychrome mosaic of the Antiquarium Comunale, but the rendering of the subject matter is slightly different since on the sarcophagus the theme of navigation is central; however, as previously noted in the analysis of the Ostia mosaics, the lighthouse is the only element that suggests the representation of a port complex in the scene.[55] As a port building, it plays a central role in evoking directly water and harbour activities, and in alluding to the owner's involvement in the shipping business, to his wealth and the success of his trade, which were also ensured by improved port infrastructure.

---

[54] Giardina 2010.
[55] Pensa 1997; 1999.

The symbolic significance of the Roman lighthouse in iconography

The iconographic depictions of Roman lighthouses in visual media can be studied through a comparison of lighthouse scenes: the Torlonia relief, the Ostia mosaics, the Antiquarium Comunale and the Ny Carlsberg Gliptotek sarcophagus are all studied here, as they constitute valid evidence that may be used to decipher the messages behind these harbour representations.[56] As previously noted, we do not think it fruitful or necessary to reconstruct the topographic elements. The evidence for lighthouses being surrounded by ships, sailors and other facilities or port structures stems from both archaeological and iconographic sources. This is the case at Portus, where the archaeological evidence for the lighthouse of Claudius has survived and fieldwork has partly identified the site and its layout. Of course, aspects of style should be taken into account when examining iconographic representations. However, even taking constraints of style into account, the most visible details in such artworks are the lighthouses, then the quay structures, and then the ships in the harbour scene; other elements of note include deities, people, sea monsters and animals and, occasionally, architectonic details such as columns or arches.[57] From our iconographic sources, we can note the complexity of the lighthouse and port. These representations primarily portray the lighthouse as a leading structure in the port complex and as a key element within the harbour complexes, at Portus and indeed across the Mediterranean. It is possible, by undertaking an iconographic analysis of lighthouse scenes, to improve our understanding of the role of the lighthouse, as well as of water control and of the relationship between control and the lighthouse; themes of identity and power, of Rome and the Mediterranean (and beyond), from the mid-1st century AD onwards, can also be noted in iconographic renderings of lighthouses.

The lighthouse is always surrounded by a number of ships in the harbour and is the only port element common to all the port representations we considered; with the sole exception of the Ny Carlsberg Glyptotek sarcophagus, the representations include the same model and even the same engineering techniques. We can also relate the iconographic depictions to the descriptions by ancient authors, including those of Diodorus of Sicily, Suetonius and Pliny, of Alexandria, Portus, Ostia and Ravenna. Often, in these lighthouse's artworks, the entrances to the harbour lie to east side of the lighthouse. Also, the statue at the top of the lighthouse indicates the role of the building. Monumental colonnaded structures dominate the left edge of the mosaic, i.e. Antiquarium Comunale, but also of the other artworks; often such representations, i.e. the Torlonia relief, also depict a structure with a peristyle, roof and pediment at the top of the line of buildings. Sacrifice or *votum solvit* was an essential part of life in a Roman port, especially in Italy, as thanksgiving for safe navigation and arrival at port.[58] Sacrifice appears in iconographic representations of Roman ports dating to the 1st and 2nd centuries AD: e.g. Commodus' medallion, the Rimini mosaics, the scenes from the Column of Trajan and the Torlonia relief.[59] Portrayed in a very evocative style, scenes of slaughtering a bull and a burning brazier should be noted in this context of sacrificial representations. Merchant ships also sail into the harbour basin, and harbour workers carry out sacrifices as thanksgiving for the safe arrival.

---

[56] Liverani 2007; De Angelis 2014.
[57] Zanker 1997, 179-180; Schneider 2015, 21-25.
[58] Gentili 1979, 50-51; Maioli 1989, 335.
[59] Cuyler 2014; Ugolini 2015; 2020.

The ritual and religious acts portrayed inform the audience of the alliance between the men and the sea, and the thanks men owe to the marine gods for their safety and prosperity; during this period, the sea helped men make their fortunes in the Roman Empire. A picture of fraternity and respect for the water is drawn, and the towering building and its leading light likely represent the empire that guided its people through the Mediterranean. The building and the light emanating from it would have guaranteed a period of harmony and prosperity after decades of naval wars and wrecks, and the emperors' endeavours to make the Mediterranean a secure and stable place would also have played a role in this.

The images of lighthouses on art and visual media are not like photographs. The portrayed lighthouse on a mosaic, coin, fresco, sarcophagus or graffito is not necessarily an accurate representation of the structure it represents.[60] In fact, it is reasonable to assume that the harbour structures in Roman mosaics are not accurately portrayed in terms of scale.[61] The close parallels between the structural remains of the Claudian lighthouse and its depiction in the mosaic of the Antiquarium Comunale, but also in the reliefs and on coinage, suggest that mosaic makers used a combination of research and imagination to reproduce their interpretation of an existing place, such as Portus, Ostia or Ravenna. Such re-interpretations provide an outcome that goes far beyond simple photographic reproduction, and we gain a different understanding of which aspects of the lighthouse at Portus were considered most relevant by commissioners and mosaic makers of such artworks.

Conclusions

The commissioners and artists in Rome, and beyond, opted for very similar choices when reproducing and visualising coastal cityscapes and port scenes but chose to depict their imaginings using very diverse media –mosaics, coins, sarcophagi and wall paintings. They used the harbour facilities of Alexandria and Portus as inspiration. The general spatial disposition of the harbour, with its access point on the same side as the lighthouse, and the quays, moles and landing points are aspects which are clearly rendered. The lighthouse structures seem to betray not necessarily the need to replicate or to associate such buildings with a specific location or coastal centre, but instead the need to represent more impressionistically huge structures with and also certain symbolic aspects. An attempt at incorporating a degree of reliability could have perhaps been viewed as pointless, and it seems that the lighthouse in such visual media was a vehicle for different messages.[62] More specifically, it seems that the aim of both commissioners and artists was not a true-to-life representation of port structures in Rome, Ostia, Leptis, Alexandria or Misenum and Ravenna involving details such as a specific number of quays, moles, porticoes, columns and stairs.[63] It seems unrealistic that these people would have had the necessary awareness of the layout and setting of the coastal centres and affiliated port structures, especially lighthouses.

In the Torlonia relief and the Antiquarium Comunale mosaic, the lighthouses are the key focus of the artwork. The reduction of loss and shipwrecks, the victory over piracy, the subsequent

---

[60] Pensa 1999, 124.
[61] Cuyler 2014.
[62] De Angelis 2014.
[63] Wolfram Thill 2012; Schneider 2015.

safety for sailors and cargo, the security of maritime routes, the prevention of accidents and, as a consequence, the prevention of shortages, were all great achievements of the early Imperial period in the Roman world.[64] The visual rendering of a monumental and huge lighthouse that towered over each harbour would have emphasised that the water was a safer place and that threats and fears were being controlled. While shipwreck data suggests a peak between the end of the Republican and the beginning of the Imperial period, the phase culminating with the works promoted by Nero, Claudius and Trajan witnessed a reduction in wrecks.[65] During this phase, Rome and other major cities across the Mediterranean largely depended on grain and other goods arriving from outside Italy, and therefore sailing for import/export purposes was a common practice which was necessary to guarantee the sustainability of the Imperial economy and that of Rome in particular. The lighthouse in visual media attests to the successes and improvements which sustained a growing population and economy and supported the crucial importation of commodities from Egypt, India and beyond.[66] The execution of artworks portraying the marine environment, coastal facilities, navigation activities, water/sailors/deities and lighthouses served to inform the audience about the safety and security of sailing and commerce, in particular the grain supply, and also emphasised control over the sea.

The lighthouse, with its stairs, statue or fire at the top and ships around the building, plays such an important role in these scenes. The storage and landing facilities are clear signs of advanced engineering technology and the techniques which were used in this phase. The centrality of the lighthouse indicates that it is an essential element of the port scene; it is also clear that because of the lighthouse the port can play its role and that all correlated port activities could likely be better performed. The visual media hint at the diffusion and popularity of port scenes which have monumental lighthouses as their centerpiece. The early Imperial period constitutes a phase of outstanding significance for a number of major infrastructural plans and construction works, in particular in Portus, Ostia and Puteoli.[67] In this context, we should note the foresight of the Imperial authority and its central interest in reinforcing marine structures and related facilities across the Mediterranean. The lighthouse was the subject of these improvement plans and its importance is reflected in varied media. The lighthouse is a key element and indeed is the main architectural building in the works of art discussed here; symbolically, it references control over maritime life and also would have brought to mind the protection of deities over water and the patronage of the emperor. The archaeological evidence clearly indicates the involvement of emperors such as Claudius, Nero and Trajan, and representations of lighthouses from the periods of these emperors' reigns may also be linked to the portrayal of the emperor as Neptune. The lighthouse, architecturally speaking, also emphasises the successful completion of Imperial works and the related homage paid by commissioners and artists in thanks for the Mediterranean and its waters being made navigable.

The evocative scenes of the Torlonia relief, the Antiquarium Comunale and Ostia mosaics imply that for the Romans the afterlife, and the perils of navigation and terrestrial life would have been important and relatable themes. This may also explain the varied meaning and

---

[64] Noreña 2011.
[65] Parker 1992.
[66] Horden and Purcell 2000.
[67] Keay 2012.

reading that could be associated to such iconographic representations, thus almost certainly the long debated topographical *raison d'être* of such representation and related scholarly association with specific place lose its importance and become clearly pointless. Although doubts have been expressed about certain details of the works discussed here, e.g. the exact location or model that inspired the subject matter portrayed, the key messages pertaining to the size, centrality and characteristics of the lighthouse within the harbour complex are clear. Full control, a sense of safety and security, but also protection and gratitude to the deities and emperors for prosperity and economic sustainability, are all emotions that viewers of these works would have felt. No more wrecks, dark waters or stormy waves: a much safer environment was now present, and had been sponsored by the emperors.[68] The role of the lighthouse was not just to act as a building that illuminated the water and guaranteed safe landing – it also ensured nocturnal navigability and safe access to harbours.

In the visual representations discussed here, the scenes are likely rendered to convey a further message: that lighthouses shed light over local waters but Rome's authority shed light over the whole Mediterranean and even beyond. The pivotal location of the lighthouse, and its light which spread in several directions, emphasises the impact of Imperial authority over water. Therefore, these visual images tell us more about the role played by the Imperial authority in contrasting the potential threat of water. The construction of a monumental port building as the lighthouse, then depicted in such artworks, is a key expression of the Imperial power that guaranteed safety and control over water. After troubled decades of wars, shortages, and wrecks, the promoter of harbour works and the commander-in-chief made Mediterranean waters and lands a better, safer place. The representations of the liminal space between land and sea, which is occupied by the lighthouse and the other harbour facilities, convey a message of power, control and authority as well as of conquest and pacification. At a time when maritime trade was key to maintaining Rome's economy, the Mediterranean was fully controlled by Rome and seas finally became a secure place owing in part to the improvement and reinforcement of harbour facilities, lighthouses and anchoring places *in primis*. Furthermore, the links to Roman authority, which are identifiable in the lighthouse scenes, would have served to remind the viewers of imperial achievements.

Bibliography

Abaecherli Boyce 1966, A. Abaecherli Boyce, Nero's Harbour Sestertii, *American Journal of Archaeology* 70, 65-66.

Bailey 1984, D.M. Bailey, Alexandria, Carthage and Ostia (not to mention Naples), *Studi Adriani* 3, 265-272.

Becatti 1961, G. Becatti, *Ostia IV - Mosaici* (Libreria dello Stato, Rome).

Belz 1978, C. Belz, *Marine Genre Mosaic Pavements of Roman North Africa* (University of California, Los Angeles).

Beresford 2012, J. Beresford, *The Ancient Sailing Season* (Brill, Leiden).

Calza 1940, G. Calza, *La necropoli di Porto di Roma nell'Isola Sacra* (Libreria dello Stato, Rome).

Casson 1971, L. Casson, *Ships and Seamanship in the Ancient World*. New York: Johns Hopkins University Press.

---

[68] Cuyler 2014; Ugolini 2020.

Clarke 1979, J. R. Clarke, *Roman Black and White Figural Mosaics* (Johns Hopkins University Press, New York).

Cuyler 2014, M. J. Cuyler, Portus Augusti: The Claudian Harbour on Sestertii of Nero, in N. T. Elkins and S. Krmnicek (eds) *'Art in the Round'. New Approaches to Ancient Coin Iconography,* (VML GmbH, Rahden), 121-135.

Dall'Olio 1995, L. Dall'Olio, I temi figurativi nella pittura parietale antica dal IV secolo a.C. al IV secolo d.C., in *Atti del convegno internazionale sulla pittura parietale antica* (Bologna University Press, Bologna), 196-198.

De Angelis 2014, F. De Angelis, Sublime Histories, Exceptional Viewers: Trajan's Column and its Visibility, in J. Elsner and M. Meyer (eds), *Art and Rhetoric in Roman Culture,* (Cambridge University Press, Cambridge), 89-114.

Delacroix 2013, B. Delacroix, Les phares romains de la façade atlantique – Manche – Mer du Nord: Amers, marqueurs d'une navigation côtière extra-méditeranéenne, in M.Y. Daire *et al.* (eds), *Anciens peuplements littoraux et relations homme/milieu sur les côtes de l'Europe Atlantique,* (Archaeopress, Oxford), 223-231.

Dunbabin 1978, K. M. D. Dunbabin, *The Mosaics of Roman North Africa: Studies in Iconography and Patronage* (Oxford University Press, Oxford).

Dunbabin 1999, K. M. D. Dunbabin, *Mosaics of Greek and Roman World* (Cambridge University Press, Cambridge).

Fraser 1972, P. M. Fraser, *Ptolemaic Alexandria II* (Oxford University Press, Oxford).

Gentili 1979, G. V. Gentili, Il mosaico dell'*Hercules bibax* o del porto canale tra i mosaici di una *domus* adrianea di Rimini, *Bollettino d'Arte* 64, 49-56.

Giardina 2010, B. Giardina, *Navigare Necesse Est. Lighthouse from Antiquity to the Middle Ages. History, Architecture, Iconography and Archaeological Remains* (Archaeopress, Oxford).

Hohlfelder 2008, R. L. Hohlfelder, ed., *The Maritime World of Ancient Rome. Memoirs of the American Academy in Rome. Supplementary Volume VI* (University of Michigan Press, Ann Arbor MI).

Horden, Purcell 2000, P. Horden and N. Purcell, *The Corrupting Sea. A Study of Mediterranean History* (Blackwell, Oxford).

Keay, Millett, Paroli, Strutt 2005, S. Keay, M. Millett, L. Paroli, and K. Strutt, *Portus* (The British School at Rome, London).

Keay 2012, S. Keay, ed., *Rome, Portus and the Mediterranean* (The British School at Rome, London).

Kolendo 1982, J. Kolendo, Le port d'Alexandrie sur une peinture de Gragnano?, *Latomus* 41.2, 305-311.

Liverani 2007, P. Liverani, Tradurre in immagini, in T. Hölscher (ed), *Römische Bilderwelten. Von der Wirklichkeit zum Bild und zurük. Verlag Archäologie und Geschichte,* (Verlag Archäologie und Geschichte, Heidelberg), 13-27.

Maioli 1989, M. G. Maioli, Civitas Classis: ipotesi di lettura del mosaico di S. Apollinare Nuovo in base agli scavi, in M. Lapucci (ed), *Studi in memoria di Giuseppe Bovini* 1 (Edizioni del Girasole, Ravenna), 335-343.

Mikocki 1990, T. Mikocki, *La perspective dans l'art romain* (Warsaw University Publisher, Warsaw).

Noreña 2011, C. F. Noreña, *Imperial Ideals in the Roman West. Representation, Circulation, Power* (Cambridge University Press, Cambridge).

Ojeda 2017, D. Ojeda, Rilievo Torlonia inv. n. 430: l'immagine sul faro, *Bullettino della commissione archeologica comunale di Roma* 118, 85-92.

Parker 1992, A. J. Parker, *Ancient Shipwrecks of the Mediterranean and the Roman Provinces* (Archaeopress, Oxford).

Pensa 1988, M. Pensa, Alcune osservazioni sulle immagini di città e porti nella documentazione numismatica, *Rivista Italiana di Numismatica* 99, 113-158.

Pensa 1997, M. Pensa, Immagini di città e porti: aspetti e problemi, *Corsi di Cultura sull'Arte Ravennate e Bizantina* 43, 689-710.

Pensa 1999, M. Pensa, Moli, fari e pescatori: la tradizione iconografica della città portuale in età romana, *Rivista di Archeologia* 23, 94-130.

Picard 1952, C. Picard, Sur quelques représentations nouvelles du phare d'Alexandrie et sur l'origine alexandrine des payseges portuaires, *Bulletin de Correspondance Hellénique* 76, 61-95.

Poulsen 1951, F. Poulsen, *Catalogue of Ancient Sculpture in the Ny Carlsberg Glyptotek* (Ny Carlsberg Foundation, Copenhagen).

Reddé 1979, M. Reddé, La représentation des phares à l'époque romaine, *Mélanges de l'École Française de Rome - Antiquité* 91, 845-872.

Salvetti 1995, C. Salvetti, Appunti sul mosaico con scena di Porto dell'Antiquarium Comunale, in *Atti del II colloquio dell'associazione italiana per lo studio e la conservazione del mosaico* (Edizioni del Girasole, Ravenna), 383-394.

Schneider 2015, H. Schneider, Infrastruktur und Politische Legitimation im Frühen Principat, in A. Kolb (ed) *Infrastruktur und Herrschaftsorganisation im Imperium Romanum*, (De Gruyter, Berlin), 21-51.

Settis, La Regina, Agosti 1988, S. Settis, A. La Regina and G. Agosti, *La Colonna Traiana* (Einaudi, Turin).

Tabarroni 1976, G. Tabarroni, La rappresentazioni del faro sulle monete di Alessandria, *Quaderni Ticinesi* 5, 191-203.

Testaguzza 1970, O. Testaguzza, *Illustrazione dei porti di Claudio e Traiano e della città di Porto a Fiumicino* (Julia Editrice, Rome).

Thylander 1952, H. Thylander, *Inscriptions du port d'Ostie* (Gleerup, Lund).

Tuck 2008, S. L. Tuck, The Expansion of Triumphal Imagery beyond Rome: Imperial Monuments at the Harbors of Ostia and Lepcis Magna, in R. L. Hohlfelder (ed) *The Maritime World of Ancient Rome. Memoirs of the American Academy in Rome. Supplementary Volume VI* (University of Michigan Press, Ann Arbor MI), 325-341.

Ugolini 2015, F. Ugolini, A New Interpretation of the Iconography of the 'Mosaic of the Ships' in the Palazzo Diotallevi, Rimini, *Mosaic* 42, 4-11.

Ugolini 2017, F. Ugolini, The Roman Ports of the Northern and Central Adriatic Sea: Form, Role and Representation (PhD diss.) (King's College London, London).

Ugolini 2020, F. Ugolini, *Visualizing Harbours in the Classical World. Iconography and Representation around the Mediterranean* (Bloomsbury, London).

Wolfram Thill 2012, E. Wolfram Thill, Cultural Constructions: Depictions of Architecture in Roman State Reliefs (PhD diss.) (University of North Carolina at Chapel Hill, Chapel Hill NC)

Zanker 1997, P. Zanker, In Search of Roman Viewer, in D. Buitron-Oliver (ed), *The Interpretation of Architectural Sculpture in Greece and Rome*, (National Gallery of Art, Washington DC), 179-192.

Roman Offensive Planning: Shaping the Lower Rhine Waterscape

Stijn Heeren and Mark Driessen

Introduction

The Netherlands has an international reputation in water management. Dutch engineers advise in matters of water containment and shoreline readjustments from North America to the Middle East, and from South Africa to Oceania. The knowledge on water management was built up in the course of centuries, when the Dutch people tried to control the risks attached to living in a lowland delta. Windmills pumping water out of areas lying below sea level are as famous as the Dutch tulips and wooden shoes and have become part of the (slightly stereotypical) historical image of the Dutch. The oldest democratic institutions to realise dikes by collective participation, called *waterschappen*, originated in the Late Middle Ages and still exist today.[1] Water as a tool for warfare - artificial flooding to stop approaching armies – was exploited since the 80-years war, the uprising against Spain, starting in the late sixteenth century.[2]

Although the historical battle against water was a reality, it is not entirely correct to look for the origins of water management in the Dutch medieval past. The oldest dikes in our regions are of Roman origin.[3] Large-scale and far-reaching measures, including the diversion of rivers and the digging of canals, were taken in the Early Roman period already (see below). In this paper we argue that the unique geographical position and the logistic potential of the coastal delta in the Low Countries, at the confluence of several important Northwestern-European waterways, was already recognised and actively exploited by the Roman military authorities. In order to tell this story, archaeological evidence will be presented, combined with written sources for the appropriate historical context.

Strategic use of the Lower Rhine delta

The Dutch river area: short survey of Roman period rivers

The Dutch coastal delta where some of the main Northwestern-European rivers merge, was an almost inextricable network of streams, wetlands and islands created by these rivers and their tributaries. Geophysical research makes clear that the courses of the riverbeds have shifted considerably over time, due to the meandering and anastomosing aspects of these channels.[4]

---

[1] In 1255 CE Count William II of Holland granted privileges to a group of officials called *heemraden* who oversaw the local dikes, following earlier regional approaches towards problems with storm floodings around Leiden and Utrecht. The original privilege of 1255 CE is still part of the collection of *Hoogheemraadschap Rijnland* in the *Gemeenlandshuis Rijnland* in Leiden

[2] De Kraker 2015.

[3] Zuidhoff and Dijkstra 2011; De Clercq and Van Dierendonck 2008.

[4] Berendsen and Stouthamer 2001; Cohen *et al.* 2012; Vos 2015.

The geophysical reconstruction of the Rhine delta in the Roman period matches very well with the antique sources,[5] which supply us with a basic description of this waterscape and the names of the rivers.[6] The Rhine, coming from the southeast, turns west and splits near the Dutch-German border into two streams (figure 1): the Rhine (*Rhenus*) and the Waal (*Wahalis*). The Rhine splits again in the Oude Rijn flowing out directly into the sea, and a northern branch (Oer-IJ and/or Vlie) discharging via the northern peat lakes called *Flevo* or *Flevum*. The Waal, the main distributary of the Rhine, flowed together with the Meuse (*Mosa*) forming the third and wide mouth called the *Helinium*. The past course of the largest rivers is more or less secure, thanks to large-scale research already mentioned. The location of the smaller streams is hard to establish. Later river activity may have eroded the physical remains of the predecessors. Therefore, not all precursors of modern rivers are identified with certainty. This applies for instance to the eastern Lake Flevum connection which is therefore indicated as a dashed line. The breadth of the individual river courses as shown does not represent their actual width, but simply indicate our ideas of their relative importance in the Roman period.

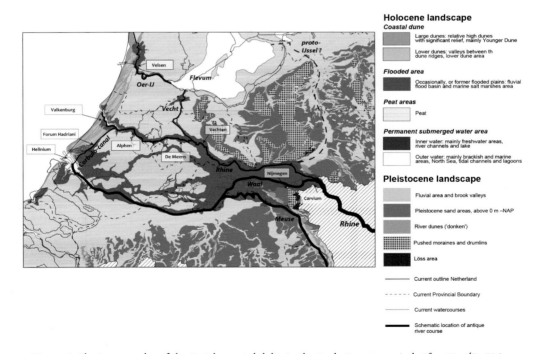

Figure 1. The topography of the Dutch coastal delta in the Early Roman period. After Vos/De Vries 2013, with modifications by the present authors.

---

[5] Caes. *BG.* 4,10; Mela 3,24; Pliny *NH.* 4.101; Tacitus *Ann.* 2,6; 2,8.

[6] See also Polak and Kooistra 2013.

Military campaigns in the northwest between 19 BCE and 43 CE

Although Julius Caesar campaigned in the Rhine delta in the 50s BCE, no Roman camp from that date has so far been found. Archaeological evidence for this episode may turn up in the future, but Caesar's presence was of a temporary and short-term nature. The oldest Roman military settlement in the Lower Rhine basin known at present is the Augustan legionary camp at Nijmegen along the river Waal. The first phase of this very large camp has been dated by numismatics to the period between 19 and 16 BCE, which coincides with the second term of Marcus Agrippa as governor of Northern Gaul.[7] Under orders from emperor Augustus, Agrippa's task was to organise civilian government and infrastructure in the north of Gaul. Since the pre-Roman *oppida*, often continued as Roman seats of power, simply did not exist here, roads and new cities were created *ex nihilo*.[8]

A new phase of expansion began in 12 BCE, when several campaigns were launched to pacify Germanic groups east and north of the Rhine. Drusus won several victories and after his untimely death in 9 BCE, Tiberius took over. The Lippe river was used as a transportation route eastwards of the Rhine into Germany. The army camps of Oberaden (11-8/7 BCE), Hedemünden (11-8/7 BCE), Olfen (11-7 BCE), Dorsten-Holsterhausen (12 BCE – 9 CE), Haltern (7 BCE – 9 CE), Wilkenburg (1-6 CE) and Anreppen (1-6 CE) show that elaborate defensive and logistical structures were built for these campaigns.[9] Expansion was now aimed towards the Weser River and in 3 BCE, the river Elbe was reached by Roman armies under Ahenobarbus.[10] Excavations at Waldgirmes an der Lahn, in the current state of Hessen east of the Rhine, have revealed a Roman style city, of which several parts were still in various stages of construction. The city is dated to the middle-Augustan period and believed to have been the planned capital for a province of Germania.[11]

Roman expansion in Germania beyond the Rhine came to a halt after the *clades Variana* of 9 CE. Three legions under Publius Quinctilius Varus were ambushed by a confederation of Germanic tribes, led by Arminius, a Roman veteran officer of Germanic descent. Three short-term effects were the abandonment of the military bases along the Lippe, the end of the building project at Waldgirmes, and the launching of several punitive campaigns (in 14 and 16 CE), aimed at recovering the legionary standards that were captured by the German tribes in 9 CE.[12] The punitive campaigns were in part naval operations that sailed via Lake Flevum to the Germanic coast. From the fact that the city of Waldgirmes was never completed, we may gather that the ambitions of a Germanic province north of the Rhine were abandoned for good. The most important and long-term effect was that from that point onwards, the Rhine was accepted as the demarcation of Roman-governed territory, although campaigns and fortified sites north of the Rhine were used into the 40s CE.

---

[7] Kemmers 2005; Driessen 2007; Niemeijer 2015.

[8] Wightman 1985, 48-52; Carroll 2000, 32-34.

[9] For a map overview of these see Grote 2012, 305. For the camp of Wilkenburg see several papers in Lehmann *et al.* 2018.

[10] Kunow 1987, 36-41; Carroll 2000, 34-37.

[11] Becker and Rasbach 2015.

[12] Timpe 1968.

The Rhine frontier was not yet guarded by many fortifications. There were, of course, large legionary bases at Bonn, Cologne, Neuss and Xanten and smaller fortifications at Nijmegen, Vechten and Velsen,[13] but this was far from a closed line of forts, which we know existed a few decades later. Until late in the 20th century it was believed that the *limes,* in the sense of a closed line of forts with defensive function, was created in 47 CE. In that year, the written sources report that Gnaeus Domitius Corbulo was campaigning in the northern Germanic areas and that he was ordered to disengage by Claudius, and to return to the Lower Rhine and to busy his men with digging a canal, the so-called Corbulo canal.[14]

However, new data regarding the date of many Lower Rhina *castella* have come to light. The felling dates of the oldest wooden defensive structures at Alphen indicated a construction date around 40 or 41 CE.[15] This ties in very well with stamped wine barrels dating to the reign of Caligula (37-41 CE) found at Valkenburg and Vechten. Based on these stamps, Wynia was already arguing in 1999 that it was very likely that the building of the Lower Rhine *limes* was organised by Caligula in the years 39-41 CE rather than by Claudius in 47 CE.[16] Coin assemblages from Alphen, Valkenburg and De Meern underline the hypothesis that the first structures of these forts were already built as part of Caligula's planned Britannia-campaign.[17] Apparently, Caligula was not simply a mad potentate as the written sources would have us believe,[18] but he was also planning a large military campaign against Britain, involving the preparation of enormous infrastructural works. The campaign was However postponed and Claudius was successful a few years later in 43 CE, receiving all the credit for adding a new province to the empire.

The relevance of the above is twofold. First, the Lower Rhine *limes* was not the creation of a defensive strategy in the late 40s CE, but rather from offensive planning around 37-40 CE. Secondly, the implication of this political context is that the Lower Rhine *limes* had a different function. Implicit in all earlier works is the assumption that the function of the *limes* was defensive, a bulwark against attacks from outside the empire. It now becomes clear that transport by water, albeit guarded by defenses, was the primary function. The Lower Germanic *limes* as aquatic barrier should be considered to have functioned as a secured transport route rather than as a purely defensive line: its primary goal was to ship men and supplies to Britain.[19]

Sites connected to naval activity

The Drusus dam

The name *Carvium ad molem* (Carvium at the dam) is mentioned in a funerary inscription dredged up in 1938 at the location Herwen-Bijlandse Waard (figure 2).[20] The dam is also

---

[13] Kunow 1987, 51.
[14] Tacitus Ann. XI, 18-20; Dio LXI, 30: 4-6.
[15] Polak, Kloosterman and Niemeier 2004, 249-252.
[16] Wynia 1999.
[17] Kemmers 2004; 2006.
[18] Suetonius 46; Dio LIX, 21.
[19] Graafstal 2002; Driessen 2007, 91-108; 2014.
[20] Année Epigraphique 1939, 107; Jongkees 1959.

Figure 2. Tombstone of Marcus Mallius mentioning the dam
(*moles*) at Carvium (for transcription of text see Jongkees 1959;
picture: Museum Het Valkhof – Nijmegen)

mentioned by Tacitus in combination with a canal, the *fossa Drusiana*. Suetonius uses the plural *fossae Drusianae*.[21] Based on this name it is very likely that the canal(s) and dam were already engineered on the orders of Drusus in the Germanic campaigns of 12-9 BCE. As the result of the recovery of quantities of building material (brick and stone) as well as military gear and brooches during dredging operations, it is assumed that a *castellum* was built later in the 1st century to guard the dam and canal.[22]

The location at the point of divergence between the rivers Rijn and Waal is important. A canal connects waterways and a dike is meant to block water. It is very likely that Drusus deflected the course of the existing waterways. What can have been the reason for this? This depends on the situation he came across, which we do not know exactly. A less desirable situation would have been that most of the water from the Rhine would have flowed into the southern branch of the fork, the Waal. The Waal connects to the Meuse, which was already navigable because it carried enough water. In the same hypothetical situation, the remaining north-western stream of the Rhine received less water, rendering it hardly navigable. The other far more desirable situation would have been that most of the water took the northern branch of the fork, the Rhine proper. This would have resulted in a navigable Rhine route towards the North Sea, which is the most direct route with more northward connections. It is therefore most logical to assume that the purpose of Drusus' dam was to limit the watershed of the Waal in favor of a larger Rhine, thus creating new logistic and strategic opportunities for expansion

---

[21] Tacitus *Ann.* XIII, 53; *Hist.* V, 19; Suetonius, *Divus Claudius* 1.
[22] Bogaers and Rüger 1974, 90-92; Willems 1986, 52-3, 257-258.

northwards, in addition to an existing connection. The canal of Drusus most likely opened up another connection. The location of this connection is contested. Either this location is close to the *moles* and connects the Rhine to a precursor of the IJssel (dashed line in fig. 1), which would open up a northeastern route via Lake Flevum, or maybe the more westward Vecht connection between the Rhine and Lake Flevum was initiated or secured by the Drusian fosse.[23]

The fortification at Vechten and possible locations of the fossa Drusiana

Although the ground plan of Vechten in its late 1st and 2nd century form looks very much like other *castella* along the Lower Rhine, it has long been suspected that Vechten was a naval base.[24] The main reason for this suspicion is the number of inscriptions from Vechten mentioning Oceanus, Neptune and Rhenus, as well as a naval officer, a *trierarchus*.[25] Additionally, a graffito on the base of a samian ware plate of a warship was found here. However, since boat houses or harbour facilities, known from other locations (see below) were not actually excavated, doubt remained about the nature of the Vechten *castellum*.[26]

In a recent article, Polak (2014) also presents the almost forgotten evidence of excavations in the 19th century, which included fragments of ships, revetments and granaries. Furthermore, Polak extensively discusses the dating of the site, mainly using coins and samian ware. He arrives at the conclusion that a date as early as the Drusus campaigns is not supported by the finds but that there are good indications for a date early in the Haltern horizon, probably 5 BCE. Vechten was most likely a naval base in its early phase, and the oldest military node west of Nijmegen.[27]

In the past, an assumed early date of Vechten has been used to support the thesis of the *fossa Drusiana* being located at the Vecht-connection between the Rhine and Lake Flevum. Now that the Drusian date cannot be supported by the finds, this thesis becomes weaker.

The other option, that the *fossa Drusiana* connected the Rhine to a precursor of the IJssel (or that parts of the proto-IJssel actually were man-made, being the *fossa Drusiana*), is not easy to confirm, since the IJssel as we know it today is of a much later date. As is the case with many older watercourses the remains can be eroded by later river meandering. The location of a proto-IJssel in figure 1 is therefore hypothetical.

The military outpost and harbor of Velsen

The Roman outpost and harbor of Velsen are also part of the Roman military reorientation after the *clades Variana*. Velsen I consisted initially of a fort, a large loading platform and four pier-like structures laid out next to the Oer-IJ. Due to the abrasive effects of the watercourse, the base was reinforced with four newly erected open quay jetties and revetments. Additionally, the basin was subsequently dredged out to keep the harbour navigable (figure 3). Two

---

[23] Willems 1986, 56-61 including references.
[24] Holwerda 1915; Cf. Polak 2014.
[25] CIL XIII 8815; 12086a.
[26] Polak 2014.
[27] Polak 2014.

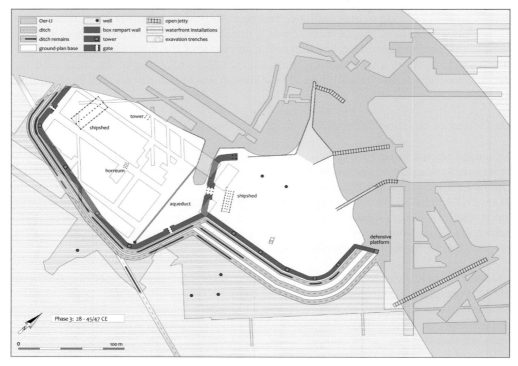

Figure 3. Phase 3 of the military outpost and harbor of Velsen (28-45/47 CE). Drawing: Jos Kaarsemaker

boathouses were discovered in the excavation, comparable to examples known from Haltern and from Mediterranean contexts, one big enough to house two small galleys.[28] Although no ships have been excavated, evidence of transshipment, provisioning and nautical artifacts have been retrieved in the harbour basin.[29]

The Roman military outpost of Velsen I was constructed around 15/16 CE and continued in use until the second half of the 40s. The initial use is frequently connected to the provisioning and controlling of Germanicus' second punitive campaign some years after the Varus disaster. This naval base most probably played a role in safeguarding the region, the northern Rhine route and coast, and the logistical organisation of military campaigns in the north.

The Corbulo canal

The Corbulo canal connects the Rhine and Meuse estuaries (see fig. 1). This canal is known from literary sources,[30] but also attested by archaeological research. Tacitus mentions that Corbulo and his troops were ordered back to the Rhine frontier by the emperor Claudius, after Corbulo had been appointed as the new legate of Germania Inferior in 47 CE and restored order

---

[28] Morel 1988.

[29] Driessen 2014.

[30] Tacitus *Ann.* XI, 18-20; Dio LXI 61 30: 4-6.

among Germanic groups in the North Sea coastal area. To keep his men busy, who were bored and on the brink of revolt, Corbulo ordered the digging of a canal connecting the Rhine and Meuse through which one could avoid the dangers of the Ocean. Dio's descriptions are similar, he only states that the canal was constructed during Corbulo's second period of command (around 50 CE), and gives a technical water management function: *'in order to prevent the rivers from flowing back and causing inundations at the flood-tide of the Ocean'*. Excavations revealed a canal with varying width of 4.5 to 15m, between 1.5 and 2 m deep (in antiquity), which partially integrated existing streams and parts of a tidal creek system.[31] Almost halfway along the canal – running parallel to the beach barrier – a portage was found, which helped to regulate a more or less constant water level and prevented the canal from silting up. Wooden revetments were dated to 49 or 50 CE by dendrochronology. The function of the Corbulo canal was – according to classical sources and recent research – most likely twofold. On the one hand, it may have served in draining water from low lying areas. A first-century wooden culvert with a one-way valve retrieved under a dike, and a sudden increase in the number of ditches laid out during wet periods both from nearby rural areas underline the existence of such drainage practices.[32] It would also seem that the canal was constructed to create a safe inland connection between the Meuse and Rhine estuaries, which can also be supported by the retrieved portage and an observed towpath next to the canal.[33]

Decades after the creation of the Corbulo canal, a new town called *Forum Hadriania (the later Municipium Aelium Cananefatium)* was founded at the banks of the canal, near the current town of Voorburg, close to The Hague. Archaeological research revealing a harbor at this town makes it clear that this canal was still or again in use during the second half of the second and repaired in the first quarter of the third century, and the harbour had a connection with Britain.[34]

Water management and offensive planning

The Drusus dam and the resulting increased watershed through the Rhine opened up several important waterways, which were invaluable for military-strategic and logistic reasons. One improved waterway was the Old Rhine, which was used for the invasion of Britain planned by Caligula and carried out by Claudius, and became the location of many fortifications on its southern bank. The fort of Vechten was an early stronghold on this route. The other new waterway was the northern route via Lake Flevum, most likely opened up by the Drusus canal. This waterway offered routes towards the coastal area of Germania Magna and was controlled by the fortification at Velsen. It is significant that the two oldest strongholds west of Nijmegen, from a period before the 'fixed' *limes* was built, were naval bases, or at least military fortifications with harbour facilities. The logistics of military campaigns were clearly a prime priority for the military staff.

Arguing from the knowledge of hindsight, several far-reaching consequences can be connected to the waterworks of Drusus. The monumental fortifications of the *limes* were built along the

---

[31] De Kort and Raczynski-Henk 2014.

[32] De Ridder 1999; Van Londen 2006.

[33] De Kort and Raczynski-Henk 2014.

[34] Driessen and Besselsen 2014; Driessen 2018.

increased watershed of the Rhine some decades after Drusus, and this *limes* formed a barrier as well as a transport link for over 350 years. The riverine routes were used well into the Middle Ages as can *inter alia* be derived from continuing archaeological research on Roman and Medieval river barges, and it can even be surmised that the formation of the IJssel river from the Late Roman period onwards could have been the result of the waterways created in the Early Roman period.

These far-reaching measures were carried out by engineers of the Roman army and were linked to the political ambition at that time to develop a new Germanic province north of the Rhine. While planning the military campaigns to achieve their political ambitions, they deemed a change in the waterways of Northern Gaul and neighboring Germania necessary, because the military made use of water transport far more often than land transportation. It is clear that the Roman authorities were very well informed about the geography of the north-western provinces and the area far beyond the frontier. In addition to the geographical information, they had the engineering skills as well as the manpower to effectuate large waterworks. Intention, knowledge and skill were thus combined and resulted in a re-shaping of the course of large rivers, meant for use by Roman armies.

Waterscapes

In the above account, a mild surprise at the scale and effect of Roman water management was expressed: the waterworks were of considerable magnitude, and their political context and geographical effects had large implications. The question arises whether or not such surprise is justified. Were such large scale and long-lasting effects uncommon, not to be expected? Northern Gaul is often looked at as being on the periphery of the Gaulish provinces, which were essentially mainland provinces. Modern scholars seem to analyze past geography implicitly in terms of land: landscape, landholding, land routes. However, when we focus on the Roman empire in its entirety, we of course observe that the core of the Empire is the Mediterranean Sea. Much of Italy is surrounded by sea, and trade routes over land are much longer than sea routes. Rome lived on Egyptian corn which was transported over sea from Alexandria on a yearly base. Mediterranean wine, olive oil and many other stocks were shipped across the Roman Empire. Shipment, and waterworks, were part of Rome's core business. Maritime connectivity was pivotal for its existence.[35] Therefore, the waterworks at the Lower Rhine are perhaps, better understood as Roman planning and business as usual, rather than as being exceptional. The Roman authorities must have recognised upon arrival the possibilities of this peripheral waterscape. An environment which was not dominated by land, but by a wide variety of interacting features connected with water such as rivers, estuaries, tidal creek systems, lakes, wetlands, changing ground water levels and the continuous influence of an omnipresent sea. These features, the natural ones as well as those created or transformed by earlier human action, formed part of an already existing socialised waterscape.[36] A waterscape that could be encountered, experienced, further used and adapted to present and future needs of the arriving Romans, whether these may have related to the conquest of new territories, the control of newly established and planned areas, local, regional and intra-provincial logistics or the threat posed by water. The Roman authorities transformed the

[35] Horden and Purcell 2000, 123-172.
[36] Rogers 2013, 1.

waterscape of the Low Countries rapidly with the establishment of different new waterfront installations. These new structures are – for us archaeologists – interesting to study from a technical-physical lens as well as from a socio-economic point of view, and on top of this, we also have to think of the immense changes for local communities in these waterscapes: their subsistence strategies and many associated social customs must have been affected as well.[37] Furthermore, these waterfront installations serve not only practical needs, but are also to be considered as landmarks of power and control and borders of cognitive zones.[38] These landmarks – monumentalised with waterfront installations and larger than life-size statues[39] – were both geographical as well as territorial markers; to guide those who traversed the waterscape and to accentuate the power of the new established central authority.

The Roman transformation of the waterscape furthermore demonstrated that the Roman Empire had subjugated the world technologically as well. This *taming of nature* aspect of Roman society was first treated by Heinrich Drerup,[40] which he illustrated predominantly by means of water installations. Structures which serve primarily the public interests symbolise, according to Drerup, the struggle between man and nature. Viewed as a struggle from which man emerges as victor, turning Rome into the centre of the subjugated world, Rome's engineers shaped and folded land- and waterscapes to their will. Mountains were pierced, valleys traversed to guide water, marshes were reclaimed and hills leveled, arid regions were turned into oases by means of subterranean water supply and even the most remote and inaccessible areas were transformed to fulfill the needs of Rome, from which all its subjects – new or old - could benefit. After the Roman conquest of the Low Countries, this attitude towards the environment became regular practice, turning the still predominantly natural waterscapes into man-made waterscapes. Waterscapes which became part of a global institution and 'machine' from which not only the elites could benefit, but also the masses as can be demonstrated by the archaeologically recorded prosperity of the 2nd century. These experiences, usages and adaptations of our waterscapes are deserving of consideration as one of the cornerstones of our current knowledge, experience and global success in water related issues.

The theme of Rome subjugating nature should not only be approached positively, along Drerup's line of thoughts, because there are serious downsides that must be stressed as well. Large-scale measures affecting the natural environment nearly always have unintended effects in a negative sense, for instance droughts, desertification, soil degradation, destruction of eco-systems, and so on. For the Netherlands, Pierik showed that man-made changes to the landscape caused serious flooding and erosion problems affecting the Dutch coastal areas centuries after the initial measures.[41]

We conclude that the earliest large-scale water management measures in the Netherlands date to the Early Roman period. These measures were taken in the framework of military offensive planning by the Roman authorities and had lasting effects on the physical geography and the

---

[37] Rogers 2013, 144-145.
[38] Westerdahl 2006; 2011.
[39] Driessen 2018, 439-441.
[40] Drerup 1966.
[41] Pierik 2017, 61-86.

people living there. The notion of waterscape and a Mediterranean perspective on land and water help us in understanding and appreciating the changes. The large scale and impact of the Roman measures may impress, but we also have to take into account that the measures caused serious problems, some of them direct as a consequence of the changed situation, some of them centuries later.

Post-script

Just before the final preparations of this volume, and several years after the current contribution was written, a PhD-thesis was completed at the Vrije Universiteit Amsterdam, entirely devoted to Roman waterworks in the Dutch river delta: Jan Verhagen, "Tussen de Dam van Drusus en de Friese Zuilen van Hercules. Romeinse waterwerken in de Rijn-Maasdelta". It presents a great deal of new knowledge on the Drusus dam, the Drusus canal(s) and the paleogeographic reconstruction of Roman watercourses. Just before publication of this volume an additional legionary base was discovered near Valkenburg further underlining the importance of Caligula's attempts to start a conquest campaign in Britain.

Acknowledgements

Hereby we would like to thank P. Vos / S. de Vries for the use of the palaeogeographical map used in figure 1, and Joanne Porck for editing our figures.

Bibliography

Ancient sources

Caesar, *De Bello Gallico*, ed. H.J. Edwards, 1917, London/Cambridge Mass. (Loeb Classical Library).
Cassius Dio, *Historia Romana, LXI-LXX* (*Roman History, books 61-70*), ed. E. Cary, 1925, London/ Cambridge Mass. (Loeb Classical Library).
Pomponius Mela, *Chronographia*, transl. F.E. Romer 1988, Ann Arbor.
Pliny the Elder, *Naturalis Historia*, ed. H. Rackham, 1938, London/Cambridge Mass. (Loeb Classical Library)
Suetonius, *De vita Caesares*, ed. J.C. Rolfe, 1914 London/Cambridge Mass. (Loeb Classical Library).
Tacitus, *Annales*, ed. J. Jackson, 1937, London/Cambridge Mass. (Loeb Classical Library).
Tacitus, *Historia*, ed. J.H. Moore, 1925, and J.H. More and J. Jackson, 1931, London/Cambridge Mass. (Loeb Classical Library).

Modern works

Becker and Rasbach 2015, A. Becker and G. Rasbach, *Waldgirmes: Die Ausgrabungen in der spätaugusteischen Siedlung von Lahnau-Waldgirmes (1993-2009). 1. Befunde und Funde*, Darmstadt (Römisch-Germanische Forschungen 71) (Zabern).
Berendsen and Stouthamer 2001, H. J. A. Berendsen and E. Stouthamer, *Palaeogeographic development of the Rhine-Meuse-delta, The Netherlands*, Assen.
Bogaers and Rüger 1974, J. E. Bogaers and C.B. Rüger , *Der niedergermanische Limes*, Köln (Kunst und Altertum am Rhein 50).

Carroll 2001, M. Carroll, *Romans, Celts & Germans. The German Provinces of Rome*, Stroud.

De Clerq and van Dierendock 2009, W. De Clerq and R.M. van Dierendock, Extrema Galliarum. Noordwest-Vlaanderen en Zeeland in het Imperium Romanum, *Zeeuws Tijdschrift* 58-3/4, 5-34.

Cohen, Stouthamer, Pierik and Geurts 2012, K. M. Cohen, E. Stouthamer, H. J. Pierik and A. H. Geurts, *Rhine-Meuse delta studies. Digital basemap for delta evolution and palaeogeography*, Utrecht. https://easy.dans.knaw.nl/ui/datasets/id/easy-dataset:52125, 14-10-2016.

De Kraker 2015, A. M. J. de Kraker, Flooding in river mouths: human caused or natural events? Five centuries of flooding events in the SW Netherlands, 1500–2000, *Hydrology and Earth System Sciences* 19, 2673-2684.

Drerup 1966, H. Drerup, Architektur als Symbol. Zur zeitgenössischen Bewertung der römischen Architektur, *Gymnasium: Zeitschrift für die Antike in der Deutschen Bildung* 73, 181-196.

Driessen 2007, M. J. Driessen, *Bouwen om te blijven: de topografie, bewoningscontinuïteit en monumentaliteit van Romeins Nijmegen,* Amersfoort (Rapportage Archeologische Monumentenzorg 151 - PhD thesis University of Amsterdam).

Driessen 2014, M. J. Driessen, The Roman Harbours of Velsen and Voorburg-Arentsburg (NL), in Kennecke, H. (ed.), *Der Rhein als europäische Verkehrsachse – Die Römerzeit*, Bonn (Bonner Beiträge zur Vor- und Frühgeschichtlichen Archäologie 16), 209-228.

Driessen 2018, M.J. Driessen, The logistic function of the Rhine-Meuse delta in the Roman period: the harbour town of Voorburg-Arentsburg as a case-study. In C. von Carnap-Bornheim, F. Daim, P. Ettel and U. Warnke (eds.) *Harbours as objects of interdisciplinary research – Archaeology + History + Geoscience*. Römisch-Germanisches Zentralmuseum 34, 437-458. Mainz, Verlag des Römisch-Germanischen Zentralmuseums.

Driessen and Besselsen (eds.) 2014, M.J.Driessen and E.Besselsen (eds), *Voorburg-Arentsburg: een Romeinse havenstad tussen Rijn en Maas,* Amsterdam (Themata 7).

Graafstal 2002, E. P. Graafstal, Logistiek, communicatie en watermanagement. Over de uitrusting van de Romeinse rijksgrens in Nederland. *Westerheem* 51, 2-27.

Grote (ed.) 2012, K. Grote (ed.), *Römerlager Hedemünden: Der augusteische Stützpunkt, seine Außenanlagen, seine Funde und Befunde.* Hannover (Veröffentlichungen der archäologischen Sammlungen des Landesmuseums Hannover 53).

Holwerda 1915, J. H. Holwerda, Vechten. Frührömisches Kastell und Flottenstation. *Römisch-Germanisches Korrespondenzblatt* 8, 57-60.

Horden and Purcell 2000, P. Horden and N. Purcell, *The Corrupting Sea. A Study of Mediterranean History*, Oxford.

Jongkees 1959, J. H. Jongkees, Notes on the Inscription from Herwen, in Wolters, J.B. (ed.), *Romana Neerlandica*, Groningen (Archaeologica Traiectina 3), 16-19.

Kemmers 2004, F. Kemmers, Caligula on the Lower Rhine: coin finds from the Roman fort of Albaniana (The Netherlands). *Revue Belge de Numismatique et de Sigillographie* 150, 15-49.

Kemmers 2005, F. Kemmers, *Coins for a legion. An analysis of the coin finds of the Augustan legionary fortress and Flavian canabae legionis at Nijmegen.* Ph.D. thesis Radboud Universiteit Nijmegen.

Kemmers 2006, F. Kemmers, Coins, countermarks and Caligula. The connection between the auxiliary forts in the Lower Rhine delta and the invasion of Britain. *Bulletin of the Hadrianic Society* 2006, 5-11.

Kort and Raczynski-Henk 2014, J. W. Kort and Y. Raczynski-Henk, The Fossa Corbulonis between the Rhine and Meuse estuaries in the Western Netherlands, *Water History* 6-1, 51-71.

Kunow 1987, J. Kunow, Die Militärgeschichte Niedergermaniens, in: Horn, H.G. (ed.), *Die Römer in Nordrhein-Westfalen*, Stuttgart, 27-109.

Lehmann, Hagemann, and Haßmann, 2018, R. Lehmann, K. Hagemann, and H. Haßmann. *Von Drusus bis Maximinus Thrax – Römer in Norddeutschland: Festschrift zum achtzigsten Geburtstag von Wilhelm Dräger*, Hannover (Freundeskreis für Archäologie in Niedersachsen Schriftenreihe 1).

Van Londen 2006, H. Van Londen, *Midden-Delfland. The Roman native landscape past and present* (unpublished Ph.D. thesis University of Amsterdam 2006).

Niemeijer 2015, R. Niemeijer, Die Straßen des großen augusteischen Lagers auf dem Hunerberg in Nijmegen. Die Ausgrabungen der Radboud Universiteit 1987-1997. *Kölner Jahrbuch* 48, 7-18.

Pierik 2017, H. J. Pierik, *Past human-landscape interactions in the Netherlands. Reconstructions from sand belt to coastal-delta plain for the first millennium AD*, Utrecht (Utrecht Studies in Earth Sciences 139).

Polak, Kloosterman, and Niemeijer 2004, M. Polak, R. P. J. Kloosterman, and R. A. J. Niemeijer, *Alphen aan den Rijn-Albaniana 2001-2002. Opgravingen tussen de Castellumstraat, het Omloopkanaal en de Oude Rijn,* Nijmegen (Libelli Noviomagenses 7).

Polak, and Kooistra 2014, M. Polak, and L. I. Kooistra, A sustainable frontier? The establishment of the Roman frontier in the Rhine delta. Part 1: From the end of the Iron Age to the death of Tiberius (c. 50 BC-AD 37), *Jahrbuch des Römisch-Germanischen Zentralmuseums Mainz* 60, 355-458.

De Ridder 1999, T. De Ridder, De oudste deltawerken van West-Europa. Tweeduizend jaar oude dammen en duikers te Vlaardingen. *Tijdschrift voor Waterstaatgeschiedenis* 8-1, 10-22.

Rogers 2013, A. Rogers, *Water and Roman Urbanism: Towns, Waterscapes, Land Transformation and Experience in Roman Britain*, Leiden (Mnemosyne supplement 355).

Timpe 1968, D. Timpe, *Der Triumph des Germanicus. Untersuchungen zu den Feldzügen der Jahre 14-16 n. Chr. in Germanien*, Bonn (Antiquitas Abhandlungen zur Alten Geschichte 16).

Vos 2015, P. C. Vos, *Origin of the Dutch coastal landscape. Long-term landscape evolution of the Netherlands during the Holocene, described and visualized in national, regional and local palaeogeographical map series*, Groningen.

Vos and de Vries 2013, P. C. Vos and S. de Vries, 2nd generation palaeogeographical maps of the Netherlands - version 2.0, Utrecht. Downloaded on 06 October 2016 from www.archeologieinnederland.nl.

Westerdahl 2011, C. Westerdahl, The Maritime Cultural Landscape. In: A. Catsambis/B. Ford/D.L. Hamilton (eds.), *The Oxford Handbook of Maritime Archaeology*, Oxford, 733–762.

Wightman 1985, E. M. Wightman, *Gallia Belgica*, London.

Willem 1986, W. J. H. Willems, *Romans and Batavians. A Regional Study in the Dutch Eastern River Area*, Amersfoort (PhD thesis University of Amsterdam).

Wynia 1999, S. Wynia, Caius was here. The Emperor Caius' Preparations for the Invasion of Britannia: New Evidence. In: H. Sarfatij/W.J.H. Verwers/P.J. Woltering (eds.), *In Discussion with the Past. Archaeological studies presented to W.A. van Es*, Zwolle, 145-147.

Zuidhoff, and Dijkstra, 2011, F.Zuidhoff and J. Dijkstra, De oudste dijk van Zeeland? Vondst van een dijkje en terp uit de Romeinse tijd op Walcheren, *Tijdschrift voor waterstaatsgeschiedenis* 20-2, 53-61.

'Springs Sumptuously Equipped':
Meanings of Water at Bath[1]

Eleri Cousins

This paper is essentially a meditation on the meaning of water, specifically the water that comes out of the hot springs at Bath – the ancient Roman *Aquae Sulis*. Bath was a sanctuary site in the Roman period, dedicated to the syncretic goddess Sulis Minerva, and it is obvious that the site's sacrality is rooted in the landscape, and specifically in the springs for which Bath continues to be famous. Understanding the role of the waters in the Roman period is necessarily central, then, if we want to understand what was happening at the sanctuary more broadly, and how what was happening fit in with the rest of Romano-British society. But the problem is that for us, too, the waters at Bath are not neutral. They have a particular place in our modern psyche as well, one that is largely formed by the town's role as a curative and social centre in the 18th and 19th centuries. So I want to start, not with the Romans, but rather with the more modern history of the Bath waters, and to explore the ways in which modern and pre-modern conceptions of the point of the hot springs have shaped our narrative for the Roman period, in particular the concept of Aquae Sulis as a healing sanctuary. I will then turn in the second half of the paper to examine what happens if we move away from our preconceived notions of what water must be doing at Bath, in particular the idea that the water is primarily intended to heal, and to explore what insights our evidence for ritual at the site may give us into what made the hot springs sacred for the Romano-British who worshiped there.

To understand the world of the 'eighteenth- and nineteenth-century spa, and of the antiquaries who lived there, we must understand the processes by which water became central to the town's identity in the post-medieval period. Bath's identity during the Middle Ages was primarily as a cathedral city and as a centre for the wool and cloth trade, not as a spa town.[2] Even so, the waters were both known and used for bathing in the medieval period. The renovation of the King's Bath at the main hot spring in the early twelfth century is likely to be attributed to John of Tours, a priest and physician who was also responsible for moving the see of the bishopric from Wells to Bath.[3] Certainly the baths were known as a place of healing by the first half of the twelfth century; the *Gesta Stephani*, c. 1138, mentions that the town is called Bath, because 'sick persons from all England go there in order to bathe in the healing waters, and the healthy as well in order to see these miraculous outpourings of hot water and to bathe in them.'[4]

---

[1]   The writing for this chapter was completed in 2017. Since then, the arguments it contains have been repeated and expanded upon in Cousins 2020, in particular in Chapters Two and Five.

[2]   Davis and Bonsall 2006: 38ff.

[3]   Davis and Bonsall 2006: 38; Cunliffe 1986: 64; 72-4.

[4]   *Quae civitas Batta vocatur, quod ex Anglicae linguae proprietate trahens vocabulum, Balneum interpretaur, eo quod ad illam ex omni Anglia infirmi causa in salubribus aquis diluendi, sani vero gratia mirabiles calidae aquae eruptiones videndi, et in eis balneandi, concurrere solent* (*Gesta Stephani* 28). My translation.

When the priory foundation was dissolved in the wake of the Reformation, and as the cloth trade waned at the same time, the town began to re-invent itself as the pre-eminent healing spa.[5] More extensive interest in the use of the waters for curative purposes had started to take off in the late sixteenth century, as physicians began to write about the health benefits of bathing, and of mineral water in particular.[6] This interest only increased during the seventeenth century, as physicians based in Bath began extolling in both books and pamphlets the ability of the springs to cure virtually every ailment. One physician at the baths, Dr Thomas Venner, proclaimed for example in 1628 that 'They be of excellent efficacy against all diseases of the head and sinews, proceeding from a cold and moist cause, as rheums, palsies, lethargies, apoplexia, cramps, deafness, forgetfulness, trembling or weakness of any member, aches and swellings of the joints.'[7]

The tireless efforts of these Bath-based physicians contributed a great deal to the rise of Bath as a resort. Physicians promoted tourism to the spa through their writings, through their positions on the town's governing board, and, many of them, through their status as landlords of lodging houses.[8] So by the mid-18th century, when Bath reached the peak of its social cachet as a resort for the elite of the kingdom, extolling the healthful qualities of the water was as ubiquitous as it was necessary for the continued life of the spa and all of the urban infrastructure and development which had accompanied Bath's rise to fame.

At the same time that the curative powers of the water became gospel, Bath's image as a 'valley of pleasure', as one writer put it,[9] was becoming entrenched both in literature and in the popular imagination. The picture of Georgian Bath, the social whirl of theatres, assembly rooms, card parties, the promenades up and down the pavement, all set against a backdrop of the both truly invalid and the merely fashionably so, remains an alluring one, as the innumerable memorials in 2017 honouring both the bicentennial of Jane Austen's death and the social world she depicted attested.

But the 'glory days' of Bath, at least from the point of view of social exclusivity, were fading by the end of the eighteenth century. Bath, in essence, had become too popular for its own good; the most fashionable ranks of society deemed the town passé and moved on to the new seaside resorts, and a more middle-class clientele took their place.[10] Bath's story in the nineteenth century, at least as it was perceived at the time by the city's burghers, was one of social and economic stagnation and slow decline.[11] By the end of the nineteenth century, Bath, with its cheap living conditions,[12] was seen as a place for retirees or impoverished spinsters: its cachet as a destination had faded.[13] Healthfulness, though, was still central to its identity – Bath was seen as a salubrious place to be.

---

[5] Hembry 1990: 26-27.

[6] Hembry 1990: 6ff; Davis and Bonsall 2006:67.

[7] Quoted in Davis and Bonsall 2006: 73.

[8] Davis and Bonsall 2006: 73.

[9] Quoted in Neale 1981: 12.

[10] Davis and Bonsall 2006: 151.

[11] Hembry 1997: 54ff.

[12] Hembry 1997: 62-63.

[13] Davis and Bonsall 2006: 154-155.

It is against this backdrop of social rise and fall centred on curative springs that we must think about the ways antiquaries and, later, archaeologists, wrote about the discoveries of the remains of Roman *Aquae Sulis.* I begin in the eighteenth century, when antiquarian interest started to be augmented by the first major archaeological finds; in fact many of these early objects came to light during the re-building of the town centre that took place in the Georgian period.

In June 1753 an inscription[14] was found that recorded the restoration of a sacred place, a *locus religiosus,* by a centurion named Severius Emeritus. A few months after the discovery, John Ward, then Gresham Professor of Rhetoric and vice-president of the Society of Antiquaries, put forward the suggestion that the *locus* in question might have been a public cemetery.[15] He was incorrect, but his justification reveals a good deal about his preconceptions about the nature of Roman Bath: '[T]here was no town, to which this could be more suitable than Bath, on account of the great number of strangers, who resorted thither for the benefit of the salutiferous springs. For as some of those, who came from distant parts, may be supposed from time to time to have died there; a public cemetery for the burial of them was highly requisite.'[16] Forty years later, shortly after the discovery of the pediment of the temple of Sulis Minerva and of an inscription with the phrase *pro salute* on it, Governor Thomas Pownall suggested that 'there might have been erected at the Roman town Aquae Solis an *Aedes Salutis* – the very sort of place whereat to erect and dedicate such a temple...'.[17]

These two interpretations, bookending the second half of the eighteenth century, are broadly representative of eighteenth-century antiquarian writing on the Roman town. Ward, Pownall, and their contemporaries were writing at a time when knowledge of Roman Bath was extremely limited, confined to the few contextless inscriptions and reliefs which had been found by the eighteenth century. The influence of Georgian Bath's status as the preeminent place of healing in Ward's and Pownall's writings and in the propositions they made about the ancient town is consequently clear; that was, after all, all they knew. By the mid-nineteenth century, however, the local antiquary Henry Scarth in *Aquae Solis,* the first full-length work on the Roman town, was explicitly comparing the modern and ancient: 'The natural features of the country remain unchanged, the Springs pour forth their healing as they did of old, but a free, active, enlightened, united, and strong people, governed by just laws, and encouraged to active endeavours, have taken the place of an enslaved and degenerate race, the victims of oppression and cruelty.'[18] The Victorian morality inherent in the rhetoric is compelling. Nonetheless, this assumption that the nature of Bath was the same in antiquity and in the modern period quickly led scholars to dismiss the lack of evidence for a healing sanctuary. Scarth himself, for example, declared that 'It is most probable that a School of Medicine existed in Bath at an early period. The Mineral Springs being visited by many patients for their healing benefits, would naturally cause the residence of eminent Physicians in the neighbourhood. No record, however, has been found of any patients, nor have we any Votive Altar put up by a Physician, as at Chester, or any memorial to a Physician, as on the line of the

---

[14] *RIB* 152
[15] Ward 1753-4: 334.
[16] Ward 1753-4: 337.
[17] Pownall 1795: 16.
[18] Scarth 1864: viii.

Roman Wall in Northumberland.'[19] It is hard, reading Scarth's hypotheses about physicians, not to be reminded of the crowd of doctors who made their living by promoting the baths; Scarth's School of Medicine clearly comes more from the medical culture of his own day than from anything to do with Roman Britain.

As the nineteenth century came to a close, writers continued to see Roman Bath mirrored in their own contemporary experiences of the town. Emanuel Green, a Fellow of the Society of Antiquaries and prolific local scholar on Bath, wrote in 1890 that 'Some accommodation there must have been [for strangers and invalids] as the place, with such magnificent baths, must be judged to have been much what it has been and may be still, a place of ease and idleness; a mixture of groans, music, and flippancy; a resting place for humanity, old, infirm and in ruins; a comfortable thoroughfare from this world to the next.'[20] In Green's words we can easily recognise the haven for retirees which Bath had become by the late Victorian period. In the early twentieth century, Francis Haverfield, the preeminent Roman archaeologist of his day, continued the equation of modern and ancient, writing that 'No doubt a population of others than invalids dwelt round the springs, as it does to-day. But, first and foremost, Bath was a bathing place.'[21] He too continued to assume that this bathing was for curative purposes: 'The reason for the occupation of the site is simple. In the level space within the fold of the river rise mineral springs, hot, medicinal, abundant; and their waters, suitable alike for drinking and for bathing, have power over gout and rheumatism and serious skin diseases.'[22]

By the late twentieth century, these long-standing assumptions concerning the curative nature of the Bath waters and Aquae Sulis' status as a healing sanctuary continued to be unconditionally and unquestioningly accepted by modern archaeologists. In the 1970s, Barry Cunliffe, the principal modern excavator, would open his book *Roman Bath Discovered* with the words 'Throughout its two thousand years of life, the town of Bath has always been famous as a great religious centre and for its thermal springs with their curative associations',[23] and in his seminal report on the curse tablets from the reservoir of the main hot spring Roger Tomlin would write the blunt sentence that 'the waters of Bath can cure disease.'[24] In Peter Salway's words 'In Roman times the spa was middle class, respectable, and seriously dedicated to healing and recreation', we can still see the effect of Bath's modern past: such words could as easily have been written about the town Jane Austen depicts in *Persuasion*.[25]

The automatic acceptance of the waters as curative, even in the second half of the twentieth century, is unsurprising. How could anyone think otherwise, when up until as recently as 1976 a doctor's prescription was required in order to use the spa?[26] The evidence, however, concerning Bath's claim to fame is ultimately ambiguous. On the one hand, chemical and geophysical analyses of the water have concluded that 'No evidence has yet been found to show that the chemistry of the water has any particular quality which is of outstanding

---

[19] Scarth 1864: 32.
[20] Green 1890: 126.
[21] Haverfield 1906: 216.
[22] Haverfield 1906: 219.
[23] Cunliffe 1971: 1.
[24] Tomlin 1988b: 102.
[25] Salway 1981: 688.
[26] Rolls 1991: 57-58.

medicinal value'.[27] On the other hand, studies did show that immersion in hot water (of any origin) could indeed produce positive physiological changes, and both historical evidence and modern trials seemed to indicate that the Bath waters have some effect on paralysis brought on by lead poisoning.[28] The idea, however, that the waters are effective at healing a wide range of conditions, and consequently that any use of the hot springs must have healing in mind, is a cultural construct. It is a construct that for us today has behind it the weight of centuries, but there is nonetheless no reason to assume the Romano-British who venerated the spring shared this construct, or that it was the primary impetus for the worship of Sulis and the construction of her sanctuary.

Indeed, the opposite seems to be true. A straightforward examination of the archaeological evidence from the Roman period of Bath reveals no proof that the sanctuary was curative. Of the eighteen known altars and dedications set up to the principal goddess Sulis and other gods, none were explicitly given in thanks for healing, nor are any dedicated to other healing deities such as Aesculapius or Hygeia. We also do not find requests for healing anywhere in the site's large corpus of so-called 'curse tablets', the pewter petitions for justice or vengeance thrown by worshipers of Sulis into the reservoir of the town's largest hot spring. Most instead are concerned with the theft of small items and with dedicating lost objects to the goddess: they do not even ask that Sulis strike the thief down with illness. Similarly, the ex-voto objects recovered from the main spring itself evince no connection to either sickness or healing. By far the most common offerings were coins, over twelve thousand of which have been found, predominantly *aes* denominations and spanning the whole Roman period. The more than one hundred other objects from the reservoir, ranging from a catapult washer to gemstones to pewter pans, are principally characterised by eclecticism. Finally, the sculptural corpus from Bath contains no scenes of healing or depictions of healing deities.[29]

The overall assemblage from the sanctuary, then, shows no clear interest in or connection to healing or curative rituals. Is there any archaeological material at all from Bath that can be associated with healing? Three altars have occasionally been casually cited as part of healing cult.[30] All three were set up by freedmen to Sulis, for the welfare, *salus*, of their legionary former masters – one of these was the inscription Governor Pownall was referencing, when he was imagining his *Aedes salutis*.

Two of the altars are dedicated *pro salute et incolumitate* – for the welfare and safety – of the same man, Aufidius Maximus, while the third is *ob salutem sacrum* – dedicated on account of the welfare - of Gaius Iavolenus Saturnalis. But the *pro salute et incolumitate* and *ob salutem sacrum* formulae are petitions for general welfare, not just health, and are more about the continuance of well-being and the prevention of harm, than a direct reaction to illness.[31] Indeed both phrases were used frequently in routine and regular religious petitions by citizens and the state on behalf of the emperor, and are encountered on inscriptions at sites throughout the province, almost always in army contexts. Of the forty-six other inscriptions

---

[27] Kellaway 1991: 22.

[28] O'Hare et al., (1991); Heyward (1991).

[29] It has often been claimed that *CSIR* 1.2, no. 3, a carved block found in the Cross Bath, contains Aesculapian imagery; however, the arguments are unconvincing (see Cousins 2020: 42-45 for further discussion).

[30] e.g. by Salway (1981: 688).

[31] Le Glay 1982: 427; Marwood 1988: 1.

from Roman Britain dedicated *pro salute* (not including the Bath pair), twenty-nine are for the *salus* of the emperor or his family. Of the remaining seventeen, six are for the *salus* of a military unit or group of soldiers, two are dedicated by soldiers *pro salute sua suorum*, one is for the *salus* of a woman, Sanctia Gemina, three are altars from Coventina's Well at Carrawburgh Fort, and three are, like the Bath altars, dedicated by freedmen on behalf of their former masters. The final one is for the *salus* of the *vicani* of the fort at Leintwardine, but it too is linked to the emperor since the deities petitioned are Jupiter Optimus Maximus and the *numina* of the Divi Augusti.

There is, then, in almost every single case of the phrase in Britain, a connection either to the emperor or to the army or to both. It is, in fact, language more *imperial* than curative. Given the lack of other evidence for healing cult at Aquae Sulis, nothing about their texts indicates that we must read these altars as set up in search of a specific cure.

The only ex-voto from the reservoir possibly associated with healing is a pair of ivory breasts. (A second object made of bronze may also be an anatomical depiction of a single breast.) I am willing to accept that this anatomical ex-voto may well have been deposited for or after a cure.[32] But as John Scheid has pointed out for Gaul, one anatomical ex-voto does not make a healing site.[33] To pluck this object out of the ex-voto corpus and focus on it alone is to miss the point: the very variety of objects from the spring challenges our idea of Sulis Minerva as a goddess with a single primary purpose.

Finally, an oculist's stamp marking the contents of a container of eye-salve, found in 1731, has also been cited as proof of medicinal activity at the sanctuary.[34] However, over thirty oculists' stamps have been found in Britain, from a wide range of sites, mostly urban ones.[35] They are a normal and relatively frequent part of the material culture of the north-west provinces in general.[36] We would not choose to read oculists' stamps at, for instance, London or Colchester as indicative of ritual healing: why then should we do so at Bath?[37]

It seems clear, then, that had the temple and spring not been found at Bath itself, with all the modern connotations laid out above, the site would probably never have been interpreted as a healing sanctuary. As Scheid has discussed, simply because a sanctuary revolves around a spring does not mean that it is *ipso facto* a healing site. As he puts it, 'on ne saurait considérer comme sanctuaire guérisseur (dont la fonction première est de guérir) qu'un sanctuaire qui livre des témoignages parfaitement explicites de guérisons, inscriptions univoques et/ou nombreux ex-voto de toutes sortes d'organes.'[38] Bath simply does not meet these criteria.

---

[32] Anatomical votives have usually been read as offerings either asking or giving thanks for a cure of the depicted body part (Potter 1985: 34ff). Nonetheless, it is important to note that, at least for some body parts, this interpretation may not be valid; for example, votives of feet may represent a desire for a good journey, or ears a wish to be heard by the god (Scheid 1992: 30; Recke 2013: 1075-1077).

[33] Scheid 1992: 35.

[34] Scarth 1862:32ff; Sauer 1996: 73.

[35] Frere and Tomlin 1992: 46.

[36] Boon 1983: 3; Jackson 1990: 275.

[37] Scheid (1992: 28) makes the more general point that oculists' stamps, scalpels, and other medical equipment should not be taken to be indicative of a healing sanctuary, since they are found in a wide variety of public spaces.

[38] Scheid 1992:35.

So how *were* the Romans using the waters of Sulis? I turn now properly to the Roman period sanctuary.

The Roman site of Aquae Sulis lies surrounded on three sides by the River Avon, in a marshy valley at the lower extent of the Cotswold hills in Somerset. Evidence of Roman settlement has been found on both sides of the river, but the core of the site is a walled area of about 10 hectares. Within this walled area bubble up three hot springs, the largest of which is known as the King's Spring. At this spring was built in Roman times a reservoir, which contained the flow of water, and directed it to a massive bathing complex. Nearby was the temple of Sulis Minerva, offerings to whom have been recovered in quantity from the reservoir of the spring.

The reservoir which was constructed early in the Roman period to enclose the spring was a massive feat of engineering, one of the most considerable ever undertaken in Roman Britain.[39] Today the King's Spring produces around a quarter of a million gallons a day, at a temperature of 46.5°C, and geologists working on the appearance of the springs in prehistory and the Roman period have assumed that there has been no significant change in the flow since then.[40] A quarter of a million gallons a day is an extraordinarily large volume to control, and the design of the reservoir demonstrates both the detailed Roman knowledge of the workings of the spring, as well as the Roman determination to render its output tameable. The waterlogged mud which surrounded and clogged the spring was first consolidated by a wide ring of wooden piles.[41] After construction of the permanent main drain, which led out water through a gap in the pile ring, mud was dug out from the spring head. This involved a considerable amount of earth-moving, to a level at least a meter and a half below the tops of the piles.[42] The building of the massive stone wall of the reservoir was the next stage, with a sluice for the draining of the reservoir placed on the west side, and an outlet leading to the drain of the Great Bath on the south side. Finally, the interior was lined with lead sheeting, and the tops of the piles closed over with waterproof mortar, making sure that the whole remained watertight.[43]

The change that this construction would have brought about in the character of the site cannot be overstated. The area would have gone from a muddy, hot, swamp overflowing with steaming water to a controlled human space, with the previously untamed water rigidly confined by concrete, lead, and stone, and with the surrounding area, no longer in constant danger of flooding, now able to support a built-up environment.

The reservoir had no bottom or filtering mechanism by which the spring water entered it; so alongside the water would come up silt and sand from the spring's fissure. This created a quicksand-like atmosphere at the bottom of the tank, meaning that objects thrown into the reservoir could not be seen after their deposition. In thinking about worshipers' encounters with the water, therefore, we should not be imagining a wishing-well type atmosphere, with coins glinting clearly through clean water. Furthermore, the significance of the heat and

---

[39] Cunliffe 1980: 193; Cunliffe and Davenport 1985: 42.

[40] Kellaway 1985: 7-8.

[41] Cunliffe and Davenport 1985: 39.

[42] Cunliffe and Davenport 1985: 39.

[43] Cunliffe and Davenport 1985: 40.

steam of the spring should be emphasised. This would have been an exceptional quality for ancient visitors, especially those native to Britain, where hot springs are extremely rare.

As I have argued elsewhere, ritual deposition at the reservoir seems to have been in large part concerned with harnessing and controlling feelings of loss or decay through the act of giving objects, either literally or by proxy, to the goddess' waters.[44] This is particularly seen in the deposition of pewter and silver vessels - probable so-called temple plate - and of the well-known corpus of 'curse tablets'. Many of the vessels show signs of wear or even soldered repair, indicating that their deposition in the reservoir was the last act in a longer life history of the object, taking place once the vessels were too worn to be functional any longer. The tablets, meanwhile, are almost exclusively concerned with items stolen from the worshiper; crucially, they never seek to regain the object for the worshiper, but rather dedicate it to Sulis. Deposition of vessels or tablets into the water, therefore, allows victims of time or of theft to regain control of both the situation and the object, and to refashion the loss to be a willing one – a voluntary handing-over of ownership claims to the goddess.

Another, individual, votive might also reflect the reservoir's role as a place of ritual relinquishment. This object, a small bronze pan with a handle and a 'rectangular meandering decoration' which would originally have been filled with enamel, is part of a larger category of vessels, found at various sites (including on the continent), which seem to depict the line of Hadrian's Wall;[45] three of this series, the Rudge Cup, the Amiens Patera, and the Ilam Pan, have the names of several of the western Hadrian's Wall forts running in a band below the rim of the vessel.[46] The Bath pan and a similar contextless fragment from Spain (the Hildburgh Fragment) lack this; the Bath vessel, however, does bear a punched inscription on the handle, which dedicates the pan to the Dea Sulis Minerva. The second line, unfortunately fragmentary, begins 'Codon...'; Tomlin supposes this to be the name of the dedicator.[47] Both this personal dedication by an individual and the material, bronze, mark this object out as separate from the pewter and silver vessels discussed above.

Rudge-type cups have usually been presented in scholarship as soldiers' mementos, which they took with them into retirement as 'souvenirs' of their time serving on the Wall.[48] So entrenched is this interpretation that a recent volume surveying the known vessels is titled *The First Souvenirs: Enamelled Vessels from Hadrian's Wall.*[49] It is noteworthy, however, that all four vessels for which the context is known potentially come from ritual contexts. The Bath pan, of course, comes from a votive context, and indeed has a dedicatory inscription. The Rudge Cup was found in Froxfield (Wilts.) in 1725 in a well which contained a mass of other Roman material, including 'several bones of beasts, four or five human skeletons, and some medals of the lower empire.'[50] Although eighteenth- and nineteenth-century antiquaries suggested that the cup may have been deposited as a votive, Cowen, writing in 1935, dismissed this possibility on the grounds that the animal bones and human skeletons (which could 'only be attributed

---

[44] Cousins (2014).

[45] Sunter and Brown 1988: 14-16, cat. no. 23; Breeze 2012: 6-7.

[46] Holder (2012).

[47] Tomlin 1988a: 55.

[48] Cowen and Richmond 1935: 342; Heurgon (1951); Heurgon 1952: 114-115; Künzl 2012: 18ff.

[49] Breeze, ed. (2012).

[50] Cowen and Richmond 1935: 313.

to a scene of violence'), ruled out a votive interpretation.[51] Now, however, given the work done in recent decades on structured deposits in pits and wells, vast numbers of which include deliberately placed animal bone as well as ceramic and metal vessels and occasionally human remains,[52] the context of the Rudge Cup sounds distinctly 'ritual.' Meanwhile, the Amiens Patera was found buried next to a pipe-clay Dea Nutrix figurine.[53] The context of the Ilam Pan is less clear. It was found by metal detectorists on moorland overlooking the river Manifold in Staffordshire, and subsequent excavation did not reveal any sign of a site at the location.[54] However, other finds were found nearby, including at least twelve first- and second- century brooches, 'several of which were reported to have been orientated in the same direction, seemingly in some sort of extended linear arrangement,' which could possibly suggest a type of structured deposition.[55]

These find contexts have led Ralph Jackson to argue that the pans may have had a ritual component, probably water-related, in addition to being 'souvenirs'.[56] Martin Henig has gone further, arguing that they are undoubtedly ritual in purpose.[57] Problems of survival will likely be skewing our sample, with pans that were ritually deposited less likely to be destroyed or melted down for reuse than those that were not. Nonetheless, it seems clear that at least some of these pans were imbued by their depositors with ritual significance. Can we take this a step further and ask what that significance may have been? One possibility is that some of these pans may have been used in rituals at the end of military careers or even after the end of a soldier's life, obtaining ritualised closure through the burial or relinquishment of an object symbolizing the location of the soldier's military service. Similar rituals may have taken place in another area of the north-west provinces: Roymans and Aarts have argued, although their evidence is not conclusive, that Batavian soldiers (many of whom would in fact have served on Hadrian's Wall) book-ended their military service with rites at sanctuaries in their homeland, e.g. the temple of Hercules at Empel.[58] A similar interpretation would in fact work well for the Bath pan, since it ties in thematically with the interpretations of ritual closure I have put forward for the deposition of pewter vessels and tablets.

A core component of this model of ritual relinquishment is that the reservoir is a place of chthonic significance, a place where objects can disappear through the swirling steam and quicksand into the depths of the earth. Elsewhere I have suggested that the water plays a role in these rituals of closure through its ability to effect transformation in other objects or people via its own ever-changing state as an element in flux,[59] but the chthonic power of the spring emphasised by the heat and steam is likely to be as, if not more, important. This chthonic conception of Sulis' *numen* may also be supported by our one ancient literary

[51] Cowen and Richmond 1935: 313.

[52] See, e.g., Fulford's examples from Silchester alone, which include one pit with four dog skulls and at least three pits with human remains (Fulford 2001: 201ff).

[53] Heurgon 1952: 95.

[54] Jackson 2012: 42.

[55] Jackson 2012: 42.

[56] Jackson 2012: 58-60.

[57] Henig 2010/2011

[58] Roymans and Aarts 2005: 354ff.

[59] Cousins 2014: 58.

reference to Bath. Solinus, the late third- or early fourth-century[60] author of the *Collectanea rerum memorabilium*, reports that in Britain

> '*fontes calidi opiparo exculti apparatu ad usus mortalium: quibus fontibus praesul[61] est Minervae numen, in cuius aede perpetui ignes numquam canescunt in favillas, sed ubi ignis tabuit vertit in globos saxeos.*'

> 'Hot springs are sumptuously equipped for human use: the divine spirit of Minerva presides over these springs, and in her temple the perpetual fires never decay into ashes, but rather when the fire has died out it turns into rocky balls.'[62]

The consensus has long been that Solinus is referring to Aquae Sulis in this passage; not only does Aquae Sulis match his description extremely well, it is the only site in Britain which does so.[63] It has also long been pointed out that the 'rocky balls' are likely to be chunks of coal from outcroppings near to the site.[64] Solinus did seem to have sources of information concerning Britain; the rest of his discussion of Britain contains some surprisingly accurate details – for instance, that Britain is a source for jet.[65] If we accept that he is describing rituals at the sanctuary, there are two points to make: first, that coal was burned in honour of Sulis and second, this was considered to be a notable, and characteristic, feature of the goddess' temple – noteworthy and distinguishing enough that word of it reached Solinus. Indeed, the coal's behaviour would likely have been striking to anyone used to the combustion of wood; a correspondent of J.G. Frazer described his first-hand experiences with Somerset coal in this way: 'I lived some 30 years ago at Frome in Somerset, and it took me some time to get used to the peculiar behaviour of the local house-coal, which after giving off its gases in the form of flame, leaves the grate full of dead coke, which soon goes out completely unless there is a good draft.'[66]

There is a small amount of archaeological evidence supporting Solinus' statement. Although no burnt coal was found during the twentieth-century excavations,[67] the nineteenth- century antiquary J.T. Irvine noted a find of 'a quantity of coal ashes...and thrown on it a large Roman cup' in the northwest corner of the temple precinct.[68] No coal from Bath has been tested so far, but tests of coal from other sites in the region around the Severn imply that local sources

---

[60] Hofeneder 2008: 138-139. Solinus was dated by Mommsen to the mid-third century (Mommsen 1864: v-viii) but more recent scholarship has argued for a later date.

[61] It has occasionally been suggested that this line should be emended to read '*praeest Sulis Minervae numen*' (see Hofeneder 2008: 151-152 for an overview). While there is no need from a manuscript perspective for an emendation, the suggestion, according to S. Oakley (pers. comm.), is 'neither absurd nor implausible.' There is, then, a possibility, albeit faint, that Solinus had not only heard of Bath, but also knew the full syncretic name of the goddess.

[62] Solinus, *Collectanea rerum memorabilium* 22.10. My translation.

[63] Haverfield 1906: 221; Cunliffe 1969: 7, who points out that the equation goes back to Geoffrey of Monmouth in the 12th c.

[64] Lysons 1813: 3; Scarth 1864: 3; Haverfield 1906: 221.

[65] Solinus, *Coll.* 22.11.

[66] Letter, Thomas C. Cantrill to J.G. Frazer, 24th May, 1921. Recorded in a MS note by Frazer on the last page of his personal copy of T. Mommsen's edition of Solinus (held in the Classical Faculty Library, University of Cambridge).

[67] Unburnt coal was found in the period 5 layers (i.e. after the temple had fallen into disuse) (Cunliffe and Davenport 1985: 35).

[68] Cunliffe and Davenport 1985: 35.

of coal were being used by the inhabitants of the area.[69] Evidence for the use of coal in ritual contexts in Britain, however, is exceedingly rare. Coal has been found in fourth-century layers at the temple at High Nash (Glos.);[70] on the other hand, coal from the shrine at Nettleton (Wilts.), although occasionally cited as evidence of coal in a ritual context,[71] seems rather to be associated with the site's transformation into an industrial settlement.[72] While it is possible that the use of coal at other ritual sites has either gone unrecognised, or has left no archaeological trace (either because the coal was entirely consumed or it was completely cleared from the site after use), the archaeological evidence as it now stands supports the impression from Solinus that the burning of coal was a singular part of ritual practice at Aquae Sulis – not merely rare in comparison with Solinus' continental experiences, but rare within Britain itself. Perhaps, then, coal, a material emerging from the ground, was seen as a particularly appropriate fuel for Sulis' cult: taken together, both the coal and the spring place heat from the earth at the heart of worshipers' experience of Sulis.

I want to conclude with a brief word about the role of water in the bathing complex. The sanctuary at Bath was certainly designed by people thoroughly immersed in Roman cultural *mores*,[73] and given the centrality of bathing in Roman life, it is hardly surprising that they chose to exploit the hot springs in this way. The layout of the site, however, strongly suggests that there was both an increasing physical and conceptual disconnect between the waters in the reservoir and the waters once they got to the baths: despite their proximity, there was, for instance, no logical path for visitors to Aquae Sulis to get from one place to the other. In the Baths' initial phase, bathers would have had a view onto the reservoir of the spring as they passed through the central hall of the complex to the Great Bath; the experience of bathing and the experience of viewing the sacred heart of the site would thus initially have been intertwined.[74] By the second phase, however, probably at some point in the second century, these two experiences were disconnected by changes made to the layout of the central hall, which blocked the windows to the spring from view.[75] This suggests that, although the baths were technically fed by the hot water from the reservoir, as time went on the activities taking place in the baths were consciously separated from the ritual activities taking place at the reservoir edge. There is also no evidence for any ritual activity within the bathing complex itself. It is possible, then, that the hot water of the baths, although coming from the sacred spring, was not part of the ritual experience of visitors. In other words, as the water left the spring and entered the baths, perceptions of its purpose may have changed from the ritual functions I have described above, to a more mundane appreciation of the physical pleasure it could afford to bathers: the 'sumptuously equipped' waters of Solinus' description.

These pleasures of bathing bring me thematically full-circle to where I began, with the rise of the baths for healing and social enjoyment in the early modern period. There is more to say about Roman Aquae Sulis, of course. In this paper I have focused on differing perceptions of the waters through time, and not through space, but the ways in which Aquae Sulis does or

---

[69] Smith 1996: 379.

[70] Dearne and Branigan 1995: 92.

[71] Travis 2008: 159.

[72] Wedlake 1982: 68, 220; Dearne and Branigan 1995: 94.

[73] Cousins 2016: 104.

[74] Cunliffe 1969: 103.

[75] Cunliffe 1969: 104-105.

does not compare to other watery sites in Britain and Gaul is equally important – although left for another day. I hope, however, that I have shown to what degree our modern perceptions of the Bath waters have obscured the Romano-British context, and made some steps to putting that context, and in particular the chthonic force of Sulis' waters, back at the heart of discussion where it belongs.

Bibliography

Boon 1983, G. Boon, Potters, oculists and eye-troubles. *Britannia* 14: 1-12.

Breeze (ed.) 2012, D. Breeze (ed.), *The first souvenirs: enamelled vessels from Hadrian's Wall.* Cumberland and Westmorland Antiquarian and Archaeological Society Extra Series 37. Kendal.

Cousins 2014, E. H. Cousins, Votive Objects and Ritual Practice at the King's Spring at Bath. In H. Platts, J. Pearce, C. Barron, J. Lundock and J. Yoo, eds., *TRAC 2013: Proceedings of the Twenty-Third Theoretical Roman Archaeology Conference, King's College, London 2013*, pp. 52-64. London.

Cousins 2016, E. H. Cousins, An Imperial Image: The Bath Gorgon in Context. *Britannia* 47: 99-118.

Cousins 2020, E. H. Cousins, *The Sanctuary at Bath in the Roman Empire.* Cambridge.

Cowen and Richmond 1935, J. D. Cowen and I. A. Richmond, The Rudge cup. *Archaeologia Aeliana, Series 4* 12: 310-342.

Cunliffe 1969, B. Cunliffe, *Roman Bath.* London.

Cunliffe 1971, B. Cunliffe, *Roman Bath Discovered, 1st ed.* London.

Cunliffe 1980, B. Cunliffe, The Excavation at the Roman Spring at Bath 1979: a Preliminary Description. *Antiquaries Journal* 60: 187-206.

Cunliffe 1986, B. Cunliffe, *The City of Bath.* Gloucester.

Cunliffe (ed.) 1988, B. Cunliffe, *The Temple of Sulis Minerva at Bath. Volume 2: The Finds from the Sacred Spring.* Oxford.

Cunliffe and Davenport 1985, B. Cunliffe and P. Davenport, *The Temple of Sulis Minerva at Bath: Volume 1(I) The Site.* Oxford.

Davis and Bonsall 2006, G. Davis and P. Bonsall, *A History of Bath: Image and Reality.* Lancaster.

Dearne and Branigan 1995, M. J. Dearne and K. Branigan, The Use of Coal in Roman Britain. *Antiquaries Journal* 75: 71-106.

Frere and Tomlin (eds) 1992, S. S. Frere and R. S. O. Tomlin, *The Roman Inscriptions of Britain. Volume II: Instrumentum Domesticum (Personal Belongings and the like). Fascicule 4.* Stroud.

Fulford 2001, M. Fulford, Links with the Past: Pervasive 'Ritual' Behaviour in Roman Britain. *Britannia* 32: 199-218.

Green 1890, E. Green, Thoughts on Bath as a Roman City. *Proceedings of the Bath Natural History and Antiquarian Field Club* 7: 114-126.

Haselgrove and Wigg-Wolf (eds) 2005, C. Haselgrove and D. Wigg-Wolf, *Iron Age Coinage and Ritual Practices*, pp. 337-360. Mainz.

Haverfield 1906, F. Haverfield, Romano-British Somerset. In W. Page, ed. *Victoria History of the County of Somerset, Volume I*, London: 207-371.

Hembry 1990, P. Hembry, *The English Spa: 1560-1815.* London.

Hembry 1997, P. Hembry, *British Spas from 1815 to the Present: A Social History.* London.

Henig 2010/2011, M. Henig, Souvenir or votive? The Ilam Pan. *ARA: The Bulletin of the Association for Roman Archaeology* 20: 13-15.

Heurgon 1951, J. Heurgon, The Amiens Patera. *JRS* 41: 22-24.

Heurgon 1952, J. Heurgon, La patère d'Amiens. *Monuments Piot* 46: 93-115.

Heyward 1991, A. Heyward, Lead, gout and Bath Spa Therapy. In Kellaway, (ed.) 1991a: 77-88.

Hofeneder 2008, A. Hofeneder, C. Iulius Solinus als Quelle für die keltische Religion. In Sartori (ed.) 2008: 135-166.

Holder, P. 2012, P. Holder, The Inscriptions on the Vessels. In Breeze (ed.) 2012: 65-70.

Jackson 1990, R. Jackson, A New Collyrium Stamp from Cambridge and a Corrected Reading of the Stamp from Caistor-by-Norwich. *Britannia* 21: 275-283.

Jackson 2012, R. Jackson, The Ilam Pan. In Breeze (ed.) 2012: 41-60.

Kellaway 1985, G. A. Kellaway, The Geomorphology of the Bath region. In Cunliffe and Davenport 1985: 4-8.

Kellaway (ed.) 1991a, G. A. Kellaway, *Hot Springs of Bath: Investigations of the thermal waters of the Avon Valley*. Bath.

Kellaway 1991b, G. A. Kellaway, Preface. In Kellaway (ed.) 1991a: 13-22.

Künzl 2012, E. Künzl, Enamelled Vessels of Roman Britain. In Breeze (ed.) 2012 : 9-22.

Le Glay 1982, M. Le Glay, Remarques sur la notion de *Salus* dans la religion romaine. In Bianchi, U. and M. J. Vermaseren (eds) *La Soteriologia dei Culti Orientali nell'Impero Romano*, Leiden: 427-444.

Lysons 1813, S. Lysons, *Reliquiae Britannico-Romanae*. London.

Marwood 1988, M. A. Marwood, *The Roman Cult of Salus*. BAR International Series 465.

Mommsen (ed.) 1864, T. Mommsen, *C. Iulii Solini collectanea rerum memorabilium*. Berlin.

Neale 1981, R. S. Neale, *Bath 1680-1850: A Social History, or, a Valley of Pleasure yet a Sink of Iniquity*. London.

O'Hare, Heywood, Millar, Evans, Corrall and Dieppe 1991, J. P. O'Hare, A. Heywood, N. D. Millar, J. M. Evans, R. J. M. Corrall and P. Dieppe, Physiology of immersion in thermal waters. In Kellaway (ed.) 1991: 71-76.

Potter 1985, T. W. Potter, A Republican Healing-Sanctuary at Ponte di Nona near Rome and the Classical Tradition of Votive Medicine. *Journal of the British Archaeological Association* 138: 23-47.

Pownall 1795, T. Pownall, *Descriptions and Explanations of Some Remains of Roman Antiquities Dug Up in the City of Bath, in the year MDCCXC*. Cruttwell (Bath).

Recke 2013, M. Recke, Science as art: Etruscan anatomical votives. In Turfa (ed.) 2013: 1068-1085.

Rolls 1991, R. Rolls, Quest for the quintessence. In Kellaway (ed.) 1991a: 57-63.

Roymans and Aarts 2005, N. Roymans and J. Aarts, Coins, soldiers and the Batavian Hercules cult. Coin deposition at the sanctuary of Empel in the Lower Rhine region. In Haselgrove and Wigg-Wolf (eds) 2005: 337-360.

Salway 1981, P. Salway, *Roman Britain*. Oxford.

Sartori 2008, A. Sartori (ed.), *Dedicanti e Cultores nelle Religioni Celtiche: VII Workshop F.E.R.C.A.N., Gargnano del Garda (9-12 maggio 2007)*. Milan.

Sauer 1996, E. Sauer, An Inscription from Northern Italy, the Roman Temple Complex in Bath and Minerva as a Healing Goddess in Gallo-Roman Religion. *Oxford Journal of Archaeology* 15.1: 63-93.

Scarth 1862, H. N. Scarth, On Roman Remains at Bath, *Journal of the British Archaeological Association* 18: 289-305, continued from *JBAA* 17 March 1861, p.18.

Scarth 1864, H. N. Scarth, *Aquae Solis*. London.

Scheid 1992, J. Scheid, Épigraphie et sanctuaires guérisseurs en Gaule. *Mélanges de l'École française de Rome* 104.1:25-40.'

Smith 1996, A. H. V. Smith, Provenance of Coals from Roman Sites in U.K. Counties Bordering River Severn and its Estuary and Including Wiltshire. *Journal of Archaeological Science* 23: 373-89.

Sunter and Brown 1988, N. Sunter and D. Brown, Metal Vessels. In Cunliffe (ed.) 1988: 9-21.

Tomlin 1988a, R. S. O. Tomlin, Inscriptions on Metal Vessels. In Cunliffe (ed.) 1988: 55-57.

Tomlin 1988b, R. S. O. Tomlin, The Curse Tablets. In Cunliffe (ed.) 1988: 59-280.

Travis 2008, J. R. Travis, *Coal in Roman Britain*. BAR British Series 468. Oxford.

Turfa (ed.) 2013, J. M. Turfa, *The Etruscan World*, London.

Ward 1753-1754, J. Ward, An Attempt to Explain an Antient Roman Inscription, Cut Upon a Stone Lately Found at Bath. *Philosophical Transactions* 48: 332-346.

Wedlake 1982, W. J. Wedlake, *The Excavation of the Shrine of Apollo at Nettleton, Wiltshire, 1956-1971*. Society of Antiquaries of London. London.

If Swimming Was Not a Serious Activity for the Greeks and Romans, They Would Not Have Had Swimming Pools

Jenny Amphaeris and Martin Henig

Introduction

When reading the work of, or even talking to, historians about ancient swimming, one quickly detects a general impression that swimming was not important for the Greeks and Romans, due to the limited interest that historians have in this activity. At most they will admit that it was simply useful as a military training exercise. This is true of even the German specialist in ancient swimming, E. Mehl, who notes: '*Wie schon erwähnt, stand beim Schwimmen der Römer die militärische Verwendung im Mittelpunkte*'.[1] Having a personal interest in the sport and knowing how the ancient Greeks and Romans loved competitive athletics, were engaged in naval warfare, and in private life took coastal holidays, we were keen to explore the activity further and to research thoroughly the ancient attitudes to, and uses for, swimming. Finding countless and varied references to the activity in primary sources, a new view of swimming as an activity began to emerge, one in which swimming was a varied and prominent aspect of life in both ancient Greek and Roman societies. This is emphasised by the proliferation of swimming pools in the ancient world.

There are two aspects of our hypothesis. One is an attempt to prove that swimming was seriously important in the Ancient World, despite the strictures of some modern scholars. The second involves an examination of the physical aspects of swimming, and especially the locations at which it occurred, particularly the swimming pool; it is difficult to believe that people would go to the trouble of building swimming pools, if they did not take swimming itself seriously.

In this paper we will set out a detailed reasoning to support the contention that swimming *was* a serious activity in both Greece and Rome.[2] We will begin by assessing attitudes towards building swimming pools, before defining how such pools were used. In order to do this, we will examine a number of Greek and Roman swimming pools and take a case study in order to analyse at greater depth. Then we will turn to the activity of swimming itself: the strokes, its forms, and related details, and we hope to show conclusively that swimming had many facets in ancient societies, far beyond the reaches of the limiting category of martial training. In demonstrating how swimming was highly developed and the manner in which it permeated all aspects and levels of ancient society, as well as how it led to these societies constructing structures specifically for this activity, we hope to establish that swimming was both important in antiquity and that it deserves far greater scholarly attention.

---

[1]   Mehl 1927, 69
[2]   We will use, as far as possible, the Loeb and OCT texts, as well as the Perseus website, for the Greek, Latin and English in this study.

Ancient attitudes towards swimming pools

We begin by focusing on Classical attitudes towards the building of swimming pools, considering their use in a later section. These attitudes are apparent both from features of the pools themselves and from accounts of their construction. The most pertinent point to remember about ancient swimming pools is that they were designed to be permanent structures. Not only is it possible to tell this from the use of stone rather than wood and the construction of swimming pools often within or in direct proximity to other permanent structures, such as *gymnasia* or houses, but it can be proven in that when bath complexes were rebuilt, the pools too were refashioned and not destroyed, as can be seen both at Olympia and Bath (*Aquae Sulis*). Such permanence alone indicates that swimming pools were not merely a passing phase for either Greek or Roman societies.

The next aspect demanding consideration is why the Greeks and Romans built swimming pools at all. Why did they go to the trouble when it was possible to swim in the sea, rivers, even lakes? In fact Vegetius tells us in his account on the Roman army that the *Campus Martius* site was chosen specifically as it was beside the Tiber so that soldiers could swim for training and exercise:

> *Ideoque Romani veteres [...] ad omnem rei militaris erudiverant artem, campum Martium vicinum Tiberi delegerunt, in quo iuventus post exercitum armorum sudorem pulveremque dilueret ac lassitudinem cursus natandi labore deponeret.*

> Therefore the ancient Romans, who were trained in the whole art of warfare [...] selected a Campus Martius next to the Tiber in which the youth might wash off sweat and dust after training in arms, and lose their fatigue from running in the exercise of swimming.[3]

The Greeks were not in short supply of rivers and coasts either. So why would the Romans or the Greeks need, or want, to build the pools? An obvious conclusion to reach would be that swimming was an important enough activity in itself to demand special facilities. There were even private, heated swimming pools in some rich Roman homes, as Pliny the Younger tells us in his letter to Gallus describing his Laurentine villa.[4] That could, of course, simply signify personal preference but also, more interestingly, it might indicate a widespread and strong desire by the Roman owner, perhaps also a need, to swim on a regular basis. Put together with the fact that the desire to swim could be fulfilled by using rivers, other natural locations, or public pools, this leads to the conclusion that the building of private pools is yet another indication of the importance of the wider construction of pools.

Another possible way of interpreting the building of swimming pools, at least in a Roman context, is as a manifestation of the spread of Roman culture, often termed 'Romanisation'. One of the signs of Romanisation was the bath complex: 'Other public structures of the *colonia*, particularly in the days of the Empire, might include triumphal arches, baths, theatres and [...] amphitheatres.'[5] Archaeology reveals that wherever there was a bath complex, such as Trajan's

---

[3]   Vegetius, *De Re Militari*, I.10
[4]   Pliny the Younger, *Ep.2*, XVII, 11
[5]   Salmon 1969, 28

baths in Rome, there was, with very few exceptions, a swimming pool. Woolf, in agreement, adds that in the Greek East 'the introduction of the Roman cycle of baths and the monumental building that accommodated this'[6] are signs of imperial Romanisation. Furthermore, at Bath, *Aquae Sulis*, 'The construction of a great bathing establishment, a temple, and possibly a theatre, around the sacred spring would be a project very much in keeping with what is known as Flavian Romanizing policy.'[7] It is an interesting combination, cleansing and exercise, which will be explored later, but it is clear that a swimming pool was an integral part of Roman civilisation and its image, even if it was combined with other facilities.

However, as Zanker states, in his discussion of the first public bath in Rome built by Agrippa, 'With its extensive gardens, artificial lake (*Stagnum Agrippae*) serving as a natatio, and athletic facilties, the whole complex recalls the gymnasia of Greek cities.'[8] Perhaps there was a difference between the pools connected with bath complexes and those in *gymnasia*, or perhaps the Roman identity element of building pools was less distinctive, due to their initial borrowing of Greek traditions including swimming pools.

When we turn to the ancient accounts of building work, one important feature of Classical society which must not be forgotten, is a fixation with *memoria* or 'commemoration'. Heroes like Achilles and Aeneas embodied this desire, even need, to be remembered and to live forever in the minds of others, which is one reason for the construction of lasting structures, as any triumphal arch will confirm. It is in this vein that the Classical swimming pools might be presented as monuments of civilisation, and even forever connected to a particular person, especially where the Emperors Augustus, Nero, and Trajan are concerned. A significant section of Augustus' *Res Gestae* focuses on what was built or restored during his reign, such as the *curia*, *basilica*, theatre of Pompey, and many temples.[9] Interestingly, Augustus writes using the verbs *feci* and *refeci*, 'I built' and 'I rebuilt', which are in the first person, despite it being highly unlikely that Augustus ever picked up a builder's tool in his life. It is obvious that he wishes to take credit for these building projects in this propagandist autobiography. Suetonius is also prepared to praise Augustus for his additions to the city of Rome: *excoluit adeo, ut iure sit gloriatus marmoream se relinquere, quam latericiam accepisse*, 'He so improved it that it was with justification that he boasted he had found it a city of brick and left it a city of marble.'[10] What is pertinent about his building programme for the purpose of this study is that, as part of Augustus' youth movement, he had *palaestrae* constructed across Italy, including the swimming pools uncovered at Pompeii and Herculaneum.[11] A brief look at Vitruvius' work really demonstrates the ancient attitude towards architecture:

> *Cum vero attenderem te [...] de vita communi omnium curam publicaeque rei constitutione habere [...], ut civitas per te non solum provinciis esset aucta, verum etiam ut maiestas imperii publicorum aedificiorum egregias haberet auctoritates, non putavi praetermittendum, quin primo quoque tempore de his rebus ea tibi ederem,[...]quod animadverti multa te aedificavisse et nunc aedificare, reliquo quoque tempore et publicorum et privatorum aedificiorum, pro amplitudine rerum gestarum ut posteris memoriae traderentur, curam habiturum.*

---

[6]   Woolf 1994, 126
[7]   Cunliffe 1969, 3
[8]   Zanker 1988, 139-140
[9]   *Res Gestae Divi Augusti*, 19-21
[10]   Suetonius, *Div. Aug.* 28
[11]   Balsdon 1969, 168

> But when I saw that you were giving your attention [...] to the welfare of society in general and to the establishment of public order, [...] so that not only should the State have been enriched with provinces by your means, but that the greatness of its power might likewise be attended with distinguished authority in its public buildings, I thought that I ought to take the first opportunity to lay before you my writings on this theme [...] because I saw that you have built and are now building extensively, and that in future also you will take care that our public and private buildings shall be worthy to go down to posterity by the side of your other splendid achievements.[12]

Clearly, such building work was to be encouraged and is worthy of praise, as embodying Roman identity, if not perhaps Greek culture, and one of the structures almost invariably built was a swimming pool. In summary thus far, ancient swimming pools represent permanence, their very presence being worthy of note. Furthermore, pride and identity issues aside, it is logical that there was no reason for pools to be built if they were not for the purpose of swimming and it is that activity itself which would most likely drive their construction.

Ancient swimming pools

Having established some basic ideas about ancient attitudes towards building the pools, it is appropriate to move to the swimming pool itself. First, it is necessary to cover some of the related terminology, as a major distinction between swimming pools and baths is seen in the language employed. So it is crucial to distinguish swimming pools from baths in order to establish genuine information about swimming pools. A swimming pool will most often be referred to as a *natatio* or *piscina* in Latin and a *κολυμβηθρα* in Greek, as opposed to a *therma* or *balneum* and *βαλανειον*, which all refer to bathing pools, unlike modern English which can refer to swimming pools as 'swimming baths'. In epigraphy we also find references to a *cella natatoria* or 'cold plunge pool'; an *oceanum* or 'pool room'; a *piscina* as a specifically 'cold pool'; as well as *solia* or 'heated pools' (Fagan 2002, Appendix). We also encounter *colimbum* 'plunge pool', which is an interesting development from the Greek. According to Bouet: *'le terme piscina correspond très rarement chez les auteurs anciens à une cuve aménagée dans une pièce. Dans la grande majorité des cas, il s'agit d'un bassin à l'air libre servant à la natation. C'est dans ce sens qu'on le retrouve dans toutes les inscriptions en relation avec un campus.'*[13]

We will next analyse the physical aspects of the pool, taking *Aquae Sulis*, Bath, in Somerset, dating from the late first century A.D., as a case study and then draw parallels with some other swimming pools found in the Greek and Roman world. According to Henig, who is mainly concerned with discussing the imagery of the temple pediment, the complex of Bath and temple was most probably commissioned by the client king Tiberius Claudius Togidubnus, *Rex Magnus Britanniae*, to celebrate the Roman achievement, both political and cultural.[14] We have especially selected Bath as a case study because its remains are well preserved and there has been considerable research on them; moreover, we have both been able to visit and study the site at leisure. Additionally Bath had a varied and complex history, in the Roman period alone, and it is unusual in other respects, most obviously in being a natural spa with hot

---

[12] Vitruvius, *De Architectura*, paragraphs 2-3
[13] Bouet 1999, 474
[14] Henig 1999; Henig 2000, 124-9

springs (Ptolemy calls it Ὕδατα Θερμά[15] which would correspond to *Aquae Calidae* in Latin) but also because of its location in the west of a province on the north-west frontier of the empire. It is of additional interest for its lack of symmetry within the bathing complex. Yet it holds many similarities to other pools we have examined: amongst them is the attachment of a pool to a bathing complex or in the Greek model to a *palaestra*, although it was only under Rome that pools for bathing were disseminated throughout the Mediterranean littoral and beyond; moreover the renovation of the complex, with retention of the pool over six periods of change, was by no means unique, as this was also true at Olympia in Greece, though there with less development over time.

At different periods Bath had several separate swimming pools, like the bathing complex at Side, Western Anatolia, but by the second Period, not long after the complex was built, the Great Bath was considered to be the main swimming pool. The Lucas Bath to the East might, however, still have served as a pool, which is a little unusual, as the Great Bath was the main spa and bathing centre too. Not until Period five was a new separate, albeit smaller, swimming pool built, on the site of the former *caldarium* under what is now Stall Street.

Figure 1. The Great Bath at *Aquae Sulis*, Bath. The basin measures 19.00 metres in length by 8.92 metres in breadth and is 1.52 metres deep. *Photo in the Public domain.*

---

[15]   Ptolemy, II, 13

In terms of changes, the second Period saw the destruction of the far Eastern *natatio* to make room for the Turkish bath system and the introduction of a circular plunge pool in the west, resulting in rendering the swimming pools more central, and hence unusual.[16] A comparison might be seen in Nero's bath complex in Rome, which is symmetrical, with the *natatio* at the back. Another change was the rerooting of the Great Bath in the third Period, at a time after the reign of Hadrian, thus showing a high level of maintenance and care for this bath and swimming pool.

Turning to examine the details of the individual baths will help to indicate what a swimming pool was, at least for the Romans. The pools decrease in size and temperature from the hot Great Bath (Figure 1), measuring 19m by 8.92m, 1.52m deep, with four surrounding steps and its floor covered in lead sheeting for waterproofing;[17] to the Lucas Bath, fed with the same water, measuring 13.1m by 5.95m, with 5 steps at either end; to a smaller cold *natatio* which no longer exists;[18] and in the West to a circular plunge pool, 9m in diameter and 1.22m deep,[19] but far too cold and perhaps of the wrong shape for serious swimming. The 'Stall Street pool' is a much later development and will not be considered in detail here.

All three of the separate rectangular pools to the Great Bath, the Lucas, the old *natatio*, and the Stall Street pools, were either cold or colder than the central basin, which suggests that the lower the temperature the more serious the swimming, as the cold would stimulate exercise rather than relaxation, as in the Great Bath. Mehl supports this view, that there was an ancient preference as early as the Mycenaean age for cold water in pools,[20] as perhaps does Suetonius: *refotus saepius calidis piscinis ac tempore aestiuo niuatis*; 'he was frequently refreshed by warm baths, and, in the summer time, by such as were cooled with snow',[21] though the cold water seems to have been confined to the summer for the sybaritic emperor!

With regard to depth as a feature more widely, Auberger tells us that the pool at Delphi was 1.8m deep and at Nemea it was 1m,[22] but we also find that the *natatio* of the fortress baths of *Legio II Augusta* at *Isca* (Caerleon) had a deep end sloping to 1.6m, the sloping bottom being a rare feature.[23] All of these depths are sufficient for serious swimming, even diving, particularly in the latter case. The areas of the pools differ too. Yegül tells us that the pool at Lugdunum was unusually large, at 6m by 11m,[24] and Swaddling and Drees maintain that Olympia's pool was 'unique in classical Greece' at 24m by 16m, 1.6m deep, also being rectangular and in the open air,[25] but we find plenty of larger pools, such as Nero's at 38m by 26m and the one at Ain el Hamman at 13.8m by 10.05m, 1.45m deep, both rectangular pools. There may be a tendency for pools to be larger during the Principate but without analysing every pool it is difficult to substantiate this generalisation.

---

[16]   Cunliffe 2004
[17]   Cunliffe 1969, 95-100
[18]   Cunliffe 1969,100-103
[19]   Cunliffe 1969,103-106
[20]   Mehl 1927
[21]   Suetonius, *Nero*, 27
[22]   Auberger 1996, 56
[23]   Zienkiewicz 1986, 130-137
[24]   Yegül 1992
[25]   Swaddling 1980, 30; Drees 1968

The shape of pools also differs, normally being rectangular but also coming in the form of a circle, as with Moselle, with a 17.59m diameter; oval; or apsidal, which can all still be practical if the size of the pool allows sufficient movement and also, as Vitruvius points out, the capacity is sufficient: *Magnitudines autem balneorum videntur fieri pro copia hominum.* 'The size of the baths must depend upon the size of the population.'[26]

The information presented thus far has only revealed that swimming took place in built swimming pools; this is clearly not the whole truth and Yegül, for one, certainly shows due reservation about this. However, he does take the argument a step further, writing that 'Swimming was a popular sport among the Romans, but it is hard to know if it was done in the baths' even going so far as to maintain that serious swimming was practised more in the sea or in rivers.[27] In fact the use of oil, mentioned on numerous occasions in ancient literature, supports swimming in fresh water but not how often it occurred. Horace tells us that olive oil was employed before swimming,[28] which suggests that oiling was a necessary preliminary to swimming in rivers or seas due to the temperature, if not for religious ritual: *simul unctos Tiberinis umeros lavit in undis* 'When he [Hebrus] washes his shoulders glistening with oil in Tiber's waves'. However, Decker and Thullier write about the '*calmes*' of a basin of water, natural or man-made,[29] as does Rutilius Namatianus,[30] which suggests that man-made pools, of which there is plenty of evidence, or natural pools were preferable for swimming to rivers or the ocean. This would support the building of pools, as they would not have continued to be built if they were not used and, like temples and theatres, they are both tangible and explicit evidence, not only for the activity itself but also for its prominence in ancient society.

Returning to the definition of an ancient swimming pool, van Leeuwen warns us, when discussing swimming pools, that 'particularly with regard to Roman *thermae*, swimming is often confused with adventurous bathing. Most *frigidaria* (the German *Bewegungsbad* comes closest to their original meaning) were hardly deeper than 1-1.1m, encouraging a swimming style that children tend to practice when they are not yet able to go into the deep – 'swimming with ground contact'.[31] However, based upon what we have now learned about Bath and as one looks at bathing facilities, *gymnasia,* and pools across the Roman Empire and Greece, one can see that this vast generalisation is just that, a generalisation. Depth is indeed an important factor in distinguishing a swimming pool from a bath but it is by no means the only feature and, as Nielsen points out, a *natatio* could in fact be 1-2m in depth or have varying depths,[32] and depth itself, amongst other features, varies so much that there are many contradictory off-hand statements about the 'standard' ancient swimming pool. According to Tzachou-Alexandri, 'Swimming pools were used in antiquity [... although] Swimming was not included in the contests of Classical athletics [...] The most representative example is the swimming pool in the gymnasium at Delphi which was round, with a diameter of 10m and a depth of about 1.90m. It is thought that the Lyceum at Athens had a swimming pool, and also other gymnasia will have had them for the athletes.'[33]

---

[26] Vitruvius, *De Arch.* 5. 10
[27] Yegül 1992, 37
[28] Horace, *Od.* III.xii
[29] Decker and Thullier 2004, 170
[30] Rutilius Namatianus, *De Reditu suo*, lines 245-8
[31] van Leeuwen 1998, 17
[32] Nielsen 1992, vol I
[33] Tzachou-Alexandri 1988, 37

The pools at Olympia, Pompeii, Bath, and even Tunisia tell a different story, particularly in terms of the shape of an ancient swimming pool. However, the idea that ancient pools were connected to the *gymnasia* and *palaestra* may be correct and Mehl tells us these were the first kind,[34] although they can also be found locally at quite an early date in the Roman Empire, for example the *Piscina Publica* at Rome.[35] Perhaps serious swimming pools, as opposed to bathing pools, were for the most part only found at athletic centres, not just because of depth but because of heating too: Vitruvius tells us that heat is an important aspect for choosing the location of baths,[36] but the pool at Delphi and many others, except ones in the North due to inclement climate, were outdoors or unroofed, such as the pools of Agrippa, Caracalla, Conimbriga in Portugal, and North Africa. Maecenas may have built the first indoor heated pool in Rome,[37] but that pool and Pliny the Younger's private warm pool were a luxury, as even 'Open-air swimming-pools [in the Northern regions of the empire] were also soon abandoned, without, it seems, normally being replaced by indoor pools; the warm swimming-pools – *calidae piscinae* – which were a luxury feature, are not seen in these regions.'[38]

In the Classical world, swimming pools could be used as baths, as at Side where the pool acts additionally as a *frigidarium*, or they can be separate as is true of most other Western Anatolian pools. The number of pools varies between different bath complexes: thus in the Baths of Trajan in Rome there is a single, 50m length *natatio,* while at Gafsa, a Trajanic colony, there are two open air central pools, with the East pool measuring 15m by 6.5m and the other, a trapedzoidal pool, measuring 19m by 16 m. The *natationes* are different sizes and shapes: circular at Delphi but rectangular at Olympia and at most other complexes (Nielsen 1992, 11). Some pools were roofed as at Bath, and for some temperature was a consideration, as at the Baths of Agrippa in Rome, where one was warm and the other cold. Moreover, some pools were public, while others, as stated above, were private.

The only discernible factor common to ancient swimming pools is that they all had steps, although baths did too. However, their name differs from that of a bath and, in the Greek world, the pools were linked to *palaestrae* rather than bathing facilities, thus highlighting the sport element, where for the Romans the pool might be connected either to a *palaestra* also, as at *Le palais du Miroir* in Saint-Romain-en-Gal, measuring 169m by 19m, or at a bath complex where it usually performed no other use, as was the case of the Lucas Bath at Bath, or the pool at the Baths of Caracalla, Rome. If one were asked to pick a typical ancient pool, it might be the *Aquae Flavianae* (Aïn El Hamman), in Tunisia, which is an open air pool, rectangular in shape, 13.8m by 10.05m, 1.45m deep, with steps at three corners. However, as today, there were novelty shaped swimming pools, like the one at Herculaneum, in the centre of the *palaestra*, measuring c.49m by 31m, with an intersecting arm, to produce a shape like a Christian cross, with fountain jets at its ends, a central bronze sculpture, and a deeper rectangular pool at one end, perpendicular to the long arm.[39] In conclusion, the design of an ancient swimming pool depended upon its usage and whether swimming was regarded as merely an adjunct to bathing or as a more serious activity per se in that particular location.

---

[34] Mehl 1927, 56
[35] Decker and Thullier 2004, 169
[36] Vitruvius, *De Arch.* 5. 10
[37] Dio 55, 7, 6
[38] Nielsen 1992, 84
[39] Deiss 1985

Physical and cultural forms of swimming

It is time to turn to the activity, swimming itself, having discussed the great variety of ancient facilities in which it took place. It is by no means entirely anachronistic to liken Greek and Roman swimming to modern forms, in view of the fact that the ancient civilisations and our own are akin to each other in many other ways, including architecturally, linguistically, and philosophically.

Swimming permeated Classical society in many different ways. It is referenced in literature, with Homeric references, for example in the *Iliad* where the Trojans rush into the river Xanthus;[40] in mythology, there is the tale of Hero and Leander, recounted by Ovid in his *Heroides*, and actually re-enacted in amphitheatres: *Quod nocturna tibi, Leandre, pepercerit unda desine mirari: Caesaris unda fuit.* 'Do not be surprised, Leander, that the sea spared you; it was Caesar's sea.'[41] In both major and minor literature, there is evidence for swimming, which either takes priority, as with the story of Julius Caesar escaping across a river single-handed, cited below, or is mentioned only in passing as by Ovid when he writes of Scylla swimming after her beloved Minos,[42] and by Homer when he describes Odysseus swimming to safety at the advice of Leukothea: ἀταρ χειρεσσι νεων ἐπιμαιεο νοστου γαιης φαιηκων, ὁθι τοι μοῖρ᾽ ἐστιν ἀλυξαι 'but by swimming with your hands strive to reach the land of the Phaeacians, where it is your fate to escape'.[43]

In art there are depictions on Greek vases, as shown in Gardiner;[44] the famous diver statue, even a Greek coin, from Galatia, of Orontes swimming, figured in Mehl's pictorial catalogue.[45] There is the early fifth century Tomb of the Diver from Poseidonia (Paestum) the underside of the lid of which shows a naked youth plunging from a diving board into a pool beneath,[46] while swimmers are sometimes shown with sea-creatures, actual or mythological, on mosaics from Roman baths, for example the caldarium of the House of the Menander, Pompeii, of c.40-20 B.C.[47] and in the central hall of the Baths of Neptune, Ostia dating from A.D. 139.[48]

In other societies in the ancient world, swimming was clearly regular activity as well. Etruscan art shows people swimming in paintings on tomb walls, on vases, on relief carvings, and as revealed by bronze figures and other daily objects from about the sixth Century B.C.[49] Early Sicilian *kolymbethrai* are mentioned by Diodorus Siculus.[50] In Egypt, even the Pharaohs were expected to know how to swim and so their children were taught at an early age.[51] Swimming seems to have been a significant aspect of Egyptian life too, shown by their having a hieroglyph referring to water and a goddess of swimming, Wadjet, as well as by the Osiris cult contest

---

[40] Homer, *Iliad*, XXI. 7-11
[41] Martial, Liber de Spectaculis, 25
[42] Ovid, *Met.* 8 140ff
[43] Homer, *Od.* V. 333ff.
[44] Gardiner 1930, fig. 61
[45] Mehl 1927
[46] Pedley 1990,89-94,pl.VII
[47] Dunbabin 1999,57 and 59, fig.57
[48] Dunbabin 1999,61-3,fig.62
[49] Olivová 1984
[50] Nielsen 1992, vol I, 11
[51] Decker 1975

between Horus and Seth 'which was to be decided by a feat of underwater endurance'.[52] Eastern influence is an important factor in understanding this topic, as according to Boutros at least, there was a link between Tyre and Olympia, where Baal Shamim, a god similar to Zeus, was worshipped, the first Olympic games being held in his honour c.1600-1200 B.C. and so being borrowed from the East.[53] The Amrit games, described in Egyptian texts, show that worship of Baal even included water sports.

Unfortunately, evidence for the practical side of swimming is not as forthcoming, and whilst we have some evidence of different strokes, for example, it is still uncertain whether the Romans and Greeks swam in unisex pools and whether they wore clothes or not. We have brief references to swimming clothes in the later empire,[54] and we have the facts that swimmers used oil to conserve heat and that because many pools were connected with baths and gymnasia, where nudity was regular, nude swimming was still probable, but we can at best surmise until further evidence is found.

Where women are concerned, whilst we do not have ratios of men to women, we have clear, varied evidence that women at all levels of society swam, such as the story of Agrippina when she was the victim of an attempted murder: *sed ut diversa omnia nandoque evasisse eam comperit* 'on learning that everything had gone wrong and that she had escaped by swimming';[55] and the story of the equally proficient Cloelia, who not only competently swam across the Tiber but also led a group of female captives away from the enemy Etruscans, as recounted by Livy.[56] Both Nausicaa[57] and Semele[58] were competent in the water, though they are described rather as bathing than as swimming. Suetonius describes prostitutes in a passage which also alludes to the 'leisure' aspect of swimming.[59] Pausanias also writes of Hydna, being depicted as being a diver from a great diving father, although it is unclear whether it is her skill or her sex which makes her stand out in this passage.[60]

Another important practical issue in the case of swimming is how it was taught. There are very few references to teaching, and there is no 'Digby guide' to it, which might mean that it was not regarded as important, or alternatively that it was as habitual as walking.[61] The references we do find are about parents, slaves, and the army teaching Romans and Greeks how to swim.[62] Thus Vegetius writes *natandi usum aestivis mensibus omnis aequaliter debet tiro condiscere. Non enim semper pontibus flumina transeuntur*; 'Every recruit without exception should in the summer months learn the art of swimming, for rivers are not always crossed by bridges';[63] Suetonius notes, taking on board Morgan's argument[64] that it is 'swimming' and not 'note-making' which Suetonius means: *Nepotes et litteras et natare aliaque rudimenta per se*

[52] Olivová 1984, 49
[53] Boutros 1981
[54] Mehl 1927, 60
[55] Suetonius, *Nero* XXXIV
[56] Livy, II xiii.6
[57] Homer, *Odyssey* VI. 96
[58] Nonnos VII. 184-9
[59] Suetonius, *Domitian* XXII
[60] Pausanias, X xix 1
[61] Gardiner, 1930, 93
[62] Mehl 1927
[63] Vegetius, I, 10
[64] Morgan 1974

plerum que docuit, ac nihil aeque elaboravit quam ut imitarentur chirographum suum; 'He himself taught his grandsons to read, to swim, and many other skills, particularly insisting that they take his handwriting as their model.'[65] Ovid also remarks *hic artem nandi praecipit* 'that one teaches swimming',[66] despite the fact that swimming is listed with dubious entertainments such as gambling. These quotations all substantiate Mehl's point and show that swimming was, indeed, taught.

A teaching aid which many Romans and Greeks used was the floatation device. Horace's father says to his son *simul ac duraverit aetas membra animumque tuum, nabis sine cortice* 'When years have brought strength to body and mind, you will swim without the cork.'[67] Plautus writes of rush floats: *quasi pueri qui nare discunt scirpea inditur ratis, /qui laborent minus, facilius ut nent et moveant manus*, 'Just as a float of bulrushes is placed beneath boys who are learning to swim, by means of which they may labour less, so as to swim more easily and move their hands.'[68] Caesar apparently used bladders himself: *laboris ultra fidem patiens erat...si flumina morarentur, nando traiciens vel innixus inflatis utribus*. 'He was of incredible powers of endurance...swimming the rivers which barred his path or crossing them on inflated skins.'[69] There are also Eastern reliefs showing the use of floats: 'On an Assyrian relief two men are swimming fully clad; one is using an inflated skin, the other a swimming stroke rather like modern crawl. On another relief there are three naked men, one sitting on the shore blowing up a bladder, one swimming with a bladder, and one doing the crawl.'[70]

The depictions of swimming strokes are also very important when trying to discern how the Greeks and Romans swam, for they not only show their methods but also how developed the activity had become. Front crawl is well attested and features in one of the oldest known swimming pictures in the world, from Egypt in the fifth century B.C.[71] Mehl states that sidestroke and treading water were common too. The other strokes, however, seem to vary in frequency. Breaststroke is described by Statius, of Leander swimming: *in latus ire manus mutatur usque videtur/ brachia, nec siccum speres in stamina crinem*; 'His hands seem to move sideways, he seems about to alternate his arms, you would think his hair in the thread would not be dry';[72] by Nonnus, with Semele bathing with 'paddling hands' or χεῖρας ἐρετμώσασα and στερνον ἐπιστορέσασα ῥεέθρῳ ποσσιν ἀμοιβαιοισιν ὀπιστερον ὤθεεν ὑδωρ. 'Breasting the current and treading the water back with alternate feet';[73] and by Manilius, whose description is quoted below. Backstroke is alluded to only by Ovid (see the section below on life-saving) and by Manilius, where he describes floating on one's back, showing confidence in the water. The stroke known as Butterfly was not officially created until 1950 according to the 'worldwide aquatics website'[74] and, according to Harris, the Greeks and Romans would not have 'practised so ugly and unnatural an exercise'.[75] Yet, we remain sceptical about the factual element of this statement. For a start, dolphins swim like this and with stories of Arion and

---

[65] Suetonius, *Div. Aug.* 64
[66] Ovid, *Trist.* 2, 485
[67] Horace, *Sat.* I.iv.120
[68] Plautus, *Aul.* 595-6
[69] Suetonius *Div. Jul.* LVII
[70] Olivová 1984, 38
[71] Mehl 1927, 96
[72] Statius, *Thebaid* VI. 542-5
[73] Nonnus, VII. 184-9
[74] http://www.worldwideaquatics.com/historyswim.htm
[75] Harris 1972, 124

the dolphin, with 'the boy on the dolphin' mosaic at Fishbourne Roman Palace, and with the dolphin zodiac of Manilius, which describes people imitating the dolphin movement, as well as the fact that people certainly dove, which involves this very wave-like movement, it strikes us as implausible that people would not swim like this also.

Sport

We will now explore the different cultural forms that swimming took in ancient society, beginning by discussing swimming as a sport, which it must be considered to be, based primarily upon the explicit reference to its competitive nature by Pausanias:

> πλησιον δε αὐτοῦ Διονυσου ναος Μελαναιγιδος· τουτῳ μουσικῆς ἀγῶνα κατα ἐ τος ἑκαστον ἀγουσι, και ἁμιλλης κολυμβου και πλοιων τιθεασιν ἆθλα·

> Near the latter is a temple of Dionysus of the Black Goatskin. In his honour every year they hold a competition in music, and they offer prizes for swimming-races and boat-races.[76]

Here κολυμβου could refer either to swimming or diving but it is difficult to establish how well the two activities were distinguished in the ancient world, and diving will not be discussed here except underwater in relation to work, although no doubt people did both for leisure if not sport. The event is annual. Hermione is situated on a very sheltered bay at the extremity of the Argolid, and 'so admirably adapted as a site for swimming races and for races of small boats'.[77] Pausanias remarks on many facts and anecdotes briefly on his virtual tour of the coast, without much comment or opinion, as with his list of sanctuaries and his note on sharks round the Methana peninsula, which are dangerous to bathers - another swimming reference. Moreover, the reference here to this sporting event is in passing. All of this collectively suggests that competitive swimming was a common event, despite Golden's statement to the contrary: 'We may be reminded that there is very little evidence for swimming races.'[78]

Either Pausanias has little time or inclination to go into too much detail, or, as today we do not advertise all local sports events unless they become national or even international, like the Olympics. Furthermore, the Olympic events seem to have been a fun form of martial training, of which swimming was not prominent for the Greeks, and they seem to have descended, as a tradition, from Homer's funeral games as featured in the *Iliad*. The Romans did not have their own equivalent to the Olympics and so would not publicise their own local sporting events much either. Moreover, as swimming is to an extent an everyday activity, as it still is for us, it is appropriate to expect a certain lack of reference to swimming in the Classical world, just as one would not expect to constantly read about Romans and Greeks washing their clothes, playing board games, or shopping, and to argue *ex silentio* can be quite dangerous when discussing the past.

---

[76] Pausanias, II. xxxv.1
[77] Gardner 1881
[78] Golden 1998, 8

Another explicit reference to swimming races, which is often ignored, despite its less ambiguous nature is the race described by Nonnus, between two friends Calamos and Carpos, which unfortunately ends in tragedy:

> καὶ διερῆς βαλβῖδος ἔην δρόμος· ἤρισαν ἄμφω, τίς τινα νικήσειεν, ὅπως παλινόστιμος ἔλθῃ ὄχθης ἀμφοτέρης διδυμάονα νύσσαν ἀμείβων γαῖαν ἐς ἀ ντιπεραίαν ἐρεσσομένων παλαμάων. Καὶ προχοὴν ὁδὸν εἶχεν·

> 'The race began from its watery starting-point; the match was, which could beat which to swim there and back while their hands paddled them, passing round at the turning-points on each bank, first one, then crossing to the other side. The flowing water was their way;'[79]

There is also the race between Dionysus and Ampelos described by Nonnos:

'Try a third match, swim against your comrade Bacchos and see if you can beat him!'[80] Whilst Nonnus is writing fiction, the fact that swimming races have been described suggests that they may have been more common than our lack of evidence would imply. The evidence of swimming races then, albeit exiguous, means that one must disregard the statement made in the *Real Encyclopädie der Klassischen Altertumswissenschaft*, that swimming was '*nur als Brauchkunst, nicht als Sport wie bei uns*'.[81] We do have to be slightly sceptical of its prominence as a sport, as Golden warns: 'Pausanias' statement about the matches at Hermione appears to be the only firm evidence for organised swimming events in antiquity',[82] but as we have seen, races are mentioned by Pausanias and Nonnus, and there are other references to competitive swimming such as Horace's *Ode* III vii on Enipeus:

> *quamvis non alius flectem equum sciens*
> *aeque conspicitur gramine Martio,*
> *nec quisquam citus aeque*
> *Tusco denatat alveo.*
> 'Although on the Campus Martius you will see
> nobody so adept at managing a horse
> and nobody swimming so fast
> down Tiber's course.'

and Pliny (in *Ep.* 9.33) on Hippo, Africa:

> *Adiacet navigabile stagnum; ex hoc in modum fluminis aestuarium emergit, quod vice alterna, prout aestus aut repressit aut impulit, nunc infertur mari, nunc redditur stagno. Omnis hic aetas piscandi navigandi atque etiam natandi studio tenetur, maxime pueri, quos otium lususque sollicitat. His gloria et virtus altissime provehi: victor ille, qui longissime ut litus ita simul natantes reliquit.*

---

[79] Nonnus, XI. 406-426
[80] Nonnus, XI. 7-16
[81] Mehl 1938, 1
[82] Golden 1998, 117

'it stands upon a navigable lake communicating with an estuary in the form of a river, which alternately flows into the lake, or into the ocean, according to the ebb and flow of the tide. People of all ages amuse themselves here with fishing, sailing, or swimming; especially boys, whom love of play brings to the spot. With these it is a fine and manly achievement to be able to swim the farthest; and he that leaves the shore and his companions at the greatest distance gains the victory.'[83]

These are all quotations which imply that swimming was a competitive activity, and it would seem careless to discount swimming as a sport: '*noch war das Wettschwimmen ein Bestandteil der grossen hellenischen oder römischen Feste*'.[84] Furthermore, 'Given that Pausanias is of necessity selective in his descriptions',[85] he *does* mention the swimming competition, which could mean that this race is either important or unusual. Either way, it does exemplify at least one ancient swimming race, which can help to classify the activity as a sport, and it does help to show how significant swimming was at least for the Greeks.

Martial

Swimming even constitutes a part of routine army exercise, as Vegetius points out. However, when Olivová discusses the Greek military – and it must be the Greeks, as we can already see that swimming was important in the Roman army – the writer points out that 'There is no record of the inclusion of swimming in the training schedules' but concludes that, since Herodotus pins the Greek success in the Battle of Salamis to their ability to swim, as opposed to the Persians, swimming must have been an active part of education to some degree, if not prescribed by the army or naval forces:[86]

> ἅτε γὰρ νέειν ἐπιστάμενοι, τοῖσι αἱ νέες διεφθείροντο, καὶ μὴ ἐν χειρῶν νόμῳ ἀ πολλύμενοι, ἐς τὴν Σαλαμῖνα διένεον. τῶν δε βαρβάρων οἱ πολλοὶ ἐν τῇ θαλάσσῃ διεφθάρησαν νέειν οὐκ ἐπιστάμενοι.

> 'For since they [the Greeks] could swim, they who lost their ships, yet were not slain in hand-to- hand fight, swam across to Salamis; but the greater part of the foreigners were drowned in the sea, not being able to swim.'[87]

Vegetius is an important source for military training of the Romans and tells us that not only about the origin of the *Campus Martius* but that all soldiers and even their horses had to learn to swim:

> *Non solum autem pedites sed et equites ipsosque equos vel lixas, quos galearios vocant, ad natandum exercere percommodum est, ne quid imperitis, cum necessitas incumbit, eveniat.*

---

[83] Pliny the Younger, *Ep.* 9.33; http://www.bartleby.com/9/4/1107.html
[84] Mehl 1927, 105
[85] Arafat 1996, 37
[86] Olivová 1984, 125
[87] Herodotus, VIII.89

'It is highly advantageous to train not just infantry but cavalry and their horses and grooms, whom they call *galearii,* to swim as well, lest they be found incapable when an emergency presses.'[88]

Suetonius' following depiction of Caesar swimming away from the enemy is a good illustration of the necessity of this skill, as mentioned by Vegetius, and it further shows us to what degree swimming was classed as important, as here Caesar is to be admired for his swimming prowess:

> *conpulsus in scapham pluribus eodem praecipitantibus, cum desiluisset in mare, nando per ducentos passus evasit ad proximam navem, elata laeva, ne libelli quos tenebat madefierent, paludamentum mordicus trahens, ne spolio pateretur hostis.*

> 'When many others threw themselves into the same boat, he plunged into the sea, and after swimming for two hundred paces, got away to the nearest ship, holding up his left hand all the way, so as not to wet some papers which he was carrying, and dragging his cloak after him with his teeth, to keep the enemies from getting it as a trophy.'[89]

Not only were great leaders and emperors good swimmers but also their auxiliaries and notably the Batavians, as Tacitus and Dio tell us: *erat et domi delectus eques, praecipuo nandi studio, arma equosque retinens integris turmis Rhenum perrumpere* 'They had also at home a select body of cavalry, who practised with special devotion the art of swimming, so that they could stem the stream of the Rhine with their arms and horses, without breaking the order of their squadrons.'[90]

> *Οὕτω γαρ καλῶς ἤσκητο το στρατιωτικον αὐτῷ ὥστε και το ἱππικον τῶν καλουμενων Βαταουων τον Ἰστρον μετα τῶν ὁπλων διενηξαντο.*

> 'So excellently, indeed, had his soldiers been trained that the cavalry of the Batavians, as they were called, swam the Ister with their arms.'[91]

Thucydides adds to the picture by describing how, in wartime, divers were required to free their city, by destroying the wooden stakes set up by the Syracusans against the Athenian ships: *κατακολυμβῶντες ἐξεπριον* 'diving under, they sawed them off',[92] and he also describes, in another situation, how:

> *ἐσενεον δε και κατα τον λιμενα κολυμβηται ὑφυδροι, καλῳ διῳ ἐν ἀσκοῖς ἐ φελκοντες μηκωνα μεμελιτωμενην και λινου σπερμα κεκομμενον.*

> 'Divers also swam in underwater from the harbour, dragging behind them by a cord skins containing poppyseed mixed with honey and pounded linseed.'[93]

---

[88] Vegetius, I.10
[89] Suetonius, *Div. Jul.* LXIV
[90] Tacitus *Historiae* 4.12
[91] Dio, 69.9
[92] Thucydides, VII. 25. 6
[93] Thucydides, IV. 26. 8

Religious ritual

Moving on from the martial sphere, an argument has been posited for connecting swimming with religion: 'the references are generally restricted to gods, heroes, deified emperors, and other mythical beings',[94] and Golden writes on the swimming race in Pausanias that 'this [is] only in connection with the cult and myth of Dionysus'.[95] However, there is reason to be sceptical about this categorisation of swimming for the following reasons. Dionysus, as mentioned later, was himself often associated with water. Furthermore, the Olympic Games were borrowed from Asia Minor as a religious festival,[96] similar to the funeral games illustrated by Homer in the *Iliad* and by later writers, which both become primarily sporting events and even an act of political diplomacy, in that Greek peace treaties tended to be contracted at festivals. Nor should we discount the race in Nonnus, which is held between two friends, with no mention of the gods, which implies that it cannot be any aspect of divine ritual. In short, whilst, as with many other activities, swimming may be *connected* with religion, it cannot be described solely as a religious act, especially in view of the fact that it takes on so many different forms.

Medical

So far, then, swimming has been seen as a sport, a military training exercise, and a religious activity but what of its other uses? Celsus, for one, describes swimming as a good exercise from a medical point of view, especially in warm water, so that the body can be supported by the water, as well as the limbs being soothed by the heat. This happens at *Aquae Sulis*, although cold water may also be recommended in summer for other medical purposes.[97]

Leisure

Swimming is also seen as a leisurely activity and a good chance to cool off after sports, 'They still swam in the Tiber after their sports in Cicero's time and later':[98]

> *Habes hortos ad Tiberim ac diligenter eo loco paratos, quo omnis iuventus natandi causa venit; hinc licet condiciones cotidie legas;*

> 'You own pleasure-gardens on the Tiber carefully sited where all the young men like to come for a swim. You can pick up whatever you fancy there any day you like'[99]

and Tisander, a famous boxer, regularly swam for exercise.

Baiae, the coastal resort for wealthy Romans, saw sea-bathing akin to that which took place in the Georgian period, and it is alluded to in the poetry of Propertius:

[94] van Leeuwen 1998, 17
[95] Golden 1998, 8
[96] Boutros 1981
[97] Celsus, 3, 24, 5
[98] Balsdon 1969, 160
[99] Cicero *Pro Caelio* 36

tu modo quam primum corruptas desere Baias:
multis ista dabunt litora discidium,

'As soon as you may, abandon decadent Baiae:
Those beaches bring so many hostile separations'.[100]

On the subject of leisure, it may be interesting to note that in the imperial period, a water-landscaping craze took off and 'Water as a life-bestowing element is the foundation for landscapes with lush vegetation and many animals',[101] for example the water staircase at Casa dell' Efebo in Pompeii, reminiscent of Nero's *Domus Aurea*, and Tiberius's sea grotto at his Sperlonga villa. This sea grotto was large and deep enough to sail around, and therefore possibly to swim in, and Suetonius recounts a lewd and surely fabricated scandal which concerns the emperor swimming with young boys on his hide-away in Capri.[102] The Sperlonga grotto, which had an island *triclinium* and detached fish-tanks, has produced no evidence to support that either the emperor or anyone else swam here. There is some evidence for swimming as an element of public entertainment in late antiquity, when ' it became fashionable, particularly in the Greek east, to convert the orchestra of a theatre into a waterproof basin, and to use it for aquatic shows, perhaps a sort of combination of mime and synchronised swimming'.[103]

Cleansing

Just as with other activities, where sometimes it could be felt more of a task than a pleasure, there are references to swimming as a part of the act of cleaning oneself, as in the case of Nausicaa and her attendants in the *Odyssey* and in the scathing essay of Seneca the Younger, *De Brevita Vitae*, (12, 6):

> *Ne illos quidem inter otiosos numeraueris qui[...] quos quando lauari debeant, quando natare,*
> *quando cenare alius admonet:*

> 'And I would not count these among the leisured class either—the men [...] who are reminded by someone else when they must bathe, when they must swim, when they must dine'.[104]

Livelihood

Furthermore, swimming could actually form as part of a paid job like sponge-fishing, as mentioned by Oppian,[105] wherein divers put white oil into their mouths to use when they reach the bottom in order to light up the sponges. A passage in Herodotus, writing about Scyllias of Scione, shows that the ability to dive was in demand, however sceptical Herodotus may be:

---

[100] Propertius, 1.11. 28-9
[101] Wikander 2000, 453
[102] Suetonius, *Tiberius* 44
[103] Wilson 1997, 157
[104] Seneca the Younger, *De Brevita Vitae* 12, 6; http://www.forumromanum.org/literature/seneca_younger/brev_e.html#12
[105] Oppian, *Hal.* V 634-50

δυτης τῶν τοτε ἀνθρωπων ἀριστος, ὁς και ἐν τῇ ναυηγιῃ τῇ κατα Πηλιον
γενομενη πολλα μεν ἐσωσε τῶν χρηματων τοῖσι Περσῃσι, πολλα δε και αὐτος
περιεβαλετο·...
θωμαζω δε εἰ τα λεγομενα ἐστι ἀληθεα. λεγεται γαρ ὡς ἐξ Ἀφετεων δυς ἐς
την θαλασσαν οὐ προτερον ἀνεσχε πριν ἠ ἀπικετο ἐπι το Ἀρτεμισιον, σταδιους
μαλιστα κη τουτοις ἐς ὀγδωκοντα δια τῆς θαλασσης διεξελθων...
περι μεντοι τουτου γνωμη μοι ἀποδεδεχθω πλοιῳ μιν ἀπικεσθαι ἐπι το Ἀ
ρτεμισιον.

'he was the best diver of the time, and in the ship-wreck at Pelion he had saved for the
Persians much of their possessions and won much withal for himself; [but he decides
to desert to the Greeks]...
If the story be true it is marvellous indeed; for it is said that he dived into the sea at
Aphetae and never rose above it till he came to Artemisium, thus passing underneath
the sea for about eighty furlongs...
it is my opinion [...] that he came to Artemisium in a boat'.[106]

This last statement is understandable when Mehl points out that the distance would have
been an astonishing 15km.[107]

Life-saving

Interestingly, even life-saving is mentioned in an ancient source, which of course requires the
ability to swim confidently: *brachia da lasso potius prendenda natanti,/ nec pigeat mento supposuisse
manum*. 'Rather extend an arm to the weary swimmer's grasp; repent not of supporting his
chin with your hand'.[108]

Astronomical

Swimming, though, does not stop at being a necessary life-skill, or a sport, for instance, but
is described in astronomical terms by Manilius, in the most complete account of ancient
swimming there is, according to Harris. We find this passage to be a very beautiful description
and one which shows a great deal of respect for the activity of swimming:

> Nam, velut ipse citis per labitur aequora pinnis
> [...]
> Et sinibus vires sumit fluctumque figurat,
> Sic, venit ex illo quisquis, volitabit in undis.
> Nunc alterna ferens in lentos bracchia tractus
> Conspicuous franget spumanti limite pontum
> Et plausa resonabit aqua, nunc aequore mersas
> Diducet palmas furtive biremis in ipso,
> [...]
> Aut immota ferens in tergus membra latusque

---

[106] Herodotus, VIII.8
[107] Mehl 1927
[108] Ovid, *Ex Ponto*, II.vi.13

Non onerabit aquas summusque accumbet in undis
Pendebitque super, totus sine remige velum.
Illis in ponto iucundum est quaerere pontum,
Corporaque immergunt undis ipsumque sub antris
Nerea et aequoreas conantur visere Nymphas,
Exportantque maris praedas et rapta profundo
Naufragia atque imas avidi scrutantur haerenas.
[...]
Adnumeres etiam illa licet cognate per artem
Corpora, quae valido salient excussa petauro
Alternosque cient motus, elatus et ante
Nunc iacet atque huius casu suspenditur ille,
Membrave per flammas orbesque emissa flagrantis,
Quae delphina suo per inane imitantia motu
Molliter ut liquidis per humum ponuntur in undis
[...]
At, si deficient artes, remanebit in illis
Materies tamen apta; dabit natura vigorem
Atque alacris cursus campoque volantia membra.

'For just as the dolphin is propelled by its swift fins through the waters [...] and derives momentum from its undulating course, wherein it reproduces the curl of the waves, so whoever is born of it will speed through the sea. Now lifting one arm after the other to make slow sweeps he will catch the eye as he drives a furrow of foam through the sea and will sound afar as he thrashes the waters; now like a hidden two-oared vessel he will draw apart his arms beneath the water; [...] else, keeping his limbs motionless and lying on his back or side, he will be no burden to the waters but will recline upon them and float, the whole of him forming a sail-boat not needing oarage. Other men take pleasure in looking for the sea in the sea itself: they dive beneath the waves and try to visit Nereus and the sea nymphs in their cave; they bring forth the spoils of the sea and the booty that wrecks have lost to it, and eagerly search the sandy bottom. [...] With them you may also reckon men of cognate skill who leap in the air, thrown up from the powerful spring-board, and execute a see-saw movement, he who was first lifted on high now finding himself on the ground and by his descent raising the other aloft; or hurl their limbs through fire and flaming hoops, imitating the dolphin's movement in their flight through space, and land as gently on the ground as they would in the watery waves [...] Even if the Dolphin's sons lack these skills, they will yet possess a physique suited to them; nature will endow them with strength of body, briskness of movement, and limbs which fly over the plain.'[109]

Not only does this passage give details on swimming strokes, as discussed beforehand, but it is a great example of literature on the activity, which eloquently shows the beauty of swimming, and it even gives us a new category of underwater diving: ancient marine archaeology.

To summarise, we can see that swimming was such a varied, developed and important activity in the ancient world that the topic makes for interesting reading, despite its striking

---

[109] Manilius, *Astronomica* 5.419-448

similarities to its modern equivalent. Perhaps this serves as a warning to anyone who studies history, not to attempt to drive a wedge between these two societies, past and present.

Analysis of perceptions

It must be noted, therefore, that swimming was a multifarious activity and cannot simply be thought of as a military exercise, as modern conceptions are too often inclined to see it. It is not even strictly a divine ritual, as van Leeuwen would have us believe. Although two of the only three explicit references to competitive swimming are in reference to the god Dionysus, there are ancient references to Dionysus as a water god and thus this can offer an opposite, or even reciprocal meaning with regard to this activity, in that it is the water, even the swimming, element which is primarily important and not the divine ritual aspect.[110]

> o(ti d'ou monon tou oi)nou Dionuson, a)lla kai pashv u(grav fusewv E(llhnev h(gountai kurpion kai a)rxhgon, a)rkei Pindarpov martuv ei)nai legwn: dendrewn de νομον Διονυσος πολυγαθης αυχανοι, ἁγνον ψεγγος ὀπωρας.

> 'To show that the Greeks regard Dionysus as the lord and master not only of wine, but of the nature of every sort of moisture, it is enough that Pindar be our witness, when he says May gladsome Dionysus swell the fruit upon the trees, The hallowed splendour of harvest time'.[111]

Having established that swimming was important and varied for the Romans and Greeks, it is worth thinking about their individual attitudes. A case can be made, in analysing ancient swimming, for a difference in Greek and Roman perceptions of swimming. According to Harris, Horace 'makes it clear that they [the Romans] did not confine themselves to the events of the narrow Olympic programme, but combined them with other sports and with traditional Roman pursuits mainly drawn from training for war. Horace's [...] Hebrus swims in the Tiber and is an expert hunter'.[112] Harris even goes on to say that some of the games were borrowed from the Greeks to include ball games, bowling of hoops and, most importantly for our purposes, swimming.[113] It would seem that as far as the Romans were concerned, at least, the Greeks invented swimming which is true certainly of the pools. It could also be said, based on the Greek adoption of Eastern practices and the creation of Olympia, aforementioned, that the Greeks borrowed swimming from the East, which might be another argument for its significance because why borrow something you will not use?

Yet it is not just in the dates that there is a Greco-Roman distinction. The place of swimming in the respective societies was slightly different as well. For the Romans, the evidence shows that swimming had an important role in military training, leisure, and health, whereas for the Greeks it seems to have been more an activity to promote livelihood and sportsmanship. However, the two societies are not irreconcilable on this issue, as swimming affected specialised

---

[110] The website http://www.xlweb.com/heritage/skanda/dionysus.htm#Water refers to Dionysus' connection with the world of water, as does the following site in the third paragraph: http://dionysia.org/greek/dionysos/thompson/dionysos.html. Also see: http://penelope.uchicago.edu/Thayer/E/Roman/Texts/Plutarch/Moralia/Isis_and_Osiris*/b.html

[111] Plutarch, *Moralia*, Volume 5. 365

[112] Harris 1972, 57

[113] Harris 1972, 74

and daily life in both societies. The fact that swimming is such a far-reaching activity can be further illustrated by the contemptuous Greek phrase, το λεγομενον μητε γραμματα μητε νεῖν ἐπιστωνται 'they spell not neither do they swim',[114] showing how much both skills were taken for granted.[115] Furthermore, the sheer amount of primary source references to swimming suggests that 'swimming became (officially or otherwise) one of the athletic skills required of the iuventus'.[116] Moreover, as Balsdon points out, the explicit references to those who could not swim indicate that 'It is evident that most Romans were able to swim, for it was thought remarkable that Gaius Caligula could not'.[117] A prime example of this surprise, even contempt, for the non-swimmer comes from the historian Suetonius:

Sed et aliorum generum artes studiosissime et diuersissimas exercuit. Thra[e]x et auriga, idem cantor atque saltator, battuebat pugnatoriis armis, aurigabat extructo plurifariam circo;...Atque hic tam docilis ad cetera natare nesciit.

'When it came to other sorts of arts, he devoted himself with great enthusiasm to the widest variety. Taking on the roles of Thracian gladiator or charioteer, sometimes even those of singer or dancer, he would engage in battle with real weapons, and drove a chariot in circuses built in various locations...However, despite being so multi-talented he never learned to swim.'[118]

Another indication of differing attitudes, which links into this discussion about the different cultural forms of swimming, is Auberger's claim that there is a difference between '*nage et natation*', the first being the practical and utilitarian side of the activity, the second being the leisure, sport, even Roman side and '*le bain romain répond à autre chose qu'au goût grec de la propreté*'.[119] This also confirms the idea that swimming was perceived differently by the Romans and Greeks, yet important still in both cultures.

Conclusion

As can be seen, therefore, just as in modern society, swimming comes in many different forms and is just as important and serious an activity in everyday ancient society as it is in more specialist contexts, such as the martial arena or sport. Beyond other literary and archaeological sources, the fact that there were ancient swimming pools across the Roman Empire and throughout Greece remain the best and most tangible pieces of evidence for the importance of swimming, due to the permanency involved in building the pools. Hence the title of this contribution: if swimming were not a serious activity for the Romans and the Greeks, they would not have had swimming pools. The pools are indicative of the prominence and frequency of swimming in Classical society, which would have been just as lost without swimming as we would be now.

---

[114] Plato, *Legg.* 689D
[115] Olivová 1984, 125
[116] Morgan 1990, 277
[117] Balsdon 1969, 221
[118] Suetonius *Gaius* 54
[119] Auberger 1996, 61

Bibliography

Arafat 1996, K.Arafat, *Pausanias' Greece*, Cambridge: Cambridge University Press

Arcellaschi 1996, A. Arcellaschi, *Rome et la natation*, Brussels, Collection Latomus, 230

Auberger 1996, J. Auberger, Quand la nage devint natation, *Latomus*, 55, 48-62

Balsdon 1969, J. Balsdon, *Life and Leisure in Ancient Rome*, London: Bodley Head.

Bouet 1998, A. Bouet, Complexes sportifs et centres monumentaux en Occident romain: les exemples d'Orange et Vienne, *RA* (1998), 33-105

Bouet 1999, A.Bouet, *Campus* et *Juventus* dans les agglomérations secondaires des provinces occidentales, *REA*, 101 , 461-86

Boutros 1981, L.Boutros, *Phoenician Sport, its influence on the origin of the Olympic games* , Amsterdam: JC Gieben

Colvin 1878, S.Colvin, *Greek athletics, Greek religion, and Greek art at Olympia : an account of ancient usages and modern discoveries*, Liverpool.

Couch 1934, H.Couch, 'Swimming among the Greeks and Barbarians', *The Classical Journal*, Vol. 29, No. 8. (May, 1934), 609-612

Cunliffe 1969, B. Cunliffe, *Roman Bath*, Oxford: Oxford University Press for the Society of Antiquaries

Cunliffe 2004, B. Cunliffe, *Roman Bath Discovered*, Stroud: Tempus

Decker 1975, W. Decker, *Quellentexte zu Sport und Körperkultur im alten Ägypten*, Sankt Augustine: Richarz

Decker 1992, W. Decker, *Sports and Games of Ancient Egypt*, trans. A. Guttmann, London: Yale University Press

Decker and Thullier 2004, W. Decker and J. Thullier, *Le Sport dans L'antiquité*, Paris: Antiqua Picard

Deiss 1985, J. Deiss, *Herculaneum*, London: Thames and Hudson

Dorwall-Smith 1996, R. Dorwall-Smith, *Emperors and Architecture: A study of Flavian Rome*, (Brussels: Collection Latomus

Drees 1968, L. Drees, *Olympia – Gods, Artists and Athletes*, London: Pall Mall Press

Dunbabin 1999, K. M. D. Dunbabin, *Mosaics of the Greek and Roman World*, ,Cambridge, Cambridge University Press

Fagan 2002, C. Fagan, *Bathing in Public in the Roman World*, USA: University of Michigan Press

Fotinos 1971, S. Fotinos, *Olympia: brief history and complete archaeological guide*, (trans. E. Pawloff) Athens

Futrell 2006, A. Futrell, *The Roman Games*, Oxford: Blackwell

Gardiner 1910, E. Gardiner, *Greek Athletic Sports and Festivals*, London: Macmillan & co.

Gardiner 1930, E. Gardiner, *Athletics of the Ancient World*, Oxford: Clarendon Press.

Gardner 1881, P. Gardner, Boat-Races at Athens, *The Journal of Hellenic Studies*, 2:, 315-317.

Golden 1998, M. Golden, *Sport and Society in Ancient Greece*, Cambridge: Cambridge University Press.

Harris 1972 , H. Harris, *Sport in Greece and Rome*, London: Thames and Hudson.

Henig 1999, M. Henig, A new star shining over Bath, *Oxford Journal of Archaeology* 18, 419-425.

Henig 2000, M. Henig, From Classical Greece to Roman Britain: Some Hellenic themes in Provincial Art and Glyptics, in G. R. Tsetskhladze, A. J. N. W. Prag and A. M. Snodgrass, *Periplous. Papers on Classical Art and Archaeology presented to Sir John Boardman.* London, Thames and Hudson 2000, 124-135.

König 2005, J. König, *Athletics and Literature in the Roman Empire*, Cambridge: Cambridge University Press.

van Leeuwen 1998, T. van Leeuwen, *The Springboard in the Pond*, London: MIT Press.

Manderscheid 2004, H. Manderscheid, Ancient Baths and Bathing: A bibliography for the years 1988-2001, *Journal of Roman Archaeology*, supp. 55 Rhode Island.

Maniscalco 1995, F. Maniscalco, *Il Nuoto Nel Mondo Greco-Romano*, Napoli: Graphotronic Melito.

Mehl 1927, E. Mehl, *Antike Scwimmkunst*, München: Ernst Heimeran.

Mehl 1938, E.Mehl, *Realenzyklopädie der Klassischen Altertums-Wissenschaft* Stuttgart, 1-9.

Morgan 1990, C. Morgan, *Athletics and Oracles*, Cambridge: Cambridge University Press.

Morgan 1974, M. Morgan, Suetonius and Swimming: A Note on Div. Aug. 64.3, *Classical Philology*, Vol. 69, No. 4. (Oct., 1974), 276-278.

Nielsen 1992, I. Nielsen, *Thermae et Balnea: the architecture and cultural history of Roman public baths*, vol I, (Aarhus: Aarhus University Press.

Olivová 1984, V. Olivová, *Sports and Games in the Ancient World*, London: Orbis

Pedley 1990 J.G.Pedley, *Paestum. Greeks and Romans in Southern Italy*, London, Thames and Hudson

Sanders 1925, H.Sanders, 'Swimming among the Greeks and Romans', *The Classical Journal*, 20, No. 9. (Jun., 1925), 566-568.

Salmon 1969 E. Salmon, *Roman Colonization under the Republic*, London: Thames and Hudson

Sansone 1988, D. Sansone, *Greek Athletics and the Genesis of Sport*, London: University of California Press.

Swaddling 1980, J. Swaddling, *The Ancient Olympic Games*, London: British Museum.

Sweet 1987, W. Sweet, *Sport and Recreation in Ancient Greece*, Oxford: Oxford University Press.

Tzachou-Alexandri 1988, O. Tzachou-Alexandri, *Mind and Body: Athletic Contests in Ancient Greece*, Athens: National Hellenic Committee.

Watson 1969, G. Watson, *The Roman Soldier*, London: Thames and Hudson.

Wikander 2000, O. Wikander, *Handbook of Ancient Water Technology*, Netherlands: Brill.

Wilson 1997, A. Wilson, Water management and usage in Roman North Africa: a social and technological study (Oxford: D. Phil. Thesis, 1997).

Woolf 1994, G. Woolf, Becoming Roman, Staying Greek, *PCPS*, 40, 116-143.

Yegül 1992, F. Yegül, *Baths and Bathing in Classical Antiquity*, London: MIT Press.

Zanker 1990, P. Zanker, *The Power of Images in the Age of Augustus,* USA: University of Michigan Press.

Zienkiewicz 1986, J. D. Zienkiewicz, *The Legionary Fortress Baths at Caerleon I. The Buildings* Cardiff, National Museum of Wales and CADW.

'Athletics' in *Oxford Classical Dictionary*[3], (1996)

http://en.wikipedia.org/wiki/Batavians

http://en.wikipedia.org/wiki/History_of_swimming

http://en.wikipedia.org/wiki/Hero_and_Leander

http://www.worldwideaquatics.com/historyswim.htm

http://hb.syl.com/theevolutionofswimmingfromancienthistorytothe present.html

http://www.theoi.com/Cult/DemeterCult.html

http://www.tkline.freeserve.co.uk/OvidTristiaBkTwo.htm#_Toc35314589

http://www.perseus.tufts.edu/cache/perscoll_Greco-Roman.html

'Creating the Imperial Thermae' Lectures, by Dr Janet DeLaine, 2007

'The Ancient Greek Olympics' written, produced and directed by A. Thomas, Channel 4, (7pm, 28/07/07)

Acknowledgements

Jenny Amphaeris expresses warm thanks to Jo and Michael Darbyshire for all their support and encouragement; Mr Michael Clarke, a great mentor and friend; as well as Dr Katharine Clarke, Dr Janet DeLaine, Dr Andrew Wilson, Miss Barbara Levick, and Ms. S Fox, Collections Manager, Roman Baths and Pump Room, Heritage Services for their helpful suggestions and contributions to this bibliography. Martin Henig is in addition very grateful to Professor Barry Cunliffe for his encouragement even prior to beginning his research in 1967 and inviting him to contribute to his report on Roman Bath (Cunliffe 1969).

The Social Lives of Wells in Roman Britain and Beyond

James Gerrard

For those of us fortunate enough to live in the world's richest, securest and most 'developed' nations, water is a benign influence. It has been cleaned, piped and brought into our homes. Tamed by the tap (or faucet), the stream of clean water descending into the sink is ours to command with a minimum of effort. We can drink it (although many of us eschew 'tap water' in favor of bottled products of supposedly better quality or taste), cleanse our bodies with it or we can wash our car with it, water the lawns, or use it to swim in. We can even play with it in our swimming pools. This consumption of drinking water is both enormous and profligate: daily per capita estimates of usage amount to 150 litres (33 gallons) in the UK and approximately 575 litres (126 gallons) in the US.[1] Yet at the same time much of the world's population continues to survive without easy access to clean water and in many regions water stress is already exacerbating geopolitical tensions. This is the world of Sedlak's 2014 publication *Water 4.0*.

In the popular imagination, the Roman Empire is inextricably associated with hydrological engineering. Monty Python's *Life of Brian* place aqueducts, sanitation and irrigation top the list of the things that the 'People's Front of Judea' feel the Romans have brought to Jerusalem. This iteration - Water 1.0[2] - of humanity's relationship with 'dihydrogen monoxide' is one that is often consumed implicitly by scholars and laity alike. Pictures of the Pont du Gard, the Baths of Caracalla or the *Kaiserthermen* grace our text books about the Roman Empire and, as a consequence, water has become, much like it is in our modern dwellings, an over-looked part of living in the temperate provinces of the Roman Empire.

The purpose of this paper is to place the supply of water at the forefront of discussions about social life.[3] The supply of water across the Roman Empire is, of course, an enormous topic and one which cannot be dealt with in its entire multifaceted complexity here.[4] Instead, I choose to focus on the use of wells to supply water to a range of Roman sites in Britain and beyond. Even this is a tall order as recent studies have so far identified over 350 Roman period wells in Britain,[5] 200 in the Netherlands[6] and nearly 500 in the Roman province of *Raetia*.[7] In order to interpret the social lives and life-cycles of these wells, a broad range of analogies from both modern and ancient societies are utilised. These provide perspectives that show how entangled and contentious water supplies might have been in the past. Inevitably this

---

[1]   UN 2006, Fig 1.2
[2]   Sedlak 2014
[3]   for instance Roche 2001, 135-165
[4]   for instance Wikander 2000; Burgers 2001; Jones and Robinson 2005
[5]   Burgers 2001, 46
[6]   van Haasteren and Groot 2013
[7]   Albrecht 2014

approach is selective, but it goes far beyond my earlier attempts in this area,[8] and presents wells and water as a critical locus for understanding social life in the north-western provinces of the Roman Empire.

Wells, *Brunnen* and *Waterputten*

Archaeology is all about interpretation but all too often the interpretations offered for individual archaeological features remain ambiguous.[9] A pit filled with broken pottery and animal bones might be reasonably interpreted as a rubbish pit, but was the hole dug to perform this function? Perhaps the hole was dug to extract some clay to make bricks and then used fortuitously to dispose of some noisome waste. Similarly, a line of postholes might be the remnants of a fence or the wall of a building. These examples, facile though they are, remain the meat and drink of interpretation in the field. There are, of course, a wide variety of other scenarios in which specific interpretations are more or less likely. In contrast, the construction of a well leaves material traces that are relatively unambiguous and this is especially true if the well is fully excavated.

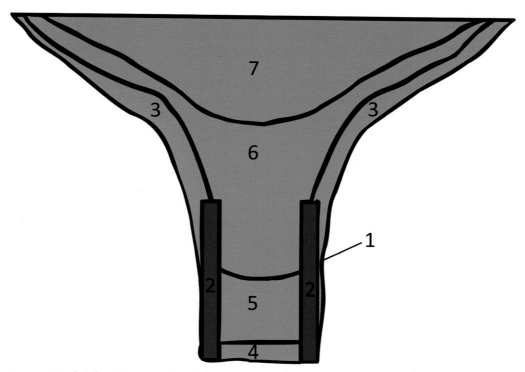

Figure 1. A sketch section showing the life-cycle of a well (after van Haasteren and Groot 2013, Figure 2). 1: construction pit; 2: lining; 3: backfill of construction pit; 4: silt during use of well; 5: abandonment deposits; 6: robbing of the lining and further abandonment deposits; 7: post-abandonment deposits.

---

[8] Gerrard 2009, 2011

[9] Roskams 2001

The construction, use and disuse of a well can each be manifested as a series of identifiable stratigraphic events (Figure 1).[10] At its very simplest the construction of a well will involve digging a deep pit or shaft that penetrates to the water table. Depending on the local geology, this well shaft may be fully or partially lined with timbers or brick or stone walling. The gap between the edge of the shaft and the lining will be backfilled with spoil leaving a well that can be capped and used. Only in exceptional circumstances, as at Coventina's Well (Northumberland),[11] do above-ground traces of well-head structures survive but occasionally silts at the bottom of the well are found to contain material associated with the use of the structure. The disuse of the well might be marked by the complete or partial robbing of its lining and its subsequent infilling through either human or natural agency. Finally, the deposits filling the well may settle over time leaving a depression at the surface. This depression may in turn be infilled either naturally or through human action long after the well itself was abandoned.

This fourfold division of the life-cycle of a well is a simplistic model. Examples can always be found that have more or less stages. Nevertheless, the simplicity underlines the model's elegance: the basic sequence of construction, use, disuse and post-abandonment are discernible at many sites across the Roman Empire, whether those sites be in Britain, Germany, or further afield. This allows the role that wells played in social life to be investigated in geographical and chronological terms.

The construction of wells

For most of human history people sourced their water from natural sources: springs, rivers, streams, pools and bogs.[12] In temperate Europe, naturally occurring water is rarely in short supply or, with a few exceptions, far away. The needs of individuals, families and communities were met by locating settlements in close proximity to a water source. Contemporary ethnography provides a powerful reminder that 'close proximity' is a relative term: today women in Africa and Asia walk on average 6km a day carrying 20kg (44lbs) of water.[13]

Wells in north-western Europe were not a Roman innovation but it seems clear that the expansion of the Roman Empire brought about the proliferation of this form of water technology. What prompted the large-scale adoption of wells? Changes in perceptions of taste and hygiene are possible. Both are culturally specific and not all groups prefer 'pure' or 'clean' water. It is claimed that some traditional societies prefer the taste of swamp water to well water[14] and pre-industrial Parisians bickered over whether well, fountain or river water made the best tasting bread.[15] Imported Mediterranean notions of water purity and hygiene[16] may have had some influence and the spread of these ideas could have had an impact on the provision of water related infrastructure. It can also be noted that the early Roman period (first and second centuries AD) saw significant changes in the forms of material culture

---

[10] van Haasteren and Groot 2014, 28-32
[11] Allason Jones and Mckay 1985
[12] Thomas 2000
[13] Loughborough University 2005
[14] Thomas 2000, 10
[15] Roche 2001, 148-149
[16] Hodge 2000a

used for styling and grooming the body,[17] and this might be related to similar changes in perceptions about hygiene.

Constructing wells could also be a response to pressure on water resources. An increasing population and *per capita* consumption might lead to a requirement for a well or wells. So might changes in the way that water rights were managed. We have only a limited and partial notion of how land tenure was organised in the peripheries of the Roman world. It does, however, seem possible that the imposition of the Roman legal system had the potential to fundamentally alter traditional socio-economic structures relating to the use and consumption of water. Given this, digging a well could provide a community with independence and water security. This latter point is important as it also allows a well to be constructed in response to an interruption in supply.

An individual, family or community who undertook to construct a well would not have done so lightly. As a starting point, a position had to be selected to locate the well. The underlying geology would play an important role in site selection and so would the height of the water table Here seasonality would play an important role. Digging a well shaft in the rainy season would encounter water higher than one dug during the dry season. Well users required a constant supply of water whatever the weather and for this reason Columella advises that wells should be dug in September at the end of the dry season so that the water table is reached at its lowest level.[18]

In towns, which were invariably sited close to rivers, and other similar locations the water table was generally relatively high and its depth could be ascertained by looking down a neighbour's well.[19] In the cramped confines of a city the main considerations would have been whether the location was suitable to the users of the well. Elsewhere topography and geology made locating the water table a more challenging task. Finding a suitable spot may have involved both the use of a water diviner (*aquilex*) and local knowledge about vegetation and rock types.

The selection of a location for a well may have had a greater significance than the purely functional concern of water supply. Given that kitchens, animals and baths all required water in considerable quantities it may be the case that structures associated with these activities would be positioned in close proximity to wells so as to minimise the effort required to transport the water. Other structures might then have to take their position from the location of the kitchens, barns and baths. If constructed at the beginning of a settlement's occupation the well would, in effect, become a cardinal point or focus to which the spatial organisation of a settlement was related.[20]

The role that a well may have played in the organisation of a settlement and its function as a source of fresh water also provides a link to the realm of the supernatural. Frontinus tells us that springs were venerated in Rome[21] and there is ample evidence that springs and wells

---

[17] Eckardt and Crummy 2008
[18] Columella, *On Agriculture* IX.3.8; Ash 1941, 135
[19] Hodge 2000b, 29
[20] Woodward and Woodward 2004, 68-70
[21] Frontinus, *Aqueducts* I.4; Bennett 1925, 339

were equivalenced in the ancient mind as ritual foci.[22] The very act of digging the well shaft and piercing the layers of geological strata - clay, rock, gravel – until fresh water welled up may thus have been an act with a variety of religious and cosmological connotations up to and beyond the classical notion of a *genius loci*. The *Calendar of 354* goes so far as to make *Luna Dies* (Monday) auspicious for the digging of wells, presumably because of the astrological association between the moon and water.[23]

Finally, once these considerations had been taken into account, the act of digging the well could begin. The size of wells varies but they are rarely more than two metres in diameter and more typically are only a metre or so wide.[24] Usually they were constructed in a circular or a square fashion, with the shape seemingly being a consequence of the lining.[25] Rock cut wells are generally circular as are wells with stone linings. In contrast, timber lined wells are usually square. The process of excavation, in all but the most benign of circumstances, would be an arduous task (as anyone who has archaeologically excavated a Roman well can testify!). Wooden spades equipped with iron blades would be the primary tool to remove softer sediments. When the digger reached a certain depth the process of excavation would become increasingly difficult, not to mention dangerous. The cramped, dark conditions would limit the ability to use tools effectively, loose sides could collapse and every bucket of spoil would have to be hauled out of the shaft. In deep shafts poor air may cause the diggers to faint and even die.[26] If rock was encountered then the shaft would have to be cut through the stone to reach the aquifer. All of these conditions and problems were encountered by twentieth-century well-diggers in Northern Ireland.[27]

Once the shaft was completed the lining would have to be installed. This might involve laying stone walling, or timber planks, or even recycling barrels if they were available. Either way, the evidence from excavated wells shows the care and attention that was devoted to this task. Carefully sawn and jointed planks are typical at many sites[28] and the stone linings of many wells are more than competently executed.[29] This may demonstrate no more than a desire on the part of the builders to create a solid and long-lasting well. Indeed, the reuse of barrels in London[30] and Oberaden,[31] to name but two examples, demonstrates that a convenient, ready-made well lining would do if available. What these linings do indicate is the need to bring more resources and skills to the task than the ability to dig a deep hole. Constructing a well was a major investment in time and labour and this remains true of traditional societies today.[32]

Once the well had been lined and the construction pit behind the lining backfilled, the end of the construction process would see various well-head structures built. These very rarely

---

[22] for instance Allason-Jones and McKay 1985; Heising 2013
[23] Salzmann 1990, Fig 12
[24] Wilmott 1982
[25] Wilmott 1982
[26] Burgers 2001, 46; Pliny, *Natural History* 31.49; Jones 1963, 409
[27] Murphy and Savage 1990
[28] for instance van Houtte *et al.* 2009; Wilmott 1982, Fig 19
[29] Heising 2013, Abb. 4
[30] Wilmott 1982, 10, 18 and 22
[31] Albrecht 1938, 19
[32] for instance Helland 1982, 250

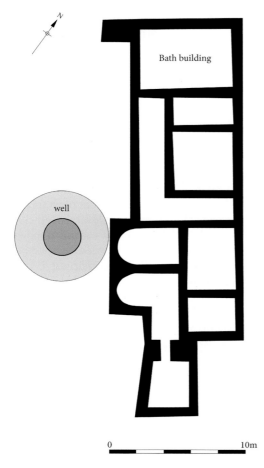

Figure 2. Plan showing the relationship between the unusually wide and deep well at Rudston and the villa's bath building (after Stead 1980, Figure 3).

survive.[33] At the most basic level we might expect a well to be planked over so that rubbish, stray animals and people did not find their way into the shaft when water was not being drawn. More typically a wall or fence to protect the well head might be anticipated. Water could then be drawn from the well using either a bucket at the end of a long rope or more complex arrangements like water lifting mechanisms.

The large number of wells that have been archaeologically investigated offer a number of insights into the processes of construction discussed above. The digging of a well shaft and its associated challenges is perhaps best exemplified by the very deep well examined during the excavation of the villa at Rudston in East Yorkshire (Stead 1980, 26-30).[34] This well was unusually large and found to be 9ft (2.75m) in diameter and 99ft (30m) deep. For virtually the entirety of its depth the shaft was cut through chalk, a reasonably soft sedimentary rock but rock nonetheless. At 69ft the archaeologists excavating the well hit the water table. With no bottom to the well shaft in sight, the excavation team made the momentous decision to lower the local water table by drilling a borehole to pump out 35,000-40,000 gallons of water per hour. This went on day and night and allowed the shaft to be fully investigated.[35]

The challenges that faced the twentieth-century excavation team highlights the enormous undertaking that constructing this well must have involved during the Roman period. The height of the modern water table would also seem to indicate that it must have been considerably lower in the Roman period. Spatially the well was located in close proximity to the bath house (Figure 2).[36] This situation is paralleled by another deep chalk cut well (this time only 86ft, 26.5m deep) at Tarrant Hinton in Dorset.[37]

---

[33] for instance Hiddink 2015, 107; Steane *et al.* 2006, Fig 9.57-9.59

[34] Stead 1980, 26-30

[35] Stead 1980, 27

[36] Stead 1980, Fig 2

[37] Graham 2006, 61-62

Figure 3. A Romano-British timberlined well from Drapers' Gardens, City of London. Note the white clay used to backfill between the edge of the construction pit and the timber planking (Reproduced by the kind permission of Pre-Construct Archaeology Ltd).

The majority of Roman period wells were not so deep. The wells at Schwanheim[38] and Kelsterbach[39] were approximately 5m and 6m deep; 2m to 10m deep seems typical for the majority of Roman period wells.[40] The excavation of these features would have been much easier than the deep shafts at Rudston and Tarrant Hinton but they remain evidence of substantial investments in time and labour. The ladders and spades found in association with some wells in the Low Countries, even if they were not themselves used in the construction of the features, serve as a reminder of the sorts of equipment required to dig a well.[41]

Typical Romano-British timber-lined wells were excavated at Drapers' Gardens in the City of London (Figure 3). The excavations, some of the largest ever undertaken in London, investigated parts of two *insulae* separated by a street. The western most *insula* was less well preserved than the easternmost but it was found to contain two timber-lined wells. One of these appears to have been constructed during the third century and was associated with

---

[38] Müller and Lange 1977, Abb 2

[39] Heising 2013, Abb 3

[40] Hodge 2000b, 30

[41] van Haasteren and Groot 2013, 28-29

the ghost of a large multi-roomed building that only survived as alignments of timber piles. Interestingly, the well was located at the rear of the building and seems to have either been contained within a room, outbuilding or fenced yard. The overall impression is of a water supply, to which access was restricted so that only the inhabitants of the building could use it. Such a provision was taken to its extreme at Kelsterbach where the well was located within a building, although here the structure and well may both have had a cult function.[42]

Another aspect of the Drapers' Gardens well, relevant to this discussion, concerns the backfill behind the lining of the well, which was found to be a clean white clay (Figure 3). Unfortunately no samples of this clay were taken but clays of this type are not local to London. They were, however, imported into *Londinium* to be used in pottery production not far from Drapers' Gardens. It seems difficult to escape the conclusion that using this clay was a deliberate choice. The intention may have been to back the timber lining with an impermeable clay lining so that the well would not be contaminated with unsanitary ground water that had percolated through the sides of the well. Here there seems to be evidence of private interest in water and concern for its taste and purity.

In the eastern *insula* wooden water pipes showed that until the late Roman period the inhabitants of this area had no need for well water. However, at some point in the fourth century the piped supply seems to have failed and this led to the construction of two new timber-lined wells. These features shared a common alignment and occupied an area of the site that had been open land. There was no evidence that access to either of these wells was restricted. This may be evidence of a communal interest in supplying water to the insula and this might go some way to explaining the ritual deposition of a hoard of bronze vessels in the southernmost well at the end of the Roman period.[43]

The completion of the well and its well-head structures marks only the beginning of the feature's life. Once completed, the well would have successfully transitioned from being a 'construction project' to a piece of useable infrastructure.

Using wells

The most important stage in a well's life-cycle is the one which is hardest to identify stratigraphically. Construction and abandonment are both processes that lead to deposition of one kind or another, whereas use only rarely leaves any traces behind. Studying the use of wells and their social lives in the Roman period therefore relies heavily on ethnography and ethnohistory. Some of these analogies will be drawn from the Classical world (although here the evidence is strongly weighted towards the Mediterranean), others will be drawn from the better documented medieval period, and a few will be taken from more exotic locations both geographically and temporally.

The well is, generally speaking, a small-scale piece of infrastructure built to serve a household or small community. The provision of a well is likely to reduce the distance travelled to collect

---

[42] Heising 2013, Abb 2
[43] Gerrard 2009

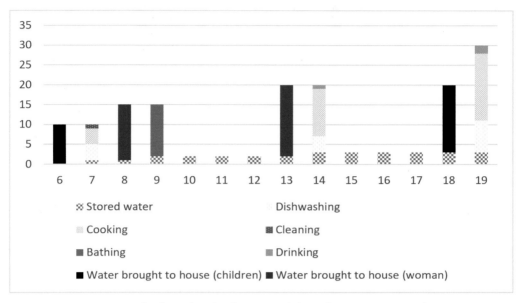

Figure 4. The diurnal cycle of water use (after White 1977, Figure 6.6).

water but ease of access often equates to an increase in usage.[44] Laurence, studying Roman Pompeii, examined the distribution of fountains within the city and found that no one lived more than eighty metres from a water source.[45] He argues that the distribution of fountains points to small-scale urban communities similar to those plotted on the famous map of the 1854 Broad Street (London) cholera epidemic.[46] This is a useful way of conceptualizing the social pull of wells and the role they may play at the heart of social life as landmarks and meeting places.

These small communities of well-users were united by their daily need to draw water with which to wash, clean, cook and drink. The diurnal rhythm of this activity would have helped to divide the day, which probably began with someone drawing water from the well (Figure 4).[47] This would have involved, at its most basic, simply casting a bucket at the end of a rope into the well and pulling it back up. The buckets, in contrast to today's strong and lightweight plastic affairs, were often stave-built wooden vessels with iron fittings. Surviving examples are known from a number of sites[48] and iron bucket fittings are a ubiquitous find. The capacity of these vessels were small, with the bucket from Heslington East thought to only hold a gallon[49] and this would necessitate drawing multiple buckets of water from the well each day. Pottery

---

[44] Narain 2014

[45] Laurence 2007, 49-50

[46] Hempel 2006, 212

[47] for instance White 1977, Fig 6.6

[48] Wrathmell and Nicholson 1990, Fig 122, Jacobi 1934

[49] Roskams *et al.* 2013

vessels were used as well and it is suspected that leather buckets may have been utilised too, although no extant Roman examples are known.[50]

Hauling the heavy, laden bucket out of the well was an onerous task, particularly with deep wells where the rope could weigh more than the bucket and the water. From the Neolithic period human ingenuity was brought to bear on this task, and well heads were equipped with a pulley, which eased the burden of drawing water significantly.[51] The next step was the provision of a windlass, which might ultimately be equipped with two buckets, so that one was descending as the other was rising.[52] This arrangement is suspected at Rudston[53] and may have been used at Saalburg.[54]

The technological solutions to drawing well water reached their ancient apogee in various water-lifting mechanisms. Force pumps have been found in Roman period wells[55] and are suspected at a number of sites.[56] Bucket-chain mechanisms were also used, as a handful of examples from across the Roman Empire (including Britain) demonstrate.[57] These devices were uncommon and still required immense effort, as anyone who has had a go at using the reconstructed bucket-chain mechanism at the Museum of London will testify! It is possible that animal power may have been harnessed to these devices, but their rarity and technological complexity suggests that they only ever supplied water in exceptional situations.

On whom in society did this back-breaking labour of fetching and drawing water fall? In many societies, both ancient and modern, this burden has been the preserve of women and girls. In the ancient world Herodotus applauded a girl for managing to carry water and spin wool at the same time.[58] A similar cultural milieu provides us with the Danaids of Classical myth, cursed to continuously carry and refill a leaky vessel with water.[59] This apparent gendered division of labour is emphasised further by black-figure pottery vessels (hydriai) where women are commonly depicted drawing water.[60] Water collection was also considered to be female labour in medieval Italy[61] and continues to be seen as such in many parts of the world, such as Bangladesh,[62] Northern Western Benin[63] and Nepal,[64] today.

[50] Quita Mould pers. comm.
[51] Hodge 2000b, 31
[52] Hodge 2000b, 31
[53] Stead 1980, 114
[54] Jacobi 1934
[55] for instance Graham 2006, 160-161; Stein 2004; 2014
[56] Hiddink 2015, 107
[57] Blair et al. 2006
[58] Herodotus, The Histories 5, 12; Godley 1922, 11
[59] March 1998, 124
[60] Lewis 2002, 75-75 and Figs 2.16 and 2.17; Waite 2000, 83-84
[61] Magnusson 2001, 137
[62] O'Reilly 2009
[63] Hadjer et al. 2005, 360
[64] Narain 2014, 209

It would be wrong to assume (in a sweeping cross-cultural generalisation) that drawing water was always a feminine role. In medieval England both men and women fetched water,[65] and drawing and managing water was a male task for the Borana pastoralists of East Africa in the 1970s.[66] However, it remains the case that those tasked with drawing water are the poor and the oppressed. It is a form of labour eschewed by those with the wealth and power to avoid it. In the patriarchal Roman world there is no reason to doubt that this burden probably fell, as it continues to fall in many parts of the world, on women and children but that is not to say that male peasants, servants and slaves did not spend their time toiling at the well head too.

The drawing of water from a well was not only hard work but a repetitive and endless toil. Yet the repetitive nature of the task made the well, fountain or pump, an ideal venue for social intercourse. For women and girls in ancient Greece and Medieval Italy drawing water was an opportunity to interact in public.[67] They were places where friends could be met, business undertaken and gossip exchanged. The well also offered an opportunity to observe life in the community and interact with members of different social groups and the opposite sex.[68] Of course, these opportunities also brought with them dangers. The well, fountain house or stream allowed men to press unwanted attentions on those fetching and carrying water.[69] In many parts of the world today harassment, sexual assault and casual violence remain dangers for the poor and the powerless venturing in search of clean drinking water.[70]

That social relationships and inequalities can be embedded in both the drawing and consumption of water is demonstrated by two examples. The first is close in time, if not geography, to the wells of Roman Britain and concerns the conversation between Jesus and the Samaritan woman at Jacob's Well:

> When a Samaritan woman came to draw water, Jesus said to her, 'Will you give me a drink?' (His disciples had gone into the town to buy food). The Samaritan woman said to him, 'You are a Jew and I am a Samaritan woman. How can you ask me for a drink?' (For Jews do not associate with Samaritans).[71]

This exchange neatly encapsulates both issues of gender and identity in the consumption of water. The second example, takes us to India where access to water may be segregated according to caste.[72] Even the consumption of stored water may be structured along these lines.[73] Our understanding of social structure in the peripheries of the Roman world is poorly understood, so it is difficult to ascertain the extent to which similar prohibitions may have existed. That said, the simplistic opposition in the late empire of the *honestiores* and the *humiliores* and the recognition of different social groups in provincial society should enable

---

[65] Goldberg 1991, fn 18

[66] Helland 1982

[67] Fantham 1995, 106-107; Magnusson 2001, 137; Waite 2000, 83-84

[68] Roche 2001, 146

[69] Fantham 1995, 108-109

[70] Crow and Sultana 2002, 721; WaterAid 2013

[71] *John* 4.7-9

[72] Ghurye 1932; Prakash and Sama 2006

[73] Freed 1970

us to postulate the existence of similar prohibitions.[74] Returning to the point made above, for some in society the ability to force others to draw water on their behalf and for their personal needs may have been a significant social distinction. Thus the well emerges not just as an arena for social interaction but also one where social division may have been clearly enacted.

A well may have performed functions other than just being a source of water during its use-life. They were in some situations literally death traps and Medieval English documents record an alarming number of accidental deaths caused by falling down wells.[75] They could even be instruments of foul-play. Medieval accusations of well poisoning aimed at Jewish populations are clearly evidence of anti-Semitic hysteria.[76] However, this hysteria gained traction because it tapped into a genuine fear that wells were vulnerable to deliberate contamination. In a similar vein, the well features as a potential instrument of murder in fourteenth-century York, when a father threatened to throw his daughter down a well if she did not go through with an arranged marriage.[77] Rather more dramatically, both the Athenians and Spartans supposedly murdered Persian ambassadors at the start of the Persian Wars by casting them into wells.[78] Perhaps more usual was the use of a well to dispose of a murder victim's body. In 1269 a woman named Ivetta was murdered by her husband who then dumped her body down a well.[79] Much earlier, the sixth-century ruler of the Frankish kingdom of Orleans, Chlodomer, supposedly killed Sigismund, King of the Burgundians and disposed of the body in the same way.[80] Sadly this phenomenon continues to this day[81] and the archaeological discovery of skeletons in wells is sometimes ascribed to this cause.[82]

A well sometimes served a more positive function. They were ready places of concealment and in 1798 Edward Fitzgerald, the Irish rebel, is reported to have hidden in a well in Dublin.[83] Wells might also offer a convenient place to conceal valuables. These sorts of deeds are sometimes invoked to explain the presence of human skeletons and collections of objects in the fills of wells.

Wells may have performed other functions during their use-lives. Perhaps the best known non-functional use is their supposed role as places of religious or spiritual significance. The 'holy well' concept is a pervasive one and the idea that wells have been venerated since prehistory has a considerable number of adherents in both popular and academic literature. Particularly seductive are the arguments that suggest contemporary folklore can be traced back to the medieval Christian veneration of earlier, Roman, prehistoric and pagan sites.[84]

[74] Gerrard 2013, 118-155
[75] Goldberg 1991, 81; Magnusson 2001, 136-137
[76] Foa 2000, 14
[77] Goldberg 1991, fn 18
[78] Herodotus, *The Histories* VII, 133; Godley 1922, 435
[79] Goldberg 1991, fn 18
[80] Gregory of Tours *History of the Franks* III.6; Thorpe 1974, 166-167
[81] Nelson 2013
[82] Hampel 2001
[83] Hinkson and West 1991, 237
[84] Varner 2009

Rattue's careful study provides a well-argued and empirical counterweight to these often fanciful invented traditions.[85]

Without presuming an ahistorical and cross-cultural interest in hydrolatory,[86] it seems clear that wells and water sources were venerated during the Roman period. Some of the textual evidence for this phenomenon has been alluded to. The archaeological evidence is rather more difficult to interpret. At Pagans Hill (Somerset, UK; the name is post-medieval) a Romano-Celtic temple was found to be associated with a deep well.[87] A rather more famous example is Coventina's Well, near Hadrian's Wall in Northumberland.[88] Here a well was built to enclose a natural spring and finds from the well shaft name a minor goddess, the eponymous Coventina. At Kelsterbach, a well containing an interesting group of finds, was found within a building and considered to be a cult focus.[89] These examples could be further enumerated. Yet once the structural evidence is discounted the basis for the function of these features come from their phases of disuse (below).

Folklore provides cautionary tales that the archaeologist considering the veneration of wells would be wise to assimilate. In post-medieval Europe many wells were considered to be 'holy' and their water thought to have medicinal, apotropaic or magical properties.[90] In some cases the veneration of a well and related depositions might leave an archaeological signature. However, often it was the water itself that was most important. Drunk, or dabbed on an afflicted part of the body with a rag that was later tied to a bush,[91] the ritual use of these sites would leave no archaeologically recoverable traces. That minor deities, *genii loci* and water nymphs may have been venerated at wells in the Roman period seems certain. Unfortunately such veneration might only be manifested archaeologically in special circumstances during the abandonment of these features.

The use-life of wells goes far beyond their functional role as water sources. A well could provide an arena for a variety of social interactions. It might also offer a place to hide, a way of indicating status, or means to conceal a crime. Some wells may even have provided hope through the real or perceived medicinal or magical benefits of their water. They might even have offered the means to venerate and communicate with supernatural beings. Wells were at the heart of their communities and social lives of individuals. Understanding and appreciating this aspect of a well's life-cycle enables us to better understand the way wells were treated during their disuse and abandonment.

Abandoning wells

The decision to abandon a well was not one that would be taken lightly, given the investment in construction and the importance of the feature in the social and economic life of the settlement. It may be hypothesised that three main factors caused well-abandonment:

[85] Rattue 1995; see also Congés 1994; Kelly 2002
[86] Rattue 1995
[87] Rahtz 1951, 1989
[88] Allason-Jones and McKay 1985
[89] Hesing 2013
[90] Hope 1893; Varner 2009
[91] Moore and Terry 1894, 217

1. That a well was surplus to requirements (water was more easily accessible from another source).
2. That the well had become 'dangerous' in some fashion. The shaft was unstable, the water was tainted or the water was perceived as being impure.
3. That the settlement had been abandoned and there was no longer a need to use the well.

Of these alternatives the first is perhaps most comprehensible to the western mind. We live in a world in which, generally speaking, wells are the residue of a bygone era of water supply. In Europe many old properties retain wells that were once vital to their occupation but have now been made redundant by the provision of mains water. In these circumstances a well is usually perceived either as a dangerous inconvenience, to be filled in, or as a charming addition to a property's character (and price tag).

A well may also become irrelevant and be abandoned if it dries up, or if the water became tainted. The failure of a water supply could be due to a variety of factors. The extraction of too much groundwater could lead to the water table being lowered and this might be expected in settlements with high population. It can also be a consequence of environmental changes. Work on climate records and proxies for the Roman period has, for instance, identified a number of periods of sustained drought in Europe that could have caused wells to fail.[92]

The abandonment of 'dangerous' wells bears closer scrutiny. There are, for instance, examples of Roman period repairs to wells, as at Breda in the Netherlands.[93] These repairs demonstrate a concern to maintain wells and imply that in other circumstances a well might be abandoned because it had become unsafe. In other situations well-water might have become tainted. This could have happened because of increased precipitation or the contamination of groundwater from nearby activities (perhaps most likely in an urban center). Alternatively the water may have been poisoned or cursed. Such happenings may have been real, or imagined (although no less potent in the minds of those imagining). In any of these circumstances the response may have been to abandon a water source.

Finally, the disuse of a well as a natural consequence of the decision to abandon a settlement needs to be considered. Various scenarios might be imagined. A population could abandon a settlement leaving the well to silt up naturally. This would almost certainly be the consequence of a hurried abandonment, or one made under duress. There is also the possibility that if the end of occupation came about because of some trauma, for instance violence or disease, that another group of individuals could use a well to dispose of corpses and waste. A more cautious, or measured procedure of abandonment might see a well carefully filled in. Given the suggested importance of these wells in the social lives and cosmologies of their settlement, the infilling of a well could be marked in some fashion. What follows is a discussion and interpretation of a handful of wells and their abandonment phases. It is not and cannot be a comprehensive and detailed discussion of the abandonment of wells, which is a topic worthy of examination in its own right.

[92] McCormick *et al.* 2012
[93] Hoegen 2004, 254

Rebelling against inequality at the end of Roman Britain?

The Roman Empire was, without a doubt, formed of deeply unequal societies and the Dominate was, if anything, even more unequal than the Principate. In the crudest sense society was divided between the *honestories* (the honest men) and the *humiliores* (the humble men)[94] and, although further gradations of status and identity were available, the terms give a flavour of social stratification.[95] The *honestiores* can probably be equated with the 'natural leaders of society' most visible archaeologically through villas. Often lauded by scholars as a reservoir of Classical values in provincial society, it should not be forgotten that their place at the top of the dunghill was a product of the manipulation of law and custom, wealth, landownership and the control of people through clientage, slavery and various mechanisms of legalistic bondage (perhaps best known to us through the late Roman social class known as *coloni*).

Britain was one of the earliest regions of the Roman Empire to be cast adrift and, whatever happened in the generations between the usurpation of Constantine III in AD 407 and the 'Groans of the Britons' in AD 446, the villa owning elements in society would have been confronted by a variety of challenges.[96] Indeed, our only contemporary account of this period, the writings of St Patrick, are concerned, albeit obtusely, with this very issue, as are other late antique authors in the west (such as Sidonius Apollinaris). At least one of those issues might have been recalcitrant clients, slaves, and unfree tenants – a phenomenon arguably visible historically as the so-called *Bagaudae*. What impact might this have had on the abandonment of wells? The following discussion suggests that two wells associated with villas at Rudston and Dalton Parlours might reflect the challenges that went hand-in-hand with the end of the Roman Empire.

Much was made above of the labour that would have gone into constructing and drawing water from the wells at Rudston, Dalton Parlours and Tarrant Hinton. From the depths of their deep, chalk cut shafts water was drawn, at various times, by both simple bucket and pulley systems and more complex mechanisms. The proximity of these wells to bath complexes was indicative of the role these wells played in the profligate use of water at the chalkland sites. It is not too much of an interpretive leap to believe that the individuals drawing the water from these wells, either by force pump or bucket, were not of the same social status as those bathing with it and enjoying the comforts of the sumptuous villa buildings.

At Rudston the end of the Roman period was manifested in the well by a series of remarkable deposits (Figure 5).[97] The shaft, it may be remembered, was 30m deep. The lowest 6ft or so was a deposit of chalk rubble, containing ironwork derived from buckets, and possibly winding gear, as well as a couple of late third century coins and a large group of late third- or early fourth-century pottery, which was dominated by vessels associated with the carrying of water. The excavators thought that this deposit marked the abandonment of the well. Above this was a layer of clay containing a complete pot and then from a depth of 92ft to 85ft was a thick, smelly 'peaty deposit' (actually layers of moss), interleaved with deposits of chalk

---

[94] Garnsey 1970
[95] Flannery and Marcus 2012
[96] Gerrard 2013
[97] Stead 1980, 26-30

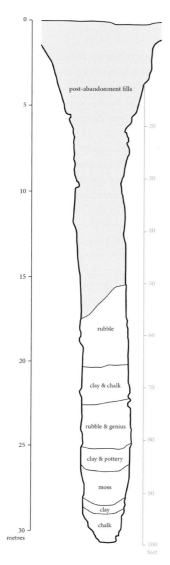

and clay. Overlying this was a layer of clay containing huge quantities of pottery (mainly vessels that could be used to carry water), dating to the late fourth century and coins of AD 364-378. Over this were a thick series of deposits of rubble and building stone. These extended from 81ft to 73ft and included a sculptural fragment of a *Genius* and stone water troughs. Further deposits of clay and chalk were sealed by another massive rubble deposit between a depth of 66ft and 50ft. Fills above this point seem to relate to the post-abandonment activity.

How can this sequence be interpreted? Climate evidence now suggests that the years around AD 300 saw drier conditions in north eastern France[98] and probably Britain too. This may have led to the water-table at Rudston falling and this could have caused the well to either fall from use, or be far less efficient as a water source. With the well no longer a reliable source of water the baths would also have fallen from use. For the *dominus* and his family this would have been a major inconvenience and, far worse, a blow to their very identity. Bathing, grooming and styling the body were a critical component of late antique elite culture.[99]

The evidence suggests that the nearby bath, even if it no longer functioned literally as a bathhouse, continued as a focus for toilet activities. The 10m³ of moss, collected from forests some distance away, may have been used as toilet paper and some associated excrement-loving insect remains may support this hypothesis.[100] The moss may also have served in another bathroom capacity as sponges.[101] Its presence in the well shows that the shaft was little more than a convenient repository for this noisome waste. Water, however, would have remained a critical element in daily life and those who had previously laboured to draw it from the depths of the rock cut shaft, now had to travel a kilometre to collect it from a nearby stream called the Gypsy Race, which is a hundred feet below the villa.[102] This was a marked deterioration in conditions for all involved.

With the end of the Roman period the position of the villa owning class was tenuous. Without the security offered by

Figure 5. Simplified sketch section of the well at Rudtson showing the various deposits mentioned in the text. Depths are in feet (after Stead 1980, Figure 16).

[98] McCormick *et al.* 2012, Fig 5b
[99] Eckardt and Crummy 2008, Gerrard 2013
[100] Stead 1980, 163-164
[101] Stead 1980, 164
[102] for the landscape context of the Rudston villa see Stoertz 1997, Map 2 and Wilson 2015, Fig 8

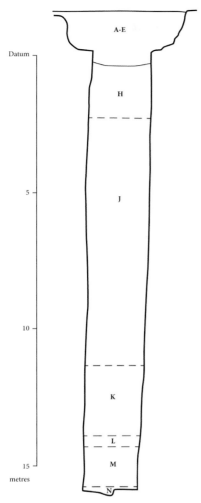

Figure 6. Simplified sketch section of the well at Dalton Parlours showing the various deposits mentioned in the text. Depths are in metres) (after Wrathmell and Nicholson 1990, Figure 115).

the Roman state the bonds that connected patron and client could be weakened.[103] It may be that the massive dump of broken pottery, mainly vessels that could have been used for transporting water, represents this very process. Freed from the yoke of fetching and carrying water for the *dominus*, his family, lackeys and herds, the peasants and tenants may have cast their vessels, which were both tools and symbols of their labour and oppression in the service of their *dominus*, his family and their beauty regime, into the disused well and followed it, for good measure, with the water troughs and the broken and burnt statue of the family's *Genius* who functioned as 'a guardian spirit... [and] as the perpetuator and protector of a family'.[104]

The sequence at Dalton Parlours lends itself to a similar interpretation.[105] At this late Roman villa complex a well was excavated just south-east of a large aisled structure, which had been extended in the fourth century to incorporate a range of heated rooms. The well at this site was not conveniently positioned near a bath building[106] but instead occupied a location close to a building 'probably devoted to non-domestic uses'.[107]

The well, some 16m deep, was divided into a series of stratigraphic units given letter codes (Figure 6).[108] The earliest of these was 'N', a shallow layer of sediment at the base of the well, over which was 'M', a layer of silt about a metre thick. Above this, another deposit of silt 'L', was sealed by a thick deposit of burnt stone and roof slates ('K'). On top of this were large blocks of dressed stone, stone water troughs and fragments of columns (the lower part of 'J').

The discussion of this sequence argued that deposits N and M were both associated with the third-century use of the well and included a bucket

---

[103] Gerrard 2013

[104] Stead 1980, 129

[105] Wrathmell and Nicholson 1990

[106] Wrathmell and Nicholson 1990, Fig 158

[107] Wrathmell and Nicholson 1990, 281

[108] Wrathmell and Nicholson 1990, 195-197 and Fig 115

and jars suitable for drawing water.[109] However, deposit L contained four wooden buckets, fragments of several others, along with a large number of lug-handled jars of late fourth-century date.[110] The deposits above contained vast quantities of building debris and stone troughs, presumably from the demolition of the villa, the partial skeletons of three dogs, six horses and other assorted animal bones. The water troughs point to the destruction of any water storage or distribution network. As at Rudston, it is possible to interpret this sequence as a consequence of a fundamental shift in the way labour (and by extension society and landholding) were organised. The deliberate dumping of the equipment used to draw and transport water is an eloquent statement of the community's feelings about this onerous task. The infilling with rubble from the villa buildings not only excised those structures from the landscape but also used the rubble to decommission the well shaft. For good measure, the animal corpses and butchery waste could have been intended to appease supernatural powers or to pollute, both physically and spiritually, the well to ensure that it could not be reused.

Other interpretations of the well sequences and finds assemblages at Rudston and Dalton Parlours are possible.[111] However, by understanding the social role that the well fulfilled during its use phases allows us to better appreciate and understand the motivations of those involved in the abandonment of these wells. The possibility that such actions reflect a response at the end of the Roman period to ingrained social inequality remains attractive but it is not the only possible explanation for unusual finds associated with well abandonment.

Murder victims or 'deviant' burials?

The use of well shafts for the disposal of the dead recalls some of the earlier discussion regarding accidental deaths and murder victims. However, in most cases the human remains are clearly associated with the disuse of the feature. Unfortunately, the interpretation of these bodies and human skeletal elements is far from straightforward.[112]

Human skeletal remains from Roman wells are not common. A small number are known in Britain,[113] but rather more seem to have been found in Roman Germany and none are listed in the recent discussion of 'special deposits' in wells from the Low Countries.[114] Of the British examples we may begin with two early twentieth century excavations: that of the late Roman villa at Brislington (near Bristol) and the excavation of the late Roman fortlet at Huntcliff (North Yorkshire).

The well at Brislington achieved a certain fame in Romano-British studies[115] because the well shaft, some 11.5m deep, was found to contain, at the depth of 32ft, the bodies of three individuals.[116] As the excavator observed there has been 'abundant room for speculation as to how these remains of several specimens of the human race came to occupy this strange

---

[109] Wrathmell and Nicholson 1990, 271

[110] Wrathmell and Nicholson 1990, 271

[111] Fleming 2016

[112] for instance Little and Papadopolous 1998; Papadopoulos 2000

[113] for instance Barker 1901, Hornsby and Stanton 1912, Oliver 1992, Beasley 2006; Cool and Richardson 2013

[114] van Haastereen and Groot 2012, Appendix

[115] see the discussion in Poulton and Scott 1993, 119

[116] Barker 1901, 286

sepulchre'.[117] He went on to suggest that these people were the inhabitants of the villa, slain in a late fourth century barbarian raid. In this the excavator's opinion was followed by a number of scholars and restated by Branigan, who linked the skeletons with the 'Barbarian Conspiracy' of AD 367. Poulton and Scott have presented a detailed critique of this hypothesis and argued, rightly in my view, that the skeletons are one component of a series of actions related to the disuse of the well.[118] This sequence began with wooden buckets and was followed by building debris, the hoard of pewter vessels and the skeletons. Over this was a dump of butchery waste, on top of which was more building debris. It is difficult to see this as the result of plundering raiders, who would be unlikely to demolish a building. It is possible that this deposit represents a general clearance of the site after a raid, but if this were the case why deposit the pewter vessels? These were valuable items and easy to recycle. Most likely is that these deposits were intentionally placed in the well and mark the end of the use of the villa and its erasure from the landscape.

Conflict was also the explanation for a group of fourteen men, women and children deposited in the late fourth or early fifth century in the well at Huntcliff.[119] Yet again, the other finds from the well suggest that alternative explanations are possible. Pottery, a piece of cloth, a leather sandal, and an 'oaken wheel' were found at the base of the well. Then came three crania sealed by a large stone slab, over which were another eleven skulls, human bones and a coin. Above this was a deposit of rubble and 'earth' that seemed to be derived from the decay of the late Roman fortlet.[120] Here we might have a 'mass grave' in the aftermath of conflict, but no injury or trauma was recorded here[121] or at Brislington.[122] This may be a consequence of the age of the reports. Nevertheless, weapon trauma is often obvious and such evidence would probably have been identified even a century ago.

In Germany a number of wells have produced articulated human remains. One of the most dramatic discoveries was from within the walls of *Nida* (Frankfurt-Heddernheim, Hessen), where a well was found to contain the bodies of a man and a woman, both brutally killed and a small child.[123] These individuals were argued to be the victims of a mid-third century Alamannic raid.[124] The excavation of a villa not far away at Schwanheim revealed another well containing a seemingly violently killed individual.[125] A different region of Germany has produced another, equally gruesome, well find.[126] At a villa near Regensburg (Bavaria), two wells contained the remains of thirteen individuals, with evidence of violent injuries, scalping and even cannibalism.[127] These human remains were interpreted as having been offered to the gods in honour of a third-century Germanic victory over the Romans.[128]

---

[117] Barker 1901, 286
[118] Poulton and Scott 1993, 119-120
[119] Hornsby and Stanton 1912, 222
[120] Hornsby and Stanton 1912, 222-223
[121] Hornsby and Stanton 1912, 222-223
[122] Barker 1901, 288-289
[123] Hampel 2001, 217
[124] Hampel 2001, 218
[125] Müller and Lange 1977
[126] Schnetz 2013
[127] Osterhaus 1984; Schröter 1984, 120; Schweissing 2009; Schnetz 2013, 55-58
[128] Schröter 1984, 120

These fascinating third-century well deposits have all been interpreted as a consequence of Roman-barbarian (Alamannic) conflict.[129] There is not space here to engage with the arguments relating to the history of Alamannic conflict during the third century, although the paucity of textual evidence may be noted.[130] More problematic are the potential difficulties in correlating any archaeological deposit or find with a specific historical event. Deposits placed in a well in the middle of the third century might have been placed due to a historically recorded event, like the barbarian raids of AD 233, but could equally have been deposited years or decades earlier or later. There is a real danger here that the historical narrative is driving archaeological interpretation.[131]

Leaving these historicising interpretations aside, we can reconsider these deposits. As the excavators of the well at Regensburg noted, the presence of the skeletons above a hoard of ironwork suggests that more is at play here than the simple disposal of corpses. At Schwanheim the skeleton was found at a depth of 1.5m, but the well was over 3m deep.[132] This shows that the lower half of the well had been filled in before the skeleton was deposited. Interestingly, this lower fill contained a stone sculpture of a bull[133] and an antler.[134] Again, it is difficult to interpret this sequence as the result of hasty corpse disposal. Finally, at *Nida* the three skeletons were placed over a basal deposit containing the skeletons of a cat and a dog and sealed by a dump of rubble.[135] This situation recalls a Roman well under Southwark Cathedral (London), which contained at its base, a cat and a dog, and was subsequently filled with rubble including a number of religious sculptures.[136]

A broader approach to the interpretation of these bodies placed in wells would place greater emphasis on the contextual associations of the bodies. The juxtaposition of hoards of objects, pieces of sculpture or groups of animal bones all suggest something more than the hurried disposal of a murder victim. The British examples, already discussed, reinforce this perception. Other excavated wells from the UK, including an example at Biddenham (Bedfordshire, UK), where a deep well contained a sequence of strange deposits of animal bones and other finds, including a sculpture of a deity and a human skeleton,[137] blurs the distinction between well and 'ritual shaft'.[138] Similarly a villa near Hemel Hempstead included shallow well that contained bucket fittings, building materials, a human cranium and a pebble modified into a likeness of a human face.[139] At Swan Street (South London) the upper torso of a man was placed face down in a well, associated with a number of broken pottery vessels and dog skeletons.[140] At all of these sites religion, ritual, and cosmology seem to play an important role.

---

[129] Drinkwater 2007, 78-79

[130] for instance Okamura 1984, 361 and Scherer 2019

[131] Gerrard 2013, 17-26

[132] Müller und Lange 1977, Abb. 2

[133] Müller und Lange 1977, Abb. 5

[134] Hesing 2013, Abb. 10

[135] Hampel 2001, 218

[136] Hammerson 1978

[137] Monkhouse 1858

[138] Webster 1997

[139] Neal 1976, 14 and Fig IX

[140] Beasley 2006, 43-44

Perhaps the best way to interpret these discoveries is through the lens of 'deviant burials'. For whatever reasons, all of the individuals placed in wells were buried in a way outside of provincial Roman cultural norms. Why this was so, remains opaque to us. For some of the German examples the way the people met their ends may have led to an atypical funeral. In other cases, it was perhaps the social status of the individuals or even their physiological condition that led to them being placed in these wells.[141] Deviant burial rites are being seen as increasingly significant in the study of Roman provincial societies[142] and 'well burial' should be accepted as one component of these diverse and divergent burial traditions.

Deer for Diana? Cosmology and the abandonment of wells

The start of this paper began with a mention of my involvement in the analysis of the well at Drapers' Gardens in London.[143] I have largely avoided further discussion of this find because its definitive publication is forthcoming. Yet this late fourth-century well, in which twenty metal vessels had been placed between a deliberately broken bracelet and butchered joints from a juvenile deer, remains the inspiration for this final case study in the abandonment of wells.

At Liberchies (Belgium) deer antlers were placed at the base of a well containing the skulls of five individuals.[144] The presence of antlers in the well at Schwanheim has already been noted above and the careful arrangement of antlers in the well at Kelsterbach has been discussed by Heising.[145] Parallels for both of these situations can be found in Britain. An antler was found in a well at Staines (Surrey)[146] and a number of antlers, almost certainly of Roman date, were found in the well at Bloxham (Oxfordshire).[147] These examples aside, the presence of antlers and deer bones in wells is relatively uncommon: a study of 492 wells in Upper Germany and Raetia noted only eighteen occurrences.[148]

Martin-Kilcher has discussed the presence of antlers and deer in wells and sees them as a product of 'Romano-Celtic' cult practice.[149] Specifically, she notes the associations between deer and the Classical goddess Diana-Artemis and Cernunnos - the supposed 'Celtic' antlered god. More recently Allen's discussion of deer in Roman Britain has suggested that the 'act of killing a deer seems to have entailed a multifaceted set of communicative phenomena, interconnecting people's ideas of landownership with religious/mythological perspectives of nature'.[150]

Leaving antlers aside, deer or parts of deer, occur in a number of Romano-British wells. Given the paucity of deer bones in Romano-British faunal assemblages this pattern is noticeable.

---

[141] Papadopoulos 2000

[142] Taylor 2008; Crerar 2012

[143] Gerrard 2009 and 2011

[144] Martin-Kilcher 2007, 43 and Abb. 8

[145] Heising 2013

[146] Chapman and Smith 1988

[147] Knight 1938

[148] Albrecht 2014

[149] Martin-Kilcher 2007

[150] Allen 2014, 183

The skeletal elements of a juvenile deer at Drapers' Gardens[151] can be joined by two juvenile deer from a late fourth-century well at Baldock;[152] elements from two juvenile deer from the rubble fill of the well at Rudston along with two adult red deer from a later deposit in the same well;[153] and an adult stag from a third- to fourth-century villa well at Bays Meadow.[154]

The significance of these deer skeletons and the effort that must have gone into hunting the animals surely indicates that in particular circumstances a deer, or parts of a deer, were a necessary component of an offering or rite undertaken as part of the decommissioning of a well. The reasons for this must remain opaque to us. Nevertheless, it is tempting to see the deer as one element within a broader cosmology. Diana-Artemis was a Classical goddess closely associated with wild animals and the hunt but also with chthonic and lunar aspects.[155] In sculpture she was often depicted, as in the famous 'Diana of Versaille', with a bow, quiver and a deer. The moon, as Ptolemy reminds us, has power over water:

> The moon, too, as the heavenly body nearest the earth, bestows her effluence most abundantly upon mundane things, for most of them, animate or inanimate, are sympathetic to her and change in company with her; the rivers increase and diminish their streams with her light, the seas turn their own tides with her rising and setting, and plants and animals in whole or in some part wax and wane with her.[156]

Here it may be recalled that *Calendar of 354* saw *Luna Dies* (Monday) as auspicious for well digging.[157] Possibly it was the connection between water, the moon and Diana in her aspects *Diana venatrix* and *Luna* that made the hunt and subsequent sacrifice of deer appropriate as an element of some termination rites.

After abandonment

The final stage of the life-cycle of a well post-dates the abandonment of the feature and usually this phase has little to do with the events that preceded it. A well shaft that was not completely filled when it was abandoned in might become little more than a rubbish pit.[158] Even a completely filled in well shaft might find its fill compacting over time and this would leave a depression at the ground surface. Such depressions could form convenient places to bury things or to dispose of noisome waste. In some cases they might even become appropriate locations for burials.[159] Very occasionally an old well may even have been cleaned out and reused, as with the Roman well at St Paul in the Bail, Lincoln, which was rediscovered and reused in the fourteenth century.[160] These activities are, however, windows on later periods and part of a new story beyond our scope here.

---

[151] Gerrard 2009

[152] Stead and Rigby 1986, 410-411

[153] Stead 1980, 149-150

[154] Noddle 2006

[155] Green 2007

[156] Ptolemy *Tetrabiblos* I.2.3; Robins 1940, 7

[157] Salzmann 1990, Fig 12

[158] van Haastereen and Groot 2013, 41-42

[159] Stead 1980, 29; Prien 2003

[160] Steane *et al.* 2006, 200

Final thoughts

This paper began with our own post-industrial societies and their flagrant and usually easy relationship with water. The gulf that separates many of us inhabiting the world of Water 4.0, with that of Water 1.0,[161] is a wide one, but it can be crossed. The rich ethnographic and historic information relating to wells and water use enables us to consider wells as a focus of social interaction in the north-western Roman Empire. This allows us to rise above anachronistic views of wells as just infrastructure and to see them as arenas around which social, economic and political life was enacted.

The well also provides a mirror in which issues of gender, inequality, ritual, cosmology, hygiene, taste, community, population and environmental change are reflected. As archaeologists and anthropologists these are issues of more than passing interest to both the study of the past and the present. The rich and growing corpus of excavated Roman wells, not to mention prehistoric precursors and medieval successors, offer a detailed resource to investigate some of these issues. This paper has attempted to show what can be done. The challenge now is to take this approach forward in order to better understand these ubiquitous, but sadly under-stated, water sources.

Acknowledgements

I am grateful to Jason Lundock for the opportunity to present this piece and his patience during the editorial process. Prof Ian Haynes (Newcastle), Vicki Ridgeway (PCA) and Freya Redman (Newcastle) commented on drafts of the paper and my doctoral student, Evan Scherer, was kind enough to assist me with the German evidence. My thanks to all of these individuals. The text was largely completed in 2015. Some minor amendments were made in 2021. Any errors are my own.

Bibliography

Albrecht 1938, C. Albrecht, *Das Römerlager in Oberaden und das Uferkastell in Beckinghausen an der Lippe*. Dortmund, Verlag Fr. Wilm. Ruhfus.

Albrecht 2014, N. Albrecht, *Römerzeitliche Brunnen und Brunnenfunde im rechtsrheinischen Obergermanien und in Rätien*. University of Heidelberg, Unpublished PhD Thesis.

Allason-Jones and McKay 1985, L. Allason-Jones, and B. McKay, *Coventina's Well: A shrine on Hadrian's Wall*. Oxford, The Trustees of the Clayton Collection.

Allen 2014, M. Allen, Chasing Sylvia's stag: placing deer in the countryside of Roman Britain, in K. Baker, R. Carden and R. Madgwick (eds.) *Deer and People*. Oxford, Windgather Press, 174-184.

Ash 1941, H. Ash, (trans.), *Columella: On Agriculture*. Cambridge, Mass., Loeb.

Barker 1901, W. Barker, Remains of a Roman villa discovered at Brislington, Bristol 1899. *Transactions of the Bristol and Gloucester Archaeological Society* 24, 283-292.

Bennett 1925, C. Bennett (trans.), *Frontinus: Stratagems and Aqueducts*. Cambridge, Mass., Loeb.

---

[161] Sedlak 2014

Beasley 2006, M. Beasley, Roman boundaries, roads and ritual: excavations at the Old Sorting Office, Swan Street, Southwark, *Transactions of the London and Middlesex Archaeological Society* 57, 23–68.

Blair, Spain, Swift, Taylor, and Goodburn 2006, I. Blair, R. Spain, D. Swift, T. Taylor, and D. Goodburn, Wells and bucket-chains: unforeseen elements of water supply in Roman London. *Britannia* 37, 1-52.

Burgers 2001, A. Burgers, *The Water Supplies and Related Structures of Roman Britain*. Oxford, British Archaeological Reports (British Series) 324, Oxford.

Chapman and Smith 1988, J. Chapman and S. Smith, A Roman well at Staines. *London Archaeologist* 6, 3-6.

Congés 1994, A. Congés, Culte de l'eau et dieux guérisseurs en Gaule romaine. *Journal of Roman Archaeology* 7, 397-407.

Cool and Richardson 2013, H. Cool, and J. Richardson, Exploring ritual deposits in a well at Rothwell Haigh, Leeds. *Britannia* 44, 191-217.

Crerar 2012, B. Crerar, *Conceptualising 'deviancy': The fragmentation of the corpse and the dislocation of identity in Romano-British funerary rites*. PhD Thesis, Cambridge University.

Crow and Sultana 2002, B. Crow and F. Sultana, Gender, class and access to water: three cases in a poor and crowded delta. *Society and Natural Resources* 15(8), 709-724.

Drinkwater 2007, J. Drinkwater, *The Alamanni and Rome 213-496: Caracalla to Clovis*. Oxford, Oxford University Press.

Eckardt and Crummy 2008, H. Eckardt and N. Crummy, *Styling the Body in Late Iron Age and Roman Britain*. Montagnac, Instrumentum Monogrpah 36.

Fantham 1995, E. Fantham, *Women in the Classical World*. Oxford, Oxford University Press.

Flannery and Marcus 2012, K. Flannery, and J. Marcus, *The Creation of Inequality*. London, Harvard University Press.

Fleming 2016, R. Fleming 2016, The ritual recycling of Roman building materials in Britain in late 4th- and early 5th-century Britain. *Post-Classical Archaeologies* 6, 147-170.

Foa 2000, A. Foa, *The Jews of Europe after the Black Death*. California, University of California Press.

Freed 1970, S. Freed, Caste ranking and the exchange of food and water in a North Indian village. *Anthropological Quarterly* 43(1), 1-13.

Garnsey 1970, P. Garnsey, *Social Status and Legal Privilege in the Roman Empire*. Oxford, Oxford University Press.

Gerrard 2009, J. Gerrard, The Drapers' Gardens hoard: a preliminary account. *Britannia*, 40, 163-183

Gerrard 2011, J. Gerrard, Wells and belief systems at the end of Roman Britain: a case study from Roman London. In: L. Lavan and M. Mulryan (eds) *The Archaeology of Late Antique 'Paganism'*. Leiden: Brill, 551-572.

Gerrard 2013, J. Gerrard, *The Ruin of Roman Britain: An Archaeological Perspective*. Cambridge: Cambridge University Press

Ghurye 1932, G. Ghurye, *Caste and Race in India*. London, Routledge.

Godley 1922, A. Godley (trans) *Herodotus: The Persian Wars*. Cambridge, Mass., Loeb.

Goldberg 1991, P. Goldberg, The public and the private: women in the pre-plague economy. *Thirteenth Century England* 3, 75-90.

Graham 2006, A. Graham, *Barton Field, Tarrant Hinton, Dorset: Excavations 1968-1984*. Dorchester, Dorset Natural History and Archaeological Society Monograph 17.

Green 2007, C. Green, *Roman Religion and the cult of Diana at Aricia*. Cambridge, Cambridge University Press.

Hammerson 1978, M. Hammerson, Excavations under Southwark Cathedral, *London Archaeologist* 3(8) (1978) 206-212.

Hadjer, Klein and Schopp 2005, K. Hadjer, T. Klein, and M. Schopp, Water consumption embedded in its social context in north-western Benin. *Physics and the Chemistry of the Earth* 30, 357-364.

Hampel 2001, A. Hampel, Tatort Nida: Mordopfer in Brunnen gestürtzt, in S. Hansen and V. Pingel (eds.) *Archäologie in Hessen: Neue Funde und Befunde. Festschrift für Fritz-Rudolf Hermann zum 65. Geburstag.* Rahden, Leidorf, 213-218.

Helland 1982, J. Helland, Social organization and water control among the Borana'. *Development and Change* 13(2), 239-258.

Hempel 2006, S. Hempel, *The Medical Detective: John Snow and the Mystery of Cholera.* London, Granta.

Heising 2013, A. Heising, Deponierung mit Hirschgeweih in einem römischen Gebäude bei Kelsterbach, Kreis Gross-Gerau – Fallbeispiel einer *clausura* zur Zeit des Limes falls?, in A. Schäfer and M. Witteyer (eds.) *Rituelle Deponierungen in Heiligtürmen der Hellenistisch-Römischen Welt.* Mainz, Mainzer Archäologische Schriften Band 10, 299-316.

Hiddink 2015, H. Hiddink, The villa settlement of Hoogeloon-Kerkakken', in N. Roymans, T. Derks and H. Hiddink (eds.) *The Roman Villa of Hoogeloon and the Archaeology of the Periphery.* Amsteram, Amsterdam University Press, 87-124.

Hinkson and West 1991, P. Hinkson, and T. West, *Seventy Years Young: Memoirs of Elizabeth Countess of Fingall.* New York, Lilliputt Press.

Hodge 2000a, A. Hodge, Purity of water, in O. Wikander (ed.) *The Handbook of Ancient Water Technology.* Leiden, Brill, 95-99.

Hodge 2000b, A. Hodge, Wells, in O. Wikander (ed.) *The Handbook of Ancient Water Technology.* Leiden, Brill, 29-38.

Hoegen 2004, R. Hoegen, Bewoningssporen uit de periode Late IJzertijd-Romeinse tijd (250v. Chr.-450n. Chr.), in C. Koot and R. Berkvens (eds.), *Bredase akkers eeuwenoud. 4000 jaar bewoningsgeschiedenis op de rand van zand en klei.*, Amersfoort (Rapportage Archeologische Monumentenzorg 102/Erfgoedstudies Breda 1), 211-271.

Hope 1893, R. Hope, *The Legendary Lore of the Wells of England.* London, Elliot Stock.

Hornsby and Stanton 1912, W. Hornsby, and R. Stanton, The Roman fort at Huntcliff, near Saltburn. *Journal of Roman Studies* 2, 215-232.

Jacobi 1934, H. Jacobi, Die Be-und Entwässerung unsere Limeskastelle, *Saalburg Jahrbuch* 8, 32-60.

Jones 1893, W. Jones (trans.), *Pliny: Natural History.* Cambridge, Mass., Loeb.

Jones and Robinson 2005, R. Jones and D. Robinson, Water, wealth and social status at Pompeii: the House of the Vestals in the first century. *American Journal of Archaeology* 109(4), 695-710.

Kelly 2002, E. Kelly, Antiquities from Irish Holy Wells and their wider context. *Archaeology Ireland* 16(2), 24-28.

Knight 1938, W. Knight, A Romano-British site at Bloxham, Oxon. *Oxoniensia* 3, 41-56.

Laurence 2007, R. Laurence, *Roman Pompeii: Space and Society.* London, Routledge.

Lewis 2002, S. Lewis, *The Athenian Woman: an iconographic handbook.* London, Routledge.

Little and Papdopolous 1998, L. Little and J. Papdopolous, A social outcast in Early Iron Age Athens. *Hesperia* 67(4), 375-404.

Loughborough University 2005, *How far do you have to walk to get safe water?* http://www.lboro.ac.uk/service/publicity/news-releases/2005/24_wwd.html [accessed 30/12/2015].

March 1998, J. March, *Dictionary of Classical Mythology.* London, Cassel.

Martin-Kilcher 2007, S. Martin-Kilcher, Brunnenfüllungen aus römischer zeit mit Hirschgeweih, Tieren, Wertsachen und Menschen, in S. Groh and H. Sedlmayer (eds.) *Blut und Wein: Keltisch-römisch Kultpraktiken.* Montagnac, Protohistoire Européene 10.

McCormick, Büntgen, Cane, Cook, Harper, Huybers, Litt, Manning, Mayewski, More, Nicolussi, and Tegel 2012, M. McCormick, U. Büntgen, M. Cane, E. Cook, K. Harper, P. Huybers, T. Litt, S. Manning, P. Mayewski, A. More, K. Nicolussi and W. Tegel, Climate change during and after the Roman Empire: reconstructing the past from scientific and historical evidence. *Journal of Interdisciplinary History* 43(2), 169-220.

Moore and Terry 1894, A. Moore, and J. Terry, Water and well-worship in Man. *Folklore* 5(3), 212-219.

Monkhouse 1858, W. Monkhouse, On the well at Biddenham, Bedfordshire. *Reports and Papers of the Bedfordshire Architectural and Archaeological Society* 4, 283-290.

Müller and Lange 1977, N. Müller and G. Lange, Ein Menschliches Skelett aus dem Brunnen einer Villa Rustica bei Frankfurt a.M.-Schwanheim. *Fundberichte aus Hessen* 15, 315-326.

Murphy and Savage 1990, D. Murphy and M. Savage, Wells, *Before We Forget... The Journal of the Poyntzpass and District Local History Society* 4, 43-52.

Narain 2014, V. Narain, Shifting the focus from women to gender relations: assessing the impacts of water supply interventions in the Morni-Shiwalik hills of North-West India. *Mountain Research and Development* 43(3), 208-213.

Neal 1976, D. Neal, Northchurch, Boxmoor and Hemel Hempstead Station: the excavations of three Roman buildings in the Bulbourne Valley. *Hertfordshire Archaeology* 4, 1-135.

Nelson 2013, D. Nelson, Indian sisters aged six to 11, raped, murdered and thrown down a well. The Telegraph Online. http://www.telegraph.co.uk/news/worldnews/asia/india/9883009/Indian-sisters-aged-six-to-11-raped-murdered-and-thrown-down-well.html [accessed 13/2/2016].

Noddle 2006, B. Noddle, Animal bones, in D. Hurst (ed.) *Roman Droitwich: Dodderhill fort: Bays Meadow villa and roadside settlement.* London, Council for British Archaeology Research Report 146, 116-120.

Okamura 1984, L.Okamura, Alamannia Devicta: *Roman-German conflicts from Caracalla to the First Tetrarchy.* Unpublished PhD Thesis, University of Michigan.

Oliver 1992, M. Oliver, Excavation of an Iron Age and Romano-British settlement site at Oakridge, Basingstoke, Hampshire 1965-6, *Proceedings of the Hampshire Field Club and Archaeological Society* 48, 55-94.

O'Reilly, Halvorson, Sultana, and Laurie 2009, K. O'Reilly, S. Halvorson, F.Sultana, and N. Laurie, Introduction: global perspectives on gender-water geographies. *Gender, Place and Culture* 16(4), 381-385.

Osterhaus 1984, U. Osterhaus, Zwei römische Brunnen aus einer *Villa rustica* in Regensburg-Harting. *Das Archäologische Jahr in Bayern* 1984, 115-118.

Papadopoulos 2000, J. Papadopoulos, Ancient Greek skeletons in wells, in J. Hubert (ed.) *Madness, Disability and Social Exclusion: the archaeology and anthropology of 'difference'.* London, Routledge, 96-118.

Poulton and Scott 1993, R. Poulton and E. Scott, The hoarding, deposition and use of pewter in Roman Britain. *Proceedings of the First Theoretical Roman Archaeology Conference.* Aldershot, Worldwide Archaeology Series 4, 115-132.

Prakash and Sama 2006, A. Prakash and R. Sama, Social undercurrents in a water-scarce village. *Economic and Political Weekly* 41(7), 577-579.

Prien 2003, R. Prien, Ein Massengrab aus der Mitte des 4. Jahrhunderts n. Chr. Im Bonner Legionslager. *Bonner Jahrbucher* 202/203, 171-198.

Rahtz 1951, P.Rahtz, The Roman temple at Pagans Hill, Chew Stoke, Somerset. *Proceedings of the Somerset Archaeological and Natural History Society* 96, 112-142.

Rahtz 1989, P. Rahtz, Pagans Hill revisited. *Archaeological Journal* 146, 330-371.

Rattue 1995, J. Rattue, *The Living Stream: Holy wells in historical context.* Woodbridge, Boydell.

Robins 1940, F. Robins (trans.), *Ptolemy: Tetrabiblos.* Cambridge, Mass., Loeb.

Roche 2000, D. Roche, *A History of Everyday Things: the birth of consumption in France, 1600-1800.* Cambridge, Cambridge University Press.

Roskams 2001, S. Roskams, *Excavation.* Cambridge, Cambridge University Press.

Roskams, Neal, Richardson, and Leary 2013, S. Roskams, C. Neal, J. Richardson, and R. Leary, 'A late Roman well at Heslington East: ritual or everyday practice?'. *Internet Archaeology* 34 http://dx.doi.org/10.11141/ia.34.5.

Salzmann 1990, M. Salzmann, *On Roman Time: the codex-calendar of 354 and the rhythms of urban life in late antiquity.* Berkeley, University of California Press.

Scherer 2019, E. Scherer, Terrae amissae: *A comparative study of Transylvania and Southwest Germany in the mid-third century.* Newcastle University PhD thesis.

Schnetz 2013, M. Schnetz, Die Villa Rustica von Regensburg-Harting. *Bericht der Bayerischen Bodendenkmalpflage* 54, 45-143.

Schröter 1984, U. Schröter, Skelettreste aus zwei römische Brunnen von Regensburg-Harting aus archäologische Belege für Menschen opfer bei den Germanen der kaizerzeit'. *Das Archäologische Jahr in Bayern* 1984, 118-120.

Schweissing 2009, M. Schweissing, Die Toten im Brunnen: Regensburg-Harting: Eine anthropologische Nachuntersuchung, in S. Burmeister (ed.) (2009) *2000 Jahre Varusschlacht: Konflikt.* Stuttgart, Konrad Theiss Verlag, 290-293.

Sedlak 2014, D. Sedlak, *Water 4.0: the past, present and future of the world's most vital resource.* New Haven, Yale University Press.

Stead 1980, I. Stead, *Rudston Roman Villa.* York, Yorkshire Archaeological Society.

Stead and Rigby 1986, I. Stead, and V. Rigby, *Baldock: the excavation of a Roman and pre-Roman settlement 1968-72.* London, Britannia Monograph 7.

Steane, Darling, Jones, Mann, Vince, and Young 2006, K. Steane, M. Darling, M. Jones, J. Mann, A. Vince and J. Young, *The Archaeology of the Upper City and Adjacent Suburbs.* Oxford, Lincoln Archaeological Studies 3.

Stein 2004, R. Stein, Roman wooden force pumps: a case study in innovation. *Journal of Roman Archaeology* 17(1), 221-250.

Stein 2014, R. Stein, *The Roman Water Pump: unique evidence for the Roman mastery of mechanical engineering.* Montagnac, Monographies Instrumentum 48.

Stoertz 1997, C. Stoertz, *The Ancient Landscapes of the Yorkshire Wolds.* Swindon, Royal Commission on the Historical Monuments of England.

Taylor 2008, A. Taylor, Aspects of deviant burial in Roman Britain', in E. Murphy (ed.) *Deviant Burial in the Archaeological Record.* Oxford, Oxbow, 91-114.

Thomas 2000, R. Thomas, Geological background, climate, water resources, in O. Wikander (ed.) *The Handbook of Ancient Water Technology.* Leiden, Brill, 3-20.

Thorpe 1974, L. Thorpe (trans.), *Gregory of Tours: The History of the Franks.* Harmondsworth, Penguin Books.

UN 2006, *Human Development Report 2006: Beyond Scarcity, Power, Poverty and the Global Water Crisis*. New York, United Nations Development Programme.

van Haasteren and Groot 2013, M. van Haasteren, and M. Groot, The biography of wells: a functional and ritual life history. *Journal of Archaeology in the Low Countries* 15(1), 25-51.

van Houtte *et al.* 2009, S. van Houtte and eighteen others 'De dubbele waterput uit het laat-Romeinse *castellum* van Oudenburg (prov. West-Vlaanderen): tafonomie, chronologie en interpretatie'. *Relicta* 9, 9-142.

Varner 2009, G. Varner, *Sacred Wells: a study in the history, mythology and meaning of holy wells and water*. New York, Algora.

Waite 2000, S. Waite, *Representing Gender on Athenian Painted Pottery*. Unpublished Newcastle University PhD Thesis .

WaterAid 2013, *Violence against women and girls: written evidence submitted by WaterAid to the Commons Select Committee on International Development*. http://www.publications.parliament.uk/pa/cm201213/cmselect/cmintdev/writev/934/m18.htm [date accessed 14/2/2016].

Webster 1997, J. Webster, Text expectations: the archaeology of 'Celtic' ritual wells and shafts, in A. Gwilt and C. Haselgrove (eds.) *Understanding Iron Age Societies*. Oxford, Oxbow Monograph 71, 134-144.

White 1977, A. White, Patterns of domestic water use in low-income communities, in R. Feacham, M. McGarry and D. Mara (eds.) *Water, Wastes and Health in Hot Climates*. Chichester, Wiley, 96-112.

Wikander (ed) 2000, O. Wikander (ed.), *The Handbook of Ancient Water Technology*. Leiden, Brill.

Wilmott 1982, T. Wilmott, Excavations at Queen Street, City of London, 1953 and 1960, and Roman timber-lined wells in London. *Transactions of the London and Middlesex Archaeological Society* 33, 1-78.

Wilson 2015, P. Wilson, Roman Britain in 2014. Sites explored: Northern England. *Britannia* 46, 295-313.

Woodward and Woodward 2004, P. Woodward, and A. Woodward, Dedicating the town: urban foundation deposits in Roman Britain. *World Archaeology* 36(1), 68-86.

Wrathmell and Nicholson 1990, S. Wrathmell and A. Nicholson, *Dalton Parlours: Iron Age Settlement and Roman Villa*. Wakefield, Yorkshire Archaeology 3.

Aspects of the Iconography of River Gods in Roman Britain[1]

Penny Coombe

I do not know much about gods; but I think that the river
is a strong brown god – sullen, untamed and intractable,
patient to some degree, at first recognized as a frontier;
useful, untrustworthy, as a conveyor of commerce;
then only a problem confronting the builder of bridge.

T.S. Eliot, *from* The Dry Salvages

The image of the reclining river god was common in ancient art,[2] the frequency of depictions perhaps reflecting the importance of water in Roman society. Large rivers such as the Rhine, Danube, Tigris and Euphrates delineated major boundaries of the Empire. Favorable tides or flow afforded safe and efficient passage by ship, and thermal waters conferred health benefits. The Nile held particular importance in the cultural mindset, and its ebb and flow evoked the protean nature of water to bring devastating flood or dry up completely, emphasizing the necessity of fresh water to support settlements. These aspects translated well into religious cult, and water was itself often an important feature of ceremonial practice, for example for pouring libations and for purification. The symbolism of rivers had deep cultural roots, taking an important place within a vast range of mythological and geographical texts, on coins and in art.[3]

Yet from Roman Britain only a handful of such statues are known from the archaeological record, and just one of these is whole and securely identified. These figures have not before been reviewed together nor compared with other depictions or conceptions of water deities in Romano-British art, especially sculpture. This paper therefore considers the origins of the figurative sculptural river god type in Greek and Roman art, brings together the British evidence while elucidating problems in establishing secure identifications, and offers suggestions as to why we see different forms of river deities in the sculpture of this region. Depictions of river gods will be the primary focus, since 'rivers especially attracted personification'[4] in the ancient world, though there will be a few examples of finds from or images of pools, bogs and marshes, lakes and wells. Oceanus and Neptune are often considered as gods of the sea, but the former was in Greek mythology the father with Tethys of the three thousand rivers, his

---

[1]   I am grateful for the opportunity and encouragement from Martin Henig and Jason Lundock to present this paper, and to the peer reviewers for their valuable comments. I would also like to thank Nikki Braunton at the Museum of London, Thomas Cadbury at the Royal Albert Memorial Museum, Exeter, and Neil Holbrook of Cotswold Archaeology for their assistance with images.

[2]   Ostrowski 1991, 8-9.

[3]   Servius, in his commentary on the Aeneid, vii.84, tells us: *nullus enim fons non sacer,* 'there is no spring that is not sacred'; Campbell 2012, 150-9; Toynbee 1934, 30-3; Meissonnier 2001, 515-545

[4]   Alcock 1965, 1; Ostrowski 1991, 26.

sons, and three thousand water nymphs, his daughters,[5] and the latter can take a fresh water aspect,[6] and so they will also be included.

The river god type in Roman sculpture

The classic depiction of a personified river or river god in Roman art, especially in three-dimensional statuary, was as a middle-aged man draped below his waist. He reclined as if on a riverbank, propped up on his left elbow, which often rested on an upturned urn spilling water signifying the source. Bearded and with a moustache, his long flowing hair falling to his shoulders, sometimes he carried a reed or cornucopia. Most personified rivers were not shown with additional attributes, and it is often difficult for the modern viewer to distinguish which river, if any particular one, was intended from the iconography alone. Context and geography instead help to identify them, though the Tiber and Nile are exceptions. The former may have been shown with a wolf and suckling twins, while the latter sometimes had a sphinx, crocodile or the addition of 16 small children representing the 16 cubits the river rose during its flood.[7] While most often carved of white marble, Pliny and Pausanias both tell us that it was considered appropriate for the Nile to be sculpted in fine dark stone:[8] a Hadrianic Nile sculpture, now in the Vatican Museums, was hewn from *bigio antico*,[9] and one now in the Galleria Doria Pamphilj in Rome, made of basalt,[10] bear out the textual evidence.

Figural personification of rivers in this reclining manner were known in the Roman world from around 150-100 BC for more than five centuries, but the type was most prevalent from the Flavian period onwards and especially in the second and into the third centuries.[11] In her review of sculptural depictions of river gods, Klementa identified 21 different rivers across the Roman world that were personified and shown in this fashion.[12] The motif appeared on a range of media, from sculptures on a heroic scale to mosaics and on coins, and even on jewelry.

Alternative poses of river gods were, however, known on classical metropolitan artworks. The Danube on the columns of Trajan or Marcus Aurelius; the Tiber observing the battle of the Milvian Bridge on the Arch of Constantine; and the Jordan on the Arch of Titus were all shown in relief, emerging from the waves to watch proceedings rather than lying on their banks. In these cases, the rivers are identifiable since they form part of story of the programme of reliefs, rather than needing to be shown in typical reclining pose.

While this reclining river god type has been shown by Gais to be a Roman creation of the Hellenistic period, which retained popularity under the Empire, there was an earlier Greek

---

[5] Hesoid, *Theogony* 337-348; Homer, *Iliad* 14.200-202 describes Oceanus as the most powerful of all the gods. The sons of Oceanus and Tethys are the river gods and the 3000 daughters are Oceanids (mostly nymphs, except Styx, a river goddess).

[6] See for instance the altar at *Pons Aelius* (Newcastle) *CSIR* GB i.1, no.213, and below.

[7] Nile excavated from near St Maria Sopra Minerva, now in the Vatican Museo Pio Clementino: Klementa 1993, 24-5, no. A14, taf.11 and 12, Abb. 22 and 23; or in the Louvre, 25-6, No. A17, Taf.15.

[8] Pausanias *Guide to Greece*, 8.24.12; Pliny, *Natural History,* 36.11.58.

[9] Klementa 1993, 22-24, no. A13, Taf.11.

[10] Klementa 1993, 31-2, no. A20, cover image.

[11] Penders 2012, 6-7.

[12] Klementa 1993.

version too. These river gods were depicted often frontally, with the head or at least horns of a bull, and are found more often on coins or vase painting rather than sculpture.[13] Achelous, described by Homer as the mightiest of rivers, was the mythical originator of this bull-horned river personification and was considered as the epitome of the powerful river.[14] According to myth,[15] he was able to transform his shape and become a raging bull, presumably when water was high and floods wreaked havoc across neighboring land. It was in this guise that Hercules finally defeated the river, taking one horn that could be filled by the goddess Plenty with the fruits and vegetables of the harvest. Many ancient texts described rivers as 'horned' or 'two-horned', perhaps referring to a delta or perhaps to this savage bull-like power of nature,[16] and reliefs of rivers, such as the Rhine, were shown in this way.[17]

Examples of reclining river god sculptures in Britain

In Britain, there remain five Roman sculptures carved in the round that have been identified as river gods, which are shown reclining in classical Roman style, while a possible sixth example is now very weathered,[18] and a small bronze figurine constitutes a seventh. An eighth, published here for the first time, is a relief and probably a nineteenth-century import and so should not be considered amongst the original Romano-British corpus.

The first example, the only one that is complete, was found at the fort of Chesters on Hadrian's Wall, in Room B at the north-western corner of the Commandant's bath house. Around 55cm tall and 85cm wide (roughly one-third life size), it shows a bearded male figure, with drapery to his waist, reclining on his left elbow (Figure 1). It has been identified according to the context as the River Tyne since the northern arm of the river flows very close to the Roman fort. Rather than an upturned urn with flowing water, his left elbow more unusually rests on another bearded mask, probably also a water deity. This could be a representation of Oceanus, into which the Tyne disgorges or perhaps duplication of the imagery. Though the drapery on his lower half is rather plastic, the folds of his garment in a garland from the left shoulder of the figure to his right hip were carefully finished, and Toynbee saw in this an aspect of the sculptor's talent.[19] We can assume that this figure ornamented the bathhouse in which it was discovered: Vitruvius reminds us that decoration was chosen appropriate to the character of a place,[20] and water-related imagery was popular in bathhouse ornament and for fountainheads.[21] In such contexts, these were likely to be depictions of water more generally, rather than cult figures.[22] Walker noted that the later surviving examples of Oceanus, for

---

[13] Gais 1978, 358-362; Clarke 2005; Jones 2005, 42; de Izarra 1993, 232; *LIMC* IV, 'fluvii'

[14] Homer, *Iliad*, 21.193-4; 'Pausanias, *Guide to Greece*, 8.38.10.

[15] see Ovid, *Metamorphoses* VIII.547-610; IX.1-90.

[16] Ausonius refers to the Moselle as horned: 'corniger...exeris auratum taurinae frontis honorem' Auson. *Mos* 469-471; Caesar, *De Bello Gallico*, 4.10 notes the Rhine split at the Delta; Kern et Bergeret-Kern 2001, 497.

[17] Espérandieu VIII, no. 6258 from Bonn.

[18] Chesters: *CSIR* GB i.6, 94; London Mithraeum: *CSIR* GB i.10, no. 7; London Great Dover Street: *CSIR* GB i.10, no. 63a; Dover: *CSIR* GB i.10, no. 63b; Cirencester: *CSIR* i.7, no. 89; Bath: *CSIR* GB i.2, no. 41.

[19] Toynbee 1962, 138, no. 30, pl. 36.

[20] Vitruvius, *De Architectura*, 7.5.2.

[21] See for instance the dolphin spout from the fortress baths at Caerleon (*CSIR* GB i.5, no. 57) or Neptune languishing with nymphs on a relief from Housesteads (*CSIR* GB i.6, no. 88), also with a hole through it to accept a water pipe, with a comparable example of Neptune from Vaison, France (*Gallia* xx, 1962, 684, fig. 49).

[22] See Ostrowski 1991, 8-9 for discussion of whether depictions are personifications of the river or body of water, or

Figure 1. River god figure from Chesters fort, Hadrian's Wall. © Penny Coombe

Figure 2. Reclining river god, carved in white marble, found on the site of the Walbrook Mithraeum in London. Museum of London accession no. A16931. © Museum of London

instance, were often in a domestic setting, and that, by then, cultural aspects played more of a role than religious.[23]

The second example, the fine white marble figure from the London Mithraeum, survives only to the middle of the torso, with no drapery remaining (Figure 2). The same long hair, and bearded older male face is seen, but this time a bullrush also leans against the right-hand side of the figure's head, identifying him as a river god. Probably carved in the second century and imported from Italy, the context of the Walbrook stream associates the figure with that stream or possibly it is a personification of the nearby River Thames. The sculpture pre-dates the temple and may have been brought in by a devotee. Association between mystery religions and water has long been understood, rivers perhaps representing the boundary between life and death, or for cleansing or healing during ritual.[24] Dedications to the *fons perennis* have been found at a number of Mithraic temple sites,[25] perhaps symbolizing the god himself, and Mithras is responsible in legend for bringing forth water by shooting an arrow into a rock (the so-called water miracle). It is perhaps no coincidence that the Mithraic temples in London and at Carrawburgh are situated beside streams. The fine imported marble statue of a river god from London would be particularly appropriate for display there, as it is similar in form to a reclining figure on a Mithraic relief from Callatis, modern Mangalia in Romania, or the marble free-standing statue now in the museum at Merida, albeit in those cases he is identified as Oceanus.[26] Worship of Isis and Serapis has also been linked to power over water, especially the fertility aspects of the Nile with which they were closely associated: as well as evidence for their cult,[27] containers for Nile water have been found in Britain at Caerwent and Silchester.[28]

Three further figures survive only as tousle-haired and bearded heads: from near Great Dover Street in Southwark (opposite Londinium, on the south bank of the Thames), from Cirencester, and from Dover, discussed in turn below. Though they are broken, the position of the surviving head was such as that scholars have completed the figure with reclining body, leaning on the left side. They are all roughly life-size or a little smaller, and carved from limestone. Toynbee notes that the Cirencester head is a particularly fine example of three-dimensional provincial sculpture, comparable to statues from the Rhineland (Figure 3).[29]

Recovered from a roadside ditch, the Southwark head might be indicative of the nearby River Thames, but given the location near to a known cemetery site it could have originated from a funerary monument of the second century.[30] Water imagery is seen on many examples of funerary art: a reclining river god in this style can be seen ornamenting the spandrels in

---

the spirit/god/genius of that water being shown in human form.

[23] Walker 2014, 227-8.

[24] Toynbee 1962, 137, no. 29, pl. 35.

[25] Walters 1974, 8 and 42-9.

[26] Mangalia: Clauss 2000, fig. 39; Merida: Vermaseren 1956, no. 778.

[27] For instance, a flagon from Southwark carries a *graffito* 'Londini ad fanum Isidis', attesting a temple to Isis nearby (Royal Commission on Historical Monuments (England), *An Inventory of the Historical Monuments in London. Vol. III: Roman London*, 1928, no. 104, pl. 53), while the altar from the Riverside Wall in London commemorates the rebuilding of a temple of Isis (*CSIR* GB i.10, no. 71), and the marble head of Serapis comes from the Walbrook Mithraeum (*CSIR* GB i.10, no. 16).

[28] Boon 1981a and Boon 1981b.

[29] Toynbee 1964, 87, pl. XIX.

[30] Mackinder 2000, 61-2.

Figure 3. Tousle-haired river
god from Cirencester.
© Penny Coombe.

the upper corners of a marble sarcophagus from Reims,[31] while more generally images of dolphins (especially ridden by cupids) or shells rank amongst typical ornament on tombs.[32] Sea centaurs or tritons are seen on the *stelae* of Curatia Dionysia and another of a man, and on pieces of arcuate window head or lintel, perhaps also from funerary monuments, found reused in the walls at Chester.[33]

The archaeological context for the Cirencester river god is not known, but it could, perhaps, have been placed within a temple area[34] or bathhouse in the second or third century. The River Churn, tributary of the Thames, flows through the town, perhaps even giving it the first part of the Latin name *Corinium Dobunnorum*, and it might be personified here. Is it just possible that the head from Dover originated in a temple to Neptune or Neptune and Minerva, attested on two inscriptions from the area, both dating to the later first and early second centuries?[35] Proximity to the sea has also suggested identification as Neptune, rather than a river god, though it is often difficult to distinguish the two from iconography alone. The sculpture was reused in building the south wall of the late Roman Shore fort in approximately

[31] Espérandieu V, no. 3677.

[32] Toynbee 1973, 207-8.

[33] *CSIR* GB i.9, nos 61, 66, 106 and 107.

[34] The group of sculptures from the Ashcroft area (including two figures of the *matres*, an altar, a figure of Diana and a single mother goddess) have been identified either as the remains of a sculptor's workshop, or as a cult center. Henig argues that the different hands seen in the carving support the latter interpretation: Henig, 1995, 111.

[35] see *RIB* I, no. 66 and *RIB* I, no. 91 and Add.

the mid-third century, and so an original date no later than the early or mid-second century would seem appropriate.

The sixth Romano-British example in stone, from Bath, is all but destroyed, but may show a small reclining river god set on a plinth, somewhat in the manner of an Etruscan funerary urn with figure on its lid, or a banqueting couch.[36] It was clearly used as a fountainhead, as there is a hole running through the piece of limestone for a pipe or fitting to carry water. From Great Chesterford in Essex comes our seventh example: a small bronze figurine of a river god reclining half-draped, and mounted on a small round base.[37] Lying back, his tousled hair is thrown back with bearded head resting on his left hand. An upturned urn supports the left elbow, while the right hand is extended.

Finally, a reclining river god relief in white marble now in the Royal Albert Memorial Museum and Art Gallery in Exeter (accession no. 5/1946.577) came to Britain in the early nineteenth century, apparently brought from a garden in Alexandria by the 3rd Earl Egremont (Figures 4 and 5). It was displayed at Silverton Park in Devon, before being given to the Museum in Exeter in 1946 as part of the L. A. D. Montague bequest.[38] Broken approximately in half, only the right-hand portion of a rectangular slab, *c.* 7 cm deep, 44.5 cm wide and 31.2 cm high, remains. On it, carved in relief within a recessed panel with a decorated frame is a river god, reclining leaning on his left elbow in classical Roman style. Draped over his shoulder, his torso is bare, and the slab is broken at the tops of his legs and across the genitals. The figure holds a cornucopia, under which is carved frontally a small sphinx. This, the lotus leaves in the background and the small figure above his right shoulder (possibly one of several more) suggest identification as the personification of the river Nile, similar in iconography to the large example from Rome, noted above. Between the front paws of the sphinx is a spout-hole, which continues through to the back and may have carried water.

The paucity of these examples of river gods carved in the round in Britain is matched by the few from the other north-western provinces. The Rhine is mentioned in literature relatively often. There are inscriptions dedicated to the *Pater Rhenus*, and it is noted as being the most important river in the area; yet few depictions that are considered certainly to be personifications of the god remain.[39] The Moselle, too, about which Ausonius wrote his fourth-century poem and which acted as a main artery of the wine trade in *Gallia Belgica*, survives on just two pieces: the river was simply shown as waves around the bottom of the boat on the famous carving of wine makers from Neumagen,[40] appearing also on the funerary monument to the Secundinii family at Igel, though again not as a personification. There are more river gods shown in relief in Gaul,[41] but apart from the relief of Neptune and nymphs from Housesteads,[42] we have no additional two-dimensional reliefs with reclining male river gods of the Roman classical type in Britain to add to the count of three-dimensional figures.

---

[36] *CSIR* GB i.2, no. 41.

[37] Toynbee 1964, 88, pl. XXb.

[38] My thanks to Thomas Cadbury for this information.

[39] *LIMC* VII, 'Rhenus, Rhenos', 634; Vollkommer 1994b.

[40] Ausonius, *Mosella*; Espérandieu VI, no. 5193.

[41] For instance, at Aix (Espérandieu I no. 97) and Marseille (Espérandieu I no. 62) – of white marble, this figure reclines on his right arm.

[42] *CSIR* GB i.6, no. 88.

Figure 4. White marble relief carving of the river Nile, probably from Alexandria, now in Royal Albert Memorial Museum and Art Gallery in Exeter, accession no. 5/1946.577. Front side. © Royal Albert Memorial Museum & Art Gallery, Exeter

Figure 5. White marble relief carving of the river Nile, probably from Alexandria, Royal Albert Memorial Museum and Art Gallery in Exeter, accession no. 5/1946.577. Rear side. © Royal Albert Memorial Museum & Art Gallery, Exeter.

Destruction, reuse or loss of much original statuary over the centuries may in part explain the lack of surviving examples, though we cannot confirm to what extent.[43] Furthermore, with now often broken statuary, we may fail to recognise correctly river gods from extant fragments, especially as accompanying inscriptions are few and diagnostic elements may be lost. The key features of the river god are the bearded face, and mature male figure half-draped in reclining pose. When only a fragment remains, such as a bearded head, there are a number of possible identifications, including Jupiter, Vulcan, and sometimes Mars.[44] The similarity of a Jupiter head from Dover with the reclining river god there has already been noted.[45] Even when the pose survives, we cannot always be sure this is a river god: according to Klementa, Oceanus is seen in just this pose in three-dimensional carvings from the Iseum on the Campus Martius, Rome (now in the National Museum in Naples) and from Mérida.[46]

In fact, identifications of Oceanus, Neptune and 'a river god' can and have been ventured for the same image, sometimes without clear preference for one over another.[47] Indeed it is possible that the deities may have been somewhat interchangeable in the ancient world. Oceanus is in mythology described as the great *river* that encircles the earth,[48] and Neptune was originally an Italian god of springs and rivers, eventually becoming the equal to Poseidon and god of the sea.[49] The distinction between fresh and salt water deities may have been less important than modern sense would suggest. However, the dedicators of twin altars, one to Neptune and one to Oceanus, at *Pons Aelius* (Newcastle) must have envisaged two different deities with power over different bodies of water.[50] Set up probably on the bridge where the River Tyne was still tidal, Neptune was conceived there as a fresh water god, while Oceanus was appropriate for salt water. No sculptural carving depicting the gods themselves accompanied those inscriptions: the altar to Neptune carries a trident, while that to Oceanus (spelled here Ocianus) has an anchor.

Attributes can help to distinguish water gods, but again these are not always consistently portrayed and have been selectively identified in modern scholarship.[51] The presence or absence of a trident has been noted as the defining attribute of Neptune.[52] In three-dimensional figures, Neptune can often be seen standing, holding a fish in his right hand and a trident in his left, and perhaps the remaining small marble leg of a man with dolphin next to his feet from London is of Neptune.[53] Oceanus, by contrast, usually has crustacean (crab or lobster) claws protruding from his head, and on occasion also dolphin heads, as seen on the face of the Great Dish from the Mildenhall treasure (Figure 6).[54] However, both crab claws and

---

[43] See also Deyts 1983 for examples of wooden figures at a source site.

[44] Walker 2014, 225-8.

[45] *CSIR* GB i.10, no. 57; see also one from Trier, Espérandieu VI, no. 4923 and two from Bonn, Espérandieu VIII, nos 6223 and 6224.

[46] Klementa 1993, 74-5 no. 3 Taf.25, and nos 4 and 5, Taf 26-7; and see n. 25.

[47] Wilson 2006, 298 gives the example of the Hemsworth mosaic roundel.

[48] Hesiod, *Theogony*, 241; Homer, *Iliad*, 9.182.

[49] Smith 1977, 121; Pascal 1964, 91.

[50] *CSIR* GB i.1, no. 213 (Neptune) and no. 216 (Ocianus).

[51] de Izarra 1993, 230-1.

[52] *CSIR* GB i.6, no. 94; see also Smith 1977, 121.

[53] *CSIR* GB i.10, no. 8.

[54] Wilson 2006.

Figure 6. The great silver plate of the Mildenhall Treasure, featuring the face of Oceanus in the center, now in the British Museum, inv. no. 1946,1007.1. © The Trustees of the British Museum.

Figure 7. Head of Neptune or Oceanus as shown on the mosaic from Withington villa, Gloucestershire, now in the British Museum, inv. no. 1812,0613.1. © The Trustees of the British Museum.

a trident can be seen on the mosaic at Withington in Gloucestershire (Figure 7), while on a border of the lost scene of Bellerophon from Room B at Frampton, a water god's head with claws and dolphins swimming from his beard (i.e. the iconography of Oceanus) is labelled in the inscription as Neptune.[55]

Cornucopiae symbolised the life-giving nature of river water and its importance in irrigation, but they were often held by *genii* (spirits or deities of a particular place which hold a *patera* or libation pate in one hand and a *cornucopia*, horn of plenty, in the other), who were also shown as middle-aged male figures with drapery to the waist.[56] Anchors are also seen on some carvings, in addition to that accompanying Oceanus on the Newcastle altar above. On a relief from Corbridge, Neptune (reclining, but shown with crab claws in his hair) holds an anchor.[57] However, a relief from Metz shows a reclining figure with an anchor, identified as a river god.[58] A rudder, representing navigation, was held by Oceanus[59] but also by river gods, such as the Tiber.[60] Anchors and rudders were part of the general apparatus carried by sea-creatures.[61]

Other forms of water deities in Romano-British sculpture

Looking beyond the reclining male figure type of a river god, a range of other forms of water deities in Romano-British sculpture can be seen. In particular, there are a number of front facing male heads which have been identified as water gods and several figures of female nymphs.

First, the male faces. These have stern stare, and a flowing beard and moustache, but are otherwise stripped of attributes. An eight-sided block with one face carved with the face of a bearded man, found on the river bed at Carlisle, could have been set into a structure like the bridge, and so has been identified as the face of the River Eden.[62] The head in a pediment of a tomb monument at Chester has been identified as a conflation of a 'gorgon' with the personification of the River Dee,[63] despite the name Dee simply meaning 'the goddess'.[64] The pediment at Bath (which is discussed further below) has been described as containing an image of Neptune conflated with Medusa, standing for Minerva (Figure 8).[65] Similar faces are seen on the pediment or coping-stone for the fort at Chester[66] and on another possibly architectural relief from York,[67] where they are also described as 'male medusas' and associated with water, the latter perhaps the River Ouse. It is worth noting that gorgons were, in the classical

---

[55] Wilson 2006, 299-300, figs. 3 and 4; see also Henig, this volume, 193-4, Figure 6.

[56] The marble genius from London (*CSIR* GB i.10, no. 4) has been identified as such due to his standing position but given his attributes could also conceivably portray the River Thames.

[57] *CSIR* GB i.1, no. 46.

[58] Espérandieu V, no. 4302.

[59] Klementa 1993, 75, no. 4, Taf. 26-7.

[60] Klementa 1993, 55-7, no. B3, Taf. 12, 13, 19, 20; Penders 2012, 19.

[61] For instance rudder carried by a sea triton on *CSIR* GB i.9, no. 107 and anchor held by a triton on *CSIR* GB i.4, no. 84, possibly a distance slab.

[62] *CSIR* GB i.6, no. 510.

[63] *CSIR* GB i.9, no. 104.

[64] Alcock 1965, 7.

[65] Henig 1999; see also Henig, this volume, 175-6, Figure 1.

[66] *CSIR* GB i.9, no. 105.

[67] *CSIR* GB i.3, no. 27.

Figure 8. Male head shown frontally in the pediment of the temple at Bath.
Photo by the Late Robert Wilkins, © School of Archaeology, Oxford

canon, female and not male and the wild snake-like hair could be understood as more general reference to the shifting nature of water and the seas.[68]

This type was also employed in funerary contexts. From Stanwick villa,[69] the right half of the head of a water god was shown with long beard and heavy-lidded eye, the other half of the face presumably carved on another block that no longer survives. One of a number of relief sculptures that have been identified as a funerary monument, the stone was reused in constructing fourth century additions to the villa. While similar front facing heads of the River Rhine, for instance, have been considered as possible fountain fixtures or are from unidentified structures,[70] this one may have performed a general apotropaic function. Funerary monuments from Neumagen, near Trier, employed similar imagery of fearsome masks,[71] and an image of the Rhine also takes the form of a mask.[72] Secondly, the pediment of the tombstone of Bodicacia, recently discovered in Cirencester, contains a male face, with the now familiar moustache, beard and long hair, facing front and with crab or lobster claws

---

[68] A native or 'Celtic' aspect has also been considered in the past: Toynbee 1964, 86-8.

[69] Coombe, Hayward and Henig 2021.

[70] Vollkommer 1994b, 34-5.

[71] Espérandieu VI, nos 5174, 5177, 5181, 5182.

[72] Borger 1977, 138, figs 135-7.

Figure 9. Bodicacia tombstone with relief carving of Oceanus, his eyes scratched across in antiquity.
© Cotswold Archaeology.

sprouting from his temples (Figure 9).[73] Found face down, the slab covered the fourth century grave of a middle-aged man, the eyes of Oceanus scratched out so as not to stare down on the body in death. The slab was evidently reused for a later burial and was not found in its original context.

There are also a number of female figures or dedications to female water sources from Roman Britain, sometimes with a local aspect and British names. Nymphs were thought to govern springs, both to ensure provision of water and with some association with healing.[74] They were typically shown in Roman sculpture standing or sitting rather than reclining, and carrying an urn from which water poured forth.[75] Three such statuettes taking this form survive from Britain, though all seem to be ornamental rather than associated archaeologically with a sacred site. From Wroxeter, the figure in fine-grained sandstone carried an urn, from which water flowed as a fountain by means of a hole drilled for a pipe.[76] Venus could be understood, though she is more commonly shown in the nude. A nymph is also most likely the subject of a small figurine from Skipton Street in London,[77] since she has drapery over her lower body and legs, and holds an urn from which water pours forth. The figurine could be from a small wayside shrine associated with a cremation cemetery in Southwark, and may date from

---

[73] Adcock 2015, 4-8; Hayward, Henig and Tomlin 2017.

[74] Lee 2006, 333.

[75] Campbell 2012, 152.

[76] *CSIR* GB i.9, no. 141, pls 38 and 39.

[77] *CSIR* GB i.10, no. 65.

Figure 10 Relief carving of three nymphs, Coventina's Well, Carrawburgh, Hadrian's Wall.
© Penny Coombe.

the early second century. Finally, the white marble nymph from York holding a mask which spouts water is an unusual type, probably representing a fountain, and might even date to the first century, though its context is unknown.[78] A dolphin fountain-spout, carved in the round, from the *natatio* at the Caerleon fortress baths perhaps accompanied a statue of Venus or a nymph.[79]

From the spring near Carrawburgh on Hadrian's Wall, there survives a stone relief of the nymph of the place, Coventina, as well as inscribed dedications to her. The well also yielded altars, a large quantity of coins and shoes, a cranium, bronze masks, and a stone head of a man.[80] The deity was perhaps shown on one relief along with two other nymphs (although the three figures are not differentiated), each reclining within an arched niche flanked by columns with classical Tuscan capitals and bases (Figure 10).[81] She is certainly figured alone in similar manner on another slab, where she is identified by an inscription.[82] The fact that they are reclining, as we have seen, is appropriate for water deities, if not for nymphs. The composition of the relief with the three nymphs is somewhat awkward, the figures apparently floating in mid-air, and the appearance in triplicate calls to mind the *matres/matronae* or *genii cucullatii* seen in the north-west of the Roman Empire.

Similarly, the three nymphs from High Rochester (*Brementium*) were even more awkwardly rendered.[83] Contained within the same niche, they were all shown naked, the one on the right holding a jug, that on the left a fringed towel, while the nymph in the centre was carved

---

[78] *CSIR* GB i.3, no. 13.

[79] *CSIR* GB i.5, no. 57.

[80] Allason-Jones and McKay 1985, 6-10.

[81] *CSIR* GB, i.6, no. 93.

[82] *CSIR* GB i.6, no. 150. See also Espérandieu I no. 506; II no. 993; III no. 2486; VI no. 5135; VII no. 5791; VIII no. 6175; VIII no. 6242.

[83] *CSIR* GB i.1, no. 218.

larger and should probably be understood as Venus. The scene seems to be of bathing, with the central figure washing her hair. Found in a water tank, and dating to the second or third century, this relief probably ornamented the tank. At Lullingstone, in a different medium, three nymphs were figured on a wall painting in the cellar, perhaps relating to the nearby River Darent,[84] while a reclining nymph inhabited a capital at Corbridge.[85]

While the intention or religious purpose for most of these renditions might have been to ensure secure water supply, they have traditionally also been thought to have a healing aspect: as Allason-Jones and McKay wrote, 'as a female deity associated with a spring, Coventina can scarcely have avoided acting as a healer even if that was not her primary responsibility.'[86] While in the classical world healing centres were dominated by male gods such as Asclepius, female deities provided healing at watery places in Britain: Green even suggests there is a natural link between the female and healing water,[87] though with Cousins's article in this volume, however, we are invited to reconsider the sanctuary at Bath, the role of the goddess Sulis there, and how this link really operated for Roman viewers.

Epigraphic evidence

Complementing the sculptural remains, inscriptions also provide surviving evidence of relationship of water with the divine, like the dedication to the *Nymphis et fontibus* by *legio XX* at Chester.[88] This altar may have marked the source of a spring from which the Roman fort and town drew water, and it was therefore important to appease the nymph at this point to ensure continued supply. Soldiers called on Neptune often: he is the water deity most represented on altars from Britain. Four curse tablets mentioning Neptune have all been found in or by rivers, again emphasizing his link to fresh water.[89] On one of these, from the Hamble estuary, he was invoked along with Niskus, perhaps a native water god; while on another from the Thames at London Bridge his name has been transformed into 'Metunus'. However, as well as dedications to Brigantia and Coventina, an altar to Neine at Greta Bridge in County Durham is also known.[90] Verbeia, attested on an altar at Ilkley, might have been the goddess of the River Wharfe.[91]

Indeed, epigraphy can be crucial to our understanding of the figures as water deities: on a relief from Birrens, the goddess Brigantia, a deity apparently of fertility and water, was shown equated with Victory and Mercury, and one might only appreciate that this was a British deity, rather than Minerva perhaps, from the inscription.[92] At Bath, we know that the local goddess Sulis was venerated alongside Minerva because of the number of dedications and curses

---

[84] Henig 1984, 173.

[85] *CSIR* GB i.1, no. 36.

[86] Allason-Jones and McKay 1985, 10.

[87] Green 1995, 89-91.

[88] *RIB* I, no. 460; *CSIR* GB i.9, no.14.

[89] From the bank of the River Tas, Caistor-St-Edmund, Norfolk: Hassall and Tomlin 1982, 408-9, no. 9; from the Thames at London Bridge: Hassall and Tomlin 1987, 360-3, no. 1; from the Little Ouse, Brandon, Suffolk: Hassall and Tomlin 1994, 293-5, no. 1; from the Hamble Estuary, Hampshire: Tomlin 1997, 455-7, no. 1.

[90] *RIB* I, no. 744.

[91] *RIB* I, no. 635; Alcock 1965, 3.

[92] Ross 1967, 217.

addressed to her, but had we only the cult statue, we might presume this was a shrine to Minerva alone. Without the recent discovery of the inscriptions on the plaques of the Ashwell treasure, for instance, successful identification of the name of Senuna (a nymph?) would have been unlikely, as she is again depicted like Minerva.[93]

Rivers, water gods, power and political boundaries

Subjugation of river gods was a powerful aspect of Roman political domination, personifications of the river acting as shorthand for a geographical area or people living alongside that body of water. Triumphal processions celebrating great victories involved statues of rivers,[94] while conquests of new provinces were celebrated on coins,[95] as well as being shown on monuments such as the arch of Titus (in the case of the River Jordan) or figured as symbolic crossing points like the Danube on the columns of Trajan and Marcus Aurelius.

However, for Britain, it was Oceanus more than rivers that in the Roman psyche formed the boundary of conquest. Britain was considered to exist at the ends of the earth, beyond the great Ocean, the river that encircled the known world. Stewart highlights the *topos* of Britain as rough and inhospitable, and an important part of this was its remote position.[96] While the historical accuracy of the trope may be debated, Suetonius and Cassius Dio tell us that Caligula received the title 'Britannicus' for his conquest of the sea, after ordering his men, arrayed along the Dutch coast, to attack the water with spears, and afterwards collect shells as spoils of the defeat of Ocean.[97] The dedication at York made in around AD 80-90 to Ocean and his consort Tethys, mirrored that made by Alexander the Great at the Indus river,[98] suggesting an association with the conqueror at the limits of his quest.

Perhaps such a geopolitical reading might be seen in the famous male head in the pediment from Bath (Figure 8).[99] While more commonly understood to have an apotropaic purpose, or erroneously identified as a (fine) blend of the classical and 'native' styles of sculpture,[100] the surrounding figures of Victory with a foot on the globe, circles of oak leaves, reminiscent of the *corona civica*,[101] and tritons ornamenting the corners of the pediment, suggested dominance. It could be dominance over the province beyond the Ocean (the central head here identified as Oceanus), a symbol of the bringing of peace to the western extremity of Europe,[102] or perhaps it should be identified as the geothermal giant Typhoeus and not a Medusa as others have suggested.[103] Archaeologically and in terms of style of the carving, the temple seems to have

[93] Jackson and Burleigh 2018.

[94] Along with *simulacra oppidorum* or *simulacra gentium*: Pliny, *Natural History*, 5, 36-7; Tacitus, *Annals*, II, 41; Florus, *Epitome*, 2.13, 88.

[95] See the Hadrianic and Antonine 'province' series: Toynbee 1934, pls I-XVII.

[96] Stewart 1995.

[97] Suetonius, *Caligula*, 44 and 46; Cassius Dio, *Roman Histories*, LIX.25.1-5.

[98] *RIB* I, nos 662-3; Diodorus Siculus, xvii, 104.

[99] *CSIR* GB i.2, 32-7.

[100] Ross 1967.

[101] Pliny, *Natural History*, 16.3-5.

[102] Henig 2000, 128. He suggests that the patron responsible for erecting the temple and other works was none other than the client king Tiberius Claudius Togidubnus, though hard evidence of this is lacking.

[103] Hind 1996.

been laid out in the late first century, the architectural and sculptural elements perhaps carved by craftsmen from Gaul.[104]

More practically, *Britannia* also simply had fewer large rivers than other, nearby north-western provinces. Though surrounded by water, the capacity of the rivers in the province was significantly lower than in other locations. The discharge of the Rhine is up to 30 times, and that of the Moselle up to 5 times, that of the Thames.[105] To navigate upstream on the Rhine would have taken considerably longer than going with the current downstream, though the exact comparison would have depended on the season.[106] These rivers, therefore, not only represented geopolitical boundaries but presented serious opportunities or barriers to maintaining efficient trade and contacts in this area.

Finally, in understanding the paucity of classical river god sculpture in Britain, perhaps we may witness lack of interest in venerating water in sculpted stone in favour of less archaeologically obvious practice. The sculptural and epigraphic habit in Britain was typically confined to certain sections of the population and often geographically concentrated in towns or at military sites.[107] The reclining river god examples above were found at important Romano-British urban and military sites, more likely to be home to sculptors with sufficient demand for them to practice their craft.

Veneration of water deities may not have been marked with images, the spirits remaining perhaps nuministic and aniconic, but their power was clearly understood,[108] evidenced by deposition of sculpture *within* water. Several heads from bronze statues of emperors or important officials have been recovered from rivers,[109] *ex votos* representing the part of the body to be cured were thrown into sacred springs, and coins were and continue to be cast into wells, rivers and springs to bring fortune.[110] Alcock writes of water deities: 'the Celtic mind regarded these spirits not as major gods, but as part of the vast race of minor deities, often nameless and always ill-defined, who had to be placated and propitiated.'[111] While we cannot always be sure of the inspiration behind deposition of objects in rivers, wells or lakes, securing water supply and seeking healing may well have provided motivation for communing with water deities more often than geopolitical aspects.

---

[104] Blagg 1979, especially 106-7.

[105] Franconi 2014, figs. 2.4 and 2.5.

[106] Franconi 2014, 59-64. Duncan-Jones estimated the ratio of cost between sea, river and land transport at around 1: 4.9: 28: Duncan-Jones 1982, 366-9. Differences were even greater over poorer roads or rivers with strong currents: Peacock 1978, 49, Table III. The ORBIS project, simulating conditions in around AD 200, suggested a price ratio for moving a given unit of cargo over a given distance of 1 (sea) to 5 (downriver) / 10 (upriver) to 52 (wagon): Scheidel 2014, 9-10.

[107] Hope 2016, 286-290.

[108] Tacitus, *Histories*, 5.17: Civilis calls on German and Batavian soldiers to fight hard and reminds them of the Rhine and German gods around them with eyes on them.

[109] The head of Nero from the River Alde in Suffolk (*CSIR* GB i.8, no. 23 – though there it is identified as Claudius); the bronze head of Hadrian dredged from the Thames (*CSIR* GB i.10, no. 213); and the head of ?Trajan from the Rhine near Xanten (Zadoks-Josephus Jitta and Gerhartl-Witteveen 1983, no. 201).

[110] Pliny, *Letters*, VIII.8: 'you can count the coins which have been thrown in and the pebbles shining at the bottom'; and see Walton, this volume.

[111] Alcock 1965, 1.

Cult sites were set up at watery locations. The handle of the silver skillet from the Capheaton treasure shows not only a classical rendition of a nymph and spring, but also a small temple over the site.[112] Lydney in Gloucestershire may have been positioned to overlook the source of the Severn (or *Sabrina*), and votives there may be understood as being associated with healing.[113] Confluences were seen as powerful and important places. Here, one river subdues another, but also the two powers meet and combine. Perhaps it is notable that the monument to Drusus was set up at Koblenz, where the Rhine and Moselle meet, while the centre of the Imperial cult in Gaul was designated as Lyon, where the Rhone joins the Sâone, and where there may well have been an earlier shrine. In London, as well as the Walbrook Mithraeum, there was a temple complex in the south-western corner of the capital, near the meeting point of the Thames with its tributary the Fleet.[114]

Conclusion

Though a popular figure in ancient art, very few images of reclining water gods have been found from Roman Britain. Where some examples survive, there is often debate over the identification, since distinguishing attributes such as rudders, crustacean's claws, dolphins and bull rushes seem to have been used interchangeably. More commonly found are images of nymphs or front-facing bearded male heads that have been seen as water deities, sometimes with an apotropaic or funerary association. These were similar to the reliefs of the Rhine[115] and other funerary images from Germany and Gaul, suggesting that Britain has more in common with the other north-western provinces than with the Mediterranean corpus of sculpture. Networks of merchants or soldiers may have interacted between these areas, bringing craftsmanship and ideas from one location to another over a period of time, and no doubt long-distance trade and economic prosperity for many relied on the flow of major arteries like the Rhine and Danube. Establishment of Roman power over water and the geopolitical boundaries drawn by rivers ensured they held a particular place in the Roman cultural mindset. There may in Britain also have endured a more nuministic sense of the divine in watery locations, attracting devotion without dedications or without sculptural remains that could have survived for the archaeologist or art historian to consider.

Bibliography

Ancient texts

Ausonius, 'Mosella', *The Works of Ausonius* ed. R. P. H. Green, Clarendon Press, Oxford, 1991
L. Annaeus Florus, *Epitome of Roman History*, trans E. S. Forster, Loeb, London W. Heinemann, 1921
Diodorus Siculus, in twelve volumes, vol. VIII, with an English Translation by C. Bradford Welles, Loeb, Cambridge MA and London, 1970
Hesiod, *Theogony* in *The Homeric Hymns and Homerica* with an English Translation by Hugh G. Evelyn-White, Loeb, Cambridge MA and London, 1914

[112] Walters 1921, 50-1, no. 192, fig.52.
[113] Wheeler and Wheeler 1932, 41-2.
[114] Williams 1993.
[115] Vollkommer 1994b.

Homer, *Iliad* trans. A.T Murray, Loeb London, vols. I and II, 1924

Ovid, *Fasti*, trans. J. G. Frazer, Loeb, Cambridge MA and London, 2nd Edn. 1989

Ovid, *Metamorphoses*, Trans. with Intro. By M. M. Innes, Penguin Harmondsworth, 1955

Pausanias, *Guide to Greece* volume 2, Southern Greece. Translated with an introduction by Peter Levi, Harmondsworth, Penguin, 1971

Pliny the Elder, *Natural History*, Trans. J. Bostock and H. T. Riley, London, Vols. I-VI, 1857

Pliny the Younger, *Letters of the Younger Pliny*, trans. B. Radice, Penguin, London 1969

Servius' Commentary on book four of Virgil's Aeneid: an annotated translation, 2002 McDonough, C., Prior, R., Stansbury, M.

Tacitus, *Annals*, Trans. M. Grant, Penguin, London, revised edn. 1989

Tacitus, *Histories*, Trans. W. H. Fyfe, revised and edited D. S. Levene, Oxford University Press, Oxford, 1997

Vitruvius, *De Architectura*, Trans. R Schofield, intro by R. Tavernor Penguin, London 2009

Modern texts

Adcock 2015, K. Adcock, From the Isles of the Blessed to the empty tomb - the newly discovered Roman tombstone from Cirencester, *Association of Roman Archaeology News* 33 2015: 4-8.

Alcock 1965, J. P. Alcock, Celtic water cults in Roman Britain, *Archaeological Journal* 122: 1-12.

Allason-Jones and McKay 1985, L. Allason-Jones and B. McKay, *Coventina's Well. A shrine on Hadrian's Wall.* Oxford.

Borger 1977, H. Borger, *Das Römisch-Germanische Museum Köln.* Munich.

Blagg 1979, T. Blagg, The date of the temple of Sulis Minerva at Bath, *Britannia* 10: 101-107.

Boon 1981a, G. Boon, Vessels of Egyptian alabaster from Caerwent and Silchester, *Bulletin of the Board of Celtic Studies* 29: 354-7.

Boon 1981b, G. Boon, Roman alabaster jars from Trier and Cologne, *Bulletin of the Board of Celtic Studies* 29: 847-9.

Campbell 2012, B. Campbell, *Rivers and the power of ancient Rome.* Chapel Hill.

Clarke 2005, M. Clarke 'An Ox-fronted River God' Sophocles *Trachiniae* 12-13, *Harvard Studies in Classical Philology* 102: 97-112.

Clauss 2000, M. Clauss, *The Roman cult of Mithras. The god and his mysteries.* Trans R. Gordon, Edinburgh.

Coombe, Hayward and Henig 2021, P. Coombe, K. M. J. Hayward and M. Henig, The sculpted and architectural stonework from Stanwick Roman villa, Northamptonshire, *Britannia* 52: 227-275.

Cunliffe 2005, B. Cunliffe, *Iron Age communities in Britain*, Oxford and New York. 4th edition.

Deyts 1983, S. Deyts, *Les bois sculptés des Sources de la Seine*, Paris

Duncan-Jones 1982, R. Duncan-Jones, *The economy of the Roman Empire.* Cambridge. 2nd edition.

Franconi 2014, T. Franconi, *The economic development of the Rhine River basin in the Roman period, 30 BC - AD 406.* DPhil thesis, University of Oxford.

Gais 1978, R. M. Gais, Some problems of river-god iconography, *American Journal of Archaeology* 82.3: 355-370.

Green 1995, M. Green, *Celtic goddesses.* London.

Hassall and Tomlin 1982, M. W. C. Hassall and R. S. O. Tomlin, Roman Britain in 1981. II: Inscriptions, *Britannia* 13: 396-422.

Hassall and Tomlin 1987, M. W. C. Hassall and R. S. O. Tomlin, Roman Britain in 1986. II: Inscriptions, *Britannia* 18: 360-377.

Hassall and Tomlin 1994, M. W. C. Hassall and R. S. O. Tomlin, Roman Britain in 1993. II: Inscriptions', *Britannia* 25: 293-314.

Hayward, Henig and Tomlin 2017, K. Hayward, M. Henig and R. Tomlin, The Tombstone. In N. Holbrook, J. Wright, E. R. McSloy and J. Geber (eds) *Cirencester Excavations VII. The Western cemetery of Roman Cirencester. Excavations at the former Bridges Garage, Tetbury Road, Cirencester, 2011-2015*, Cotswold Archaeology, Kemble: 76-83.

Henig 1984, M. Henig, *Religion in Roman Britain*. London.

Henig 1995, M. Henig, *The art of Roman Britain*. London.

Henig 1999, M. Henig, A new star shining over Bath, *Oxford Journal of Archaeology* 18: 419-425.

Henig 2000, M. Henig, From Classical Greece to Roman Britain: some Hellenic themes in provincial art and glyptics. In G. Tsetskhladze, A. Prag, A. Snodgrass (eds) *Periplous. Papers on Classical art and archaeology presented to Sir John Boardman*, London: 124-135.

Hind 1996, J. Hind, Whose head on the Bath temple-pediment?, *Britannia* 27: 358-60.

Hope 2016, V. Hope Inscriptions and identity. In M. Millet, L. Revell, and A. Moore (eds.) *Oxford Handbook of Roman Britain*. Oxford: 286-302.

De Izarra 1993, F. De Izarra, *Hommes et Fleuves en Gaule Romaine*. Paris.

Jackson and Burleigh 2018, R. Jackson and G. Burleigh, *Dea Senuna: Treasure, cult and ritual at Ashwell, Hertfordshire*. London.

Jones 2005, P. Jones, *Reading rivers in Roman literature and culture*. Oxford.

Kern and Bergeret-Kern 1999-2000, E. Kern and C. Bergeret-Kern, Elements archaeologiques pour un portrait mythologique du Rhin. In R. Bedon et A. Malissard (eds) *La Loire et les fleuves de la Gaule romaine et des régions voisines*. Limoges: 493-513.

Klementa 1993, S. Klementa, *Gelagerte Flußgötte des Späthellenismus und der römischen Kaiserzeit*. Köln.

Lee 2006, M. M. Lee, Acheloös Peplophoros: a lost statuette of a river god in feminine dress, *Hesperia* 75.3: 317-325

MacKinder 2000, A. MacKinder, *A Romano-British cemetery on Watling Street. Excavations at 165 Great Dover Street, Southwark, London*. MoLAS Archaeology Studies Series 9. London.

Meissonnier 2001, J. Meissonnier, La representation des fleuves sur les monnaies Romaines'. In R. Bedon et A. Malissard (eds) *La Loire et les fleuves de la Gaule romaine et des régions voisines*. Limoges: 515-545.

Ostrowski 1991, J. Ostrowski, *Personifications of rivers in Greek and Roman art*. Krakow.

Pascal 1964, C. B. Pascal *The cults of Cisalpine Gaul*. Collection Latomus LXXV.

Peacock 1978, D. P. S. Peacock, The Rhine and the problem of Gaulish wine in Roman Britain. In J. Du Plat Taylor and H. Cleere (eds) *Roman shipping and trade: Britain and the Rhine provinces*. CBA Research Report 24. London: 49–51.

Penders 2012, S. Penders, Imperial waters. Roman river god art in context, MA thesis, University of Leiden, https://openaccess.leidenuniv.nl/handle/1887/19796 (accessed 17 May 2016)

Ross 1967, A. Ross, *Pagan Celtic Britain*. London and New York.

Scheidel 2014. W. Scheidel, The shape of the Roman world: modeling imperial connectivity. *Journal of Roman Archaeology* 27: 7–32.

Smith 1977, D. J. Smith, Mythological figures and scenes in Romano-British mosaics. In J. Munby and M. Henig (eds), *Roman life and art in Britain. Part I*. British Archaeological Reports 4. Oxford: 105-194.

Stewart 1995, P. Stewart, Inventing Britain: The Roman creation and adaptation of an image, *Britannia* 26: 1-10.

Stewart 2010, P. Stewart, Geographies of provincialism in Roman sculpture', *Research Institutes in the History of Art Journal* http://www.riha-journal.org/articles/2010/stewart-geographies-of-provincialism (accessed 20 May 2016)

Tomlin 1997, R. S. O. Tomlin, Roman Britain in 1996: II. The inscriptions, *Britannia* 28: 455-72.

Toynbee 1934, J. Toynbee, *The Hadrianic school.* Cambridge.

Toynbee 1962, J. Toynbee, *Art in Roman Britain.* London.

Toynbee 1964, J. Toynbee, *Art in Britain under the Romans.* Oxford.

Toynbee 1973, J. Toynbee, *Animals in Roman life and art.* Baltimore and London.

Vermaseren 1956, M. J. Vermaseren, *Corpus Inscriptionum et monumentuorum religionis mithriacae,* Vol. I. The Hague.

Vollkommer 1994a, R. Vollkommer, Rhenus, Rhenos, in *LIMC* VII, 632-635.

Vollkommer 1994b, R. Vollkommer, Vater Rhein und seine römischen Darstellungen, *Bonner Jahrbücher* 194: 1-42.

Walker 2014, S. Walker, Emperors and deities in rural Britain: a copper-alloy head of Marcus Aurelius from Steane, near Brackley (Northants), *Britannia* 45: 223-242.

Walters 1921, H. Walters, *Catalogue of the silver plate (Greek, Etruscan and Roman) in the British Museum.* London.

Walters 1974, V. Walters, *The cult of Mithras in the Roman provinces of Gaul.* Leiden.

Weiss 1988. C. Weiss, Fluvii, in *LIMC* IV: 139-48.

Wheeler and Wheeler 1932, R. Wheeler and T. Wheeler, *Report on the excavation of the pre-historic, Roman and post-Roman site in Lydney Park, Gloucester,* Report of the Research Committee of the Society of Antiquaries in London, London and Oxford.

Williams 1993, T. Williams, *Public buildings in the SW quarter of Roman London.* The Archaeology of Roman London Volume 3, CBA Research Report 88.

Wilson 2006, R. J. A. Wilson, Aspects of Iconography in Romano-British Mosaics: the Rudston 'Aquatic' scene and the Brading Astronomer Revisited, *Britannia* 37: 295-336.

Zadoks-Josephus Jitta and Gerhartl-Witteveen 1983, A. N. Zadoks-Josephus Jitta and A. M. Gerhartl Witteveen, *The figural bronzes. Supplement. Description of the collections in the Rijksmuseum G. M. Kam at Nijmegen, vol. VII.* Nijmegen.

Abbreviations

CSIR GB i.1	Phillips, E. J. 1977. *Corpus Signorum Imperii Romani, Great Britain, i.1: Corbridge, Hadrian's Wall East of the North Tyne.* Oxford.
CSIR GB i.2	Cunliffe, B. W. and Fulford, M.G. 1982. *Corpus Signorum Imperii Romani, Great Britain, i.2: Bath and the Rest of Wessex.* Oxford.
CSIR GB i.3	Tufi, S. 1983. *Corpus Signorum Imperii Romani, Great Britain, i.3: Yorkshire.* Oxford.
CSIR GB i.4	Keppie, L. J. F and Arnold, B. 1984. *Corpus Signorum Imperii Romani, Great Britain, i.4: Scotland.* Oxford.
CSIR GB i.5	Brewer, R. 1986. *Corpus Signorum Imperii Romani, Great Britain, i.5: Wales.* Oxford.
CSIR GB i.7	Henig, M. 1993. *Corpus Signorum Imperii Romani, Great Britain, i.7: Roman Sculpture from the Cotswold Region with Devon and Cornwall.* Oxford.
CSIR GB i.8	Huskinson, J. 1994. *Corpus Signorum Imperii Romani, Great Britain, i.8: Eastern England.* Oxford.
CSIR GB i.9	Henig, M. 2004. *Corpus Signorum Imperii Romani, Great Britain, i.9: Roman Sculpture from the North West Midlands.* Oxford.

CSIR GB i.10	Coombe, P., Grew, F., Hayward, K, Henig, M. 2015. *Corpus Signorum Imperii Romani, Great Britain, i.10: Roman Sculpture from London and the South East.* Oxford.
Espérandieu	Espérandieu, E. 1907-66, *Recueil général des bas-reliefs, statues et bustes de la Gaule romaine*, i-xvi. Paris.
LIMC	*Lexicon Iconographicum Mythologiae Classicae*, 1981-
RIB I	Collingwood, R. G. and Wright, R. P. 1965. *The Roman Inscriptions of Britain. I. Inscriptions on stone.* Oxford.

What Lies Beneath? Interpreting the Romano-British Assemblage from the River Tees at Piercebridge, County Durham.

Philippa Walton[1] and Hella Eckardt

Introduction

In 1790, John Cade wrote to his fellow antiquary Richard Gough to report that: 'a most valuable collection of Roman silver coins has this year been taken up out of the bed of the River Tees, near Darlington. I had about a dozen sent me for inspection; some of Trajan, Gordianus, Hadrian, Severus, Antoninus, Carausius and others. Those that I saw were as perfect as if almost taken from the mint, but the treasure was dispersed into divers hands'.[2] Although it is impossible to be absolutely certain, this is perhaps an early mention of the remarkable assemblage of Roman objects found at Piercebridge, County Durham.

Separated by the passage of nearly 200 years, it was in the mid-1980s that two divers also began to retrieve coins as well as Roman pottery, military equipment and animal bone from the River Tees at Piercebridge. Today, the assemblage comprises more than 3,000 objects mostly dating to the second and third centuries AD, as well as 40kg of Roman pottery. Although finds common in 'special' or 'structured' deposits, such as coinage, items of personal adornment and toilet equipment are present in large quantities, the range of material deposited at Piercebridge is unusually broad, making the assemblage unique and therefore difficult to interpret. It was processed as potential Treasure under the Treasure Act 1997 and was acquired in 2020 by the Museum of Archaeology at Durham University. The assemblage was recently published in full as part of a research project at Reading University generously funded by the Leverhulme Trust.[3] The intention of this article is therefore to provide an insight into the composition of three categories of objects, while also exploring some of the possible motives for its deposition.[4]

[1]   The bulk of this paper was written at the Römische Germanische Kommission in Frankfurt in June 2016. The first author would like to express her gratitude to the RGK and especially to David Wigg Wolf for their hospitality. The authors would also like to thank Frances McIntosh, Matt Fittock and Eleri Cousins for drawing their attention to some parallels for the more unusual objects discussed in this article.

[2]   Robertson 2000, 216

[3]   Eckardt and Walton 2021

[4]   Walton 2008, Walton 2012, 152-166 and Walton 2016 provide summaries of some of the major categories of finds including the coins, items of personal adornment and military equipment. Casey 1989 examined the 166 coins discovered in the 1980s.

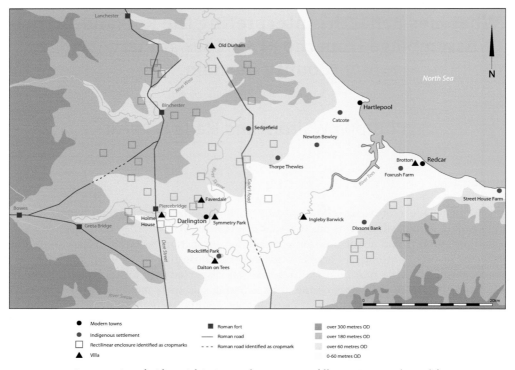

Figure 1. Piercebridge within its northern context (Illustration: Mark Hoyle)

The site

Piercebridge is part of a landscape rich in late Iron Age and Roman archaeology (Figure 1). It is to be found only four miles to the north east of the Iron Age *oppidum* of Stanwick and is situated at the point where Dere Street crosses the River Tees. Evidence of Roman occupation is found on the river's northern and southern banks, but despite its strategic location on the main thoroughfare between the legionary fortress at York and the frontier, no early Roman fort has been located at the site. Instead, excavation and survey of the substantial Romano-British 'small town' in Tofts' Field on the northern bank suggests an official or military presence from the mid to late second century AD onwards as reflected in 'a sudden and vast increase in the volume of all types of artefacts'.[5] The extant fort, visible as a series of ditches and banks surrounding the modern village, was constructed at some time in the third century AD[6] while building inscriptions, dedications and tombstones attest to the presence of soldiers from *Legio VI Victrix*,[7] *Legio II Augusta*,[8] and *Legio XXII Primigenia*.[9] On the southern bank of the river, study

[5] Cool and Mason 2008, 302

[6] Cool and Mason 2008, 302

[7] RIB I, 1205

[8] Wright 1967, 205, no. 20; RIB III, 253

[9] RIB I, 1026

has focused on an elaborately decorated early Roman *villa* and bath-house known as Holme House[10] and the masonry foundations of a large bridge thought to be Severan in date.[11]

The underwater context of the material

The assemblage was found immediately to the south of the 'small town' at Piercebridge on the bed of the River Tees (Figure 2). While some scholars argue that the assemblage simply represents settlement refuse washed from the river banks by fluvial action or the pragmatic disposal of rubbish,[12] its context does suggest more deliberate deposition in water in a manner characteristic of Roman religious and ritual practice.[13] The objects were spread over a relatively small area measuring 5 metres by 5 metres and were concentrated towards the middle of the river. Some objects were deeply buried in silt, but most were embedded in a concretion comprising burnt organic material and iron corrosion products. This concretion secured them to the riverbed and appears to have prevented their movement despite the

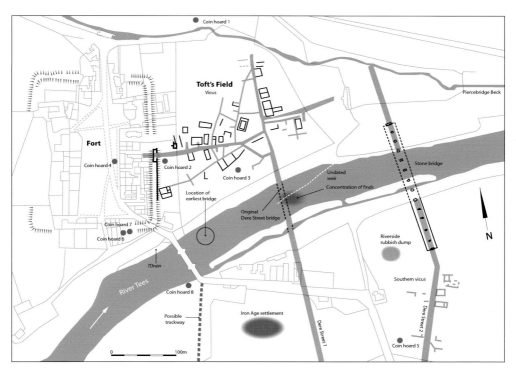

Figure 2. The location of the riverine deposit at Piercebridge, Co. Durham (Illustration: Mark Hoyle)

---

[10]   Cool and Mason 2008, 297

[11]   Fitzpatrick and Scott 1999

[12]   Fitzpatrick and Scott 1999, 117

[13]   Bradley 2000, 47-63; Smith 2015, accessed online. Horace commemorates a sacrifice he made to the spring at Bandusia (Horace Odes III, 13) and Pliny the Younger discusses the offerings made at the source of the river Clitumnus (Pliny the Younger, Letters LXXX, 8), whilst deposits of coins and finds are known from numerous European rivers including the River Liri in Italy (Frier and Parker 1970; Metcalf 1974; Houghtalin 1985), the Moselle and the Rhine in Germany (Derks 2014, 139-40) and the Saône in France (Bonnamour and Dumont 1994).

destructive force of the River Tees in flood.[14] Indeed, preliminary analysis of the pottery suggests that the average sherd weight and size is higher than that which would be expected had the assemblage been moved by water over any distance.[15]

Although the divers did not undertake detailed underwater spatial recording, they did note that some objects appeared to have been placed on the riverbed including, for example, a near complete ceramic vessel containing coins and a pipe-clay figurine. Furthermore, the presence of several iron lock mechanisms and more than 100 box fittings, mounts and studs suggests that some items may have originally been stored within wooden boxes which have not survived. Such an observation has tremendous implications for our understanding of the manner in which items came to be deposited. Were strong-boxes filled with objects actually placed on the riverbed, or on islands in the river such as are evident at the site today? Might the presence of locked boxes suggest the re-deposition of material from elsewhere at Piercebridge, perhaps the *favissa* or treasury of a nearby temple?[16] Or were these fittings, mounts and studs deposited individually and intended as symbolic items, holding 'metaphorically contrasting associations with security and access to locked places'.[17]

The findspot of the assemblage may also be significant, being immediately adjacent to the remains of an early to mid-Roman wooden bridge. Oak piles and cross members forming the foundations of the bridge's piers were exposed by drought in 1933,[18] and their continued survival was confirmed by an underwater survey in 2009.[19] Although the relationship between the bridge and the assemblage remains unclear, it is possible that it acted as a venue for, and focus of, depositional activity, as paralleled in Roman London[20] and in Trier.[21] It may even have possessed its own shrine or altars. Nearby at *Pons Aelius* (Newcastle), two altars to Neptune and Oceanus were found in the river Tyne, but originally stood on the bridge, while stonework at Chesters indicates a shrine to the Nymphs.[22] It is however odd that the chronological emphasis of deposition appears to fall in the late second and early third century, the very date at which it is argued that the wooden bridge went out of use when the substantial stone bridge further downstream was constructed. Did the timber bridge continue in use for people travelling on foot or was it perhaps converted into some sort of votive platform? Alternatively, could some of the material have eroded from the riverbanks and become caught against and between the foundations of the bridge?

---

[14] Fitzpatrick and Scott 1999, 115

[15] Gerrard 2013; Gerrard, Mills and Hudák 2021, 190-214

[16] The disposal of caches of objects thought to be associated with Roman temples is a practice known from elsewhere in Roman Britain, but these examples tends to be restricted to cult statues and priestly regalia. For example, at Leylands Farm in Norfolk, a cache of objects which included crowns and diadems were probably part of priestly regalia associated with a temple in the vicinity (Gurney 1986, 91).

[17] Hingley 2006, 237

[18] Richardson 1934-6, 230-232; Fitzpatrick and Scott 1999, 115-117

[19] Wessex Archaeology 2010, 15

[20] Rhodes 1991

[21] Cüppers 1969

[22] Rhodes 1991, 184

Figure 3. A selection of figurines recovered from the river (Photograph: Aaron Watson)

Objects associated with religious beliefs and practices

While these questions are difficult to answer without detailed survey of the riverbed, the composition of the assemblage also supports a religious or ritual motivation for deposition. For example, numerous objects directly related to religious beliefs and practices have been recovered. These include an incomplete miniature lead deity from a portable shrine,[23] a silver apotropaic amulet with the legend '*VTERE FELIX*' written both forward and backwards on each of its four sides and more than 130 rolled lead sheets, which may or may not represent curse tablets.[24]

Whilst these items cannot be attributed to the worship of any particular deity, it does appear that Mars and Mercury may have acted as something of a focus for veneration as objects specifically associated with both gods are represented. For Mars, they include a silver finger

---

[23] see Sauer 2005, 170 for a parallel

[24] The University of Cardiff's Conservation Department opened a sample of six lead rolls. Only one appeared to be inscribed with the legend 'XIV //' although there is some debate as to whether this was a deliberate epigraphic act or the result of a repetitive chopping action on the lead sheet. Subsequent research on the remaining lead rolls has established that the majority are fishing weights. However, given the resemblance of some of the smaller examples to the lead-alloy coin copies from the site, it may be that some are crudely executed coin substitutes.

ring with the dedicatory inscription 'DMART' 'To the god Mars,[25] two Cupid figurines,[26] as well as three miniaturised axes and four spears. For Mercury, they comprise an unusual pipe-clay figurine of the god wearing a winged *petasos* (see Rouvier-Jeanlin 1972, 211, no. 493 for a parallel) and two copper-alloy figurines representing a tortoise and a ram (Figure 3) As Mercury is frequently depicted with a ram, tortoise and cockerel, it is probable that these animal figurines originally formed part of a larger statue group similar to that known from *Verulamium* (Niblett 2001, 120 and Pl. 14).

The selection of Mars and Mercury is particularly appropriate given both the liminal location of the deposit and the likely military identity of at least some of the devotees. Mercury was the god of travellers, trade and boundaries, leading the newly deceased from one life to the next, whereas Mars, was both the god of war, and a protective deity who looked after the safety of soldiers during their military service.[27] An altar dedicated to *Mars Condates* (Mars of the Confluence) was discovered in 1709 at Conniscliffe near Piercebridge.[28] The riverine 'aspect' of the god makes it quite possible that this conflation of Mars with a local deity was the intended recipient of the offerings.

In addition to items naming or representing them, it has also been suggested that the general range of objects found in votive deposits may reflect the nature of the deity worshipped there.[29] It is therefore interesting that the assemblage contains a complete copper-alloy equipoise balance and a steelyard, as well as numerous items of military equipment. These could all be seen as appropriate symbolic dedications to Mercury and Mars respectively. Furthermore, as Mercury is often depicted carrying a money bag, for example on small bronzes and votive reliefs from Uley,[30] the large quantities of coinage recovered from the river may have been deemed an appropriate offering for the god of trade, commerce and commercial success.

Coinage

Although it has been argued that the assemblage is the result of refuse disposal or erosion from the adjacent 'small town', it is interesting to note that the date range of the coin assemblage from the river is not comparable with the late third and fourth century emphasis of that found during the excavations of the area.[31] It is instead dominated by issues dating to the second and early third century, with peaks in the reigns of Antoninus Pius, Septimius Severus and Severus Alexander indicating completely different patterns of deposition (Figure 4). Such high concentrations of early to mid-Roman coinage are unusual in the context of northern Britain and are usually to be found at sites with intensive urban or military activity.[32] As the first two peaks correspond with particular episodes of campaigning on the northern frontier, it may be that the deposition of coinage was associated with troop movements from the

[25] Hassall and Tomlin 1989, 337
[26] Cupid is usually considered to be the offspring of Mars and Venus, whose coupling was said to represent an allegory of love and war.
[27] Franconi 2014, 149
[28] Cool and Mason 2008, 15; RIB1024; Eckardt and Walton 2021, 270.
[29] King 2007, 191
[30] Woodward and Leach 1993, 93ff
[31] Brickstock 2008
[32] Guest 2008, 53; Moorhead 2001, 88

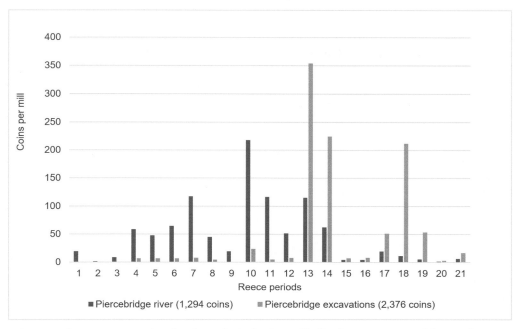

Figure 4. Histogram comparing the chronological coin profile for the riverine assemblage with coins recovered from excavations at Piercebridge

legionary fortress at York northwards. The third peak, associated with the reign of Severus Alexander is harder to explain, but could push the construction of the fort at Piercebridge, which has been tentatively dated to the period AD 260 to 280, slightly earlier.[33]

The size of the coin assemblage, comprising 1,369 coins, does suggest a deliberate process of deposition rather than casual loss or pragmatic refuse disposal. Large groups of Roman coinage are a common feature of Romano-British votive deposits on land and in water. Such groups have been argued to represent the material evidence for the ritual of the vow, an established and formulaic method of communication with a deity within the Roman world. The two parts of this vow comprised the *nuncupatio*, the promise to make an offering in return for divine intervention, and the *solutio*, whereby the offering was made.[34] Classical sources suggest that *nuncupatio* stage of the vow was often inscribed on *libelli* or wooden writing tablets.[35] The presence of 11 seal-boxes recovered from the river may provide material evidence for this practice[36] with the coinage representing the subsequent fulfilment of the vow.

---

[33] Cool and Mason 2008, 311

[34] Derks 1995

[35] See for example, Juvenal, 12, 98ff esp. 100. Cf. also *ibid.*, 27.

[36] Derks 1998, 229

Furthermore, the denominational composition of the coinage deposit from Piercebridge marks it out as unusual. While coin offerings at other watery sites such as Coventina's Well[37] and the Sacred Spring at Bath[38] are almost entirely composed of bronze denominations, suggesting that low value denominations were selected for deposition, the proportion of silver *denarii* at Piercebridge is very high. Again this may reflect the military character of activity at Piercebridge, as a larger proportion of high value coins tend to be found at military installations in comparison to civilian sites. Military provinces such as Britain, Upper and Lower Germany and Pannonia appear to have received more silver coinage than civilian ones such as Gaul and Italy.[39] It is also likely to indicate something about the status and wealth of those depositing objects as well as the value attached to the deities worshipped there. Certainly, the presence within the assemblage of more than 80 precious metal items, including two gold finger rings, eight silver finger rings, a gold earring and multiple cut gold jewellery fragments demonstrates a willingness to deposit high value artefacts, in a manner not paralleled in other votive deposits from Roman Britain.[40]

While both the date range and denominational composition of the coin assemblage are idiosyncratic, what is particularly striking is the treatment of individual coin issues. Approximately 8% of the coins in the assemblage have been subject to some form of defacement, whether that be piercing, mutilation or bending. For example, more than 46 *denarii*, ranging in date from Neronian to Severan issues, have been deliberately cut or broken into irregularly-sized pieces and a further 24 have small semi-circular cut-outs on their circumference. Although rare in Britain, defaced, cut and mutilated coins are known from other watery votive contexts such as Bourbonnes-les-Bains[41] and at sanctuary sites, particularly in Gaul and Germany.[42] This suggests a religious or ritual aspect to the practice, introduced into Britain from Gaul and the Rhine region,[43] an attractive hypothesis given the presence of soldiers from both Upper and Lower Germany at Piercebridge.[44]

The violence of the act of mutilating coins has been likened to the sacrifice of an animal,[45] and parallels may be drawn with the 'fragmentation' of objects in the Neolithic,[46] the 'ritual killing' of weaponry and other objects in the Bronze and Iron Age[47] and the dismemberment of statuary in the late Roman period.[48] Their mutilation marked them out as different, prevented

[37] Allason-Jones and Mackay 1985

[38] Walker 1988

[39] Hobley 1998, 128

[40] The assemblage of precious metal objects from Coventina's Well comprises two gold and three silver finger rings and 4 gold *aurei* (Allason-Jones and McKay 1985, 19ff) while that from the Sacred Spring includes one gold earring, one silver earring, two silver pans, two silver bosses, a silver tack, silver gilt pendant (Henig et al. 1988, 5-27) and 4 *aurei* (Walker 1988, 306ff).

[41] Sauer 2005, 79ff

[42] Aubin and Meissonnier 1994

[43] Kiernan 2001, 33

[44] Evidence includes RIB I, 1026: A tombstone of Gracilis, a centurion from Upper Germany from the Twenty Second Legion dating to AD 217 and found on the southern bank of the River Tees at Piercebridge; and RIB I,1022: an altar to Jupiter Dolichenus dedicated by Julius Valentinus, a centurion from Upper Germany.

[45] Zehnacker 1986, 54

[46] Chapman 2013

[47] Kiernan 2001, 33

[48] Croxford 2003

their re-use as currency and thus secured their passage as religious gifts. It is worth noting that the practice is not restricted to coinage, but can be observed in other classes of artefact recovered from the River Tees including jewellery, brooches and copper-alloy vessels.

There are also approximately 10 bent lead-alloy copies of Severan *denarii*, which form part of a larger group of distinctive copies in the assemblage. Along with 3 coin blanks, they may provide evidence for the production of a specific votive coinage intended for deposition. The treatment of these copies and indeed their very appearance is reminiscent of larger lead curse tablets and this may give some indication of their function. As with breaking and mutilation, the bending of coins is likely to have been a ritual act. However, no Romano-British parallels could be found, and there are few from further afield in the Roman Empire. Bent Roman coins are known from the river Liri in Italy where they were hammered into the packing of wooden bridge piles, and were interpreted as foundation deposits.[49] From an anthropological perspective, it may be relevant that in medieval England the bending of a coin was undertaken to both invoke and gain the intercession of a saint.[50]

Military dress, equipment and weaponry

As already noted, the coin assemblage and the collection of objects associated with religious beliefs both suggest a military character to activity at Piercebridge. This is confirmed by the 163 items of military dress and equipment recovered from the riverbed, which include belt and scabbard fittings, fragments of *lorica squamata* armour and four spear-heads all consistent with a second or early third century date. They were accompanied by 10 lead sealings, bearing the legends 'LVI' (*Legio VI Victrix*) and OVA (*Ala Vocontiorum* retrograde). Used to seal official documents and consignments of goods, these sealings may provide some indication of the identities of the legion and cavalry unit involved in deposition.[51]

As finds of Roman military metalwork in watery contexts are extremely rare in Britain,[52] the presence of such large quantities at Piercebridge is highly significant. Indeed, it may point to the adoption of and continued adherence to a ritual practice originating in Gaul or Germany, where numerous deposits of weaponry and military equipment have been found during dredging work, particularly along the Rhine[53] and Saône.[54] Along with deposits from temple sites such as Empel in the Netherlands, these finds have been interpreted as the offerings of veterans from auxiliary units to deities who had protected them during their service.[55] The equipment acquired great symbolic value because of the martial experiences associated with

---

[49] Houghtalin 1985, 68

[50] Kelleher 2011, 1494ff

[51] The *Ala Vocontiorum* were a cavalry unit originally stationed in Germania Inferior but moved to Britain by Hadrian in AD 122. An inscription places them at Newstead probably during the Antonine occupation of northern Britain (RIB 2121). Similar lead sealings to those recovered at Piercebridge identifying this unit have also been found at Leicester and South-Shields (RIB 2411.90 and RIB 2411.70); Walton, Humphreys and Tomlin 2021, 108-122.

[52] A small, copper-alloy catapult washer, probably dating to the first century AD, was recovered from the Sacred Spring at Bath (Henig *et al.* 1988, 8-9).

[53] Nicolay 2007, 183

[54] Bonnamour and Dumont 1994, 141ff

[55] Derks 1998, 52; Franconi 2014, 149

Figure 5. A selection of openwork belt mounts recovered from the river (Photograph: Aaron Watson)

it and signified a 'rite of passage' marking the conclusion of one stage of life and entry into the next.[56]

Although this parallel is instructive, there are some significant differences in both the chronology and type of military metalwork deposited at Piercebridge. The Continental examples mainly date to the first century AD and are characterised by large, prestige items such as helmets and swords, while the material from Piercebridge is mostly second and third century in date and is dominated by smaller pieces of metalwork associated with military dress. For example, a quarter of the brooch assemblage (24 examples) from the river is made up of Knee brooches, a type which tends to be found in military settings in Britain and is perhaps best known from the forts of the German *limes*.[57] Perhaps more striking is the number of fittings associated with second and third century military sword belts known as the *cingulum* and *balteus*.[58] As the belt was synonymous with the sword and representative of military authority,[59] their deposition should be regarded as highly symbolic. The fittings

---

[56] Derks 1998, 75ff

[57] Bayley and Butcher 2004, 179. At Catterick, twelve miles to the south of Piercebridge, the recovery of 10 Knee brooches from excavation was interpreted as representing an unusual influx of people in the period AD 150 to 225 (Mackreth 2002, 153-154).

[58] Hoss 2011, 30

[59] Hoss 2013, 322ff

include 45 strap-ends, 67 belt plates and a single buckle frame. (Figure 5). The near absence of buckle frames suggests that individual elements, rather than whole belts were selected for deposition, a *pars pro toto* gesture. A similar approach is suggested by the presence of pieces from sword scabbards including 18 copper-alloy scabbard slides, 3 baldric fittings and three chapes.

The assemblage of weaponry is restricted to a possible ballista bolt, an arrowhead and four spear-heads. None of the spear-heads appear to have been functional weapons. The first spear-head has an exaggerated leaf-shaped, blunted blade pierced with at least three semi-circular cut-outs. This treatment is reminiscent of that observed in the coin assemblage discussed above and of miniaturised spears from the temple sites of Great Walsingham, Norfolk,[60] and Uley.[61] The other three have the narrow, blunt blade and base expansion characteristic of Manning's Type 3[62] and are similar in form to the silver 'standard tip' found at Caerleon.[63] Spear-heads of this type are presumed to have had a ceremonial function connected with its use as a symbol of military might and an emblem of authority.[64] It has recently been suggested that they may have been used in exercises such as the *Hippika Gymnasia*.[65] At Chesters, the prevalence of spear-heads over other types of weaponry was linked to the cavalry presence at the fort,[66] and it is therefore possible that spearheads were selected for deposition at Piercebridge by cavalry troops.

The involvement of a cavalry unit in depositional practice at Piercebridge is supported not only by the presence of spears and lead sealings, but also by the considerable array of harness fittings recovered from the river. They include more than 147 elements associated with both the saddle and harness including strap slides and distributors, *phalerae*, as well as numerous decorative pendants and stud mounts (Figure 6). Of course, horses were not the exclusive preserve of the army and harness fittings have been found in civilian contexts both in Britain and on the Continent,[67] but the presence of so much material does suggest a cavalry presence. To gain some perspective on the size of the assemblage from Piercebridge, those from the excavations at Chesters and South Shields forts comprise 64 and 69 items respectively.[68]

Motivations for deposition

A symbolic aspect to the disposal of material culture at Piercebridge is evident and has enormous implications for our interpretation of the site. What is more difficult to establish

---

[60] Bagnall-Smith 1999, 34-35
[61] Henig 1993, 131, Find 4002
[62] Manning 1976, 19
[63] Boon 1972, 67, Fig. 38. Findspots of Manning Type 3 spear-heads in Britain are scarce, although they do appear to have a northern distribution. An example is known from Catterick (Mould 2002, 82, No 8) and an unprecedented 22 from the Clayton Collection in Chesters (McIntosh 2016, 215). A fragmentary example from South Shields was found buried with a selection of third century AD military equipment between the angle tower wall and the north east wall of the fort and appears to have been part of a votive boundary deposit (Croom 1995, 51; Haynes 1997, 122).
[64] Marchant 1990, 4
[65] McIntosh 2019, 94
[66] McIntosh 2019, 92
[67] Worrell and Pearce 2012, 387ff; Nicolay 2007, 44ff
[68] McIntosh 2019, 94

Figure 6. A selection of strap slides from horse harness recovered from the river
(Photograph: Aaron Watson)

is the motivation or motivations behind such disposal. Who deemed it necessary to deposit thousands of objects there, and why?

Clearly, the riverine location of the assemblage is significant. In the Roman world, there was a need to symbolically mark boundaries and transitions with specific rituals,[69] and crossing rivers was a potentially dangerous act that necessitated the provision of offerings to appropriate deities.[70] The concentration of material associated with Mercury may be significant in this regard. The river itself could also be unpredictable and given evidence for widespread flooding in northern Britain in the period c. AD 160 to 180,[71] it may be that on

---

[69] Smith and Brookes 2001, 6; Parker-Pearson and Richards 1994, 24-25

[70] Booth et al. 2007, 220; Braund 1996, 19; Bonnamour and Dumont 1994, 152

[71] Fitzpatrick and Scott 1999, 128, Bidwell and Holbrook 1989, 76-77

occasion, its destructive power was combatted through votive offerings intended to propitiate the appropriate gods. Indeed, some of the offerings may even represent a 'closure' deposit associated with the demolition, destruction or demise of the wooden bridge close by. At other sites, such as the Roman forts at Inchtuthil, Newstead and Bar Hill, pit deposits have been associated with the idea of abandonment and the clearing of the site, acts that are likely to have had a deeply ritual significance.[72]

Given the military emphasis of much of the material, is it is possible that much of the material represents offerings made by the military community on their way to the northern frontier, or on their return, another 'rite of passage'. It is perhaps significant that where episodes of riverine sacrifice are mentioned in Roman historical sources, they occur within the context of military campaigns and before significant battles. Lucullus sacrificed a bull to the Euphrates when he crossed with his army,[73] Cassius Dio describes the inauspicious sacrifices performed by Crassus before his defeat at Carrhae[74] and Caesar made sacrifice before crossing the Rubicon.[75] The physical boundary of the river may have acted as a sort of trigger reminding soldiers that they were entering the frontier zone, where discourse with the gods was deemed particularly appropriate, necessary or accessible. Furthermore, the very public deposition of material could be viewed as an important element in the construction of military identity and may also reflect, in part at least, something of the wider understanding of what it meant to 'act' as a Roman.[76]

Conclusion

Watery contexts are now widely accepted as having ritual significance as liminal and chtonic places, but this acceptance has been slower to emerge in Roman than in prehistoric archaeology. Over many years, spring sanctuaries and well deposits in Roman Britain have been identified and explored, often because their structural features make them easy to identify. However, there is a dispersed but growing body of evidence for Roman-period river deposits to which Piercebridge should certainly be added. As cataloguing and analysis continue, it is clear that the assemblage is a tremendously important find. It has the potential to transform our understanding not only of the development of Roman Piercebridge, but also of military identity, religion and ritual practice at the periphery of the Roman world.

Bibliography

Abbreviation RIB [here 1st edn of RIB I is cited] = Collingwood and Wright 1965, R. G. Collingwood, and R. P. Wright, *The Roman Inscriptions of Britain I.* Oxford University Press, Oxford.

Allason-Jones and McKay 1985, L. Allason-Jones, and B. McKay *Coventina's Well: a shrine on Hadrian's Wall.* Hexham: Trustees of the Clayton Collection.

Aubin and Meissonnier 1994, G. Aubin and J. Meissonnier, L'usage de la monnaie sur les sites du sanctuaire de l'ouest de la Gaule et de la Bourgogne. In: C. Godineau, I. Fauduet and

---

[72] Hingley 2006, 229
[73] Plutarch, *Luc.* 24.7
[74] Dio 14.18.5
[75] Suetonius, *Jul.* 81.2
[76] Smith 2016, accessed online

G. Coulon (eds.) *Les Sanctuaires de tradition indigene en Gaule romaine.* Actes du colloque d'Argentomagus. Paris: Errance, 143-152.

Bagnall-Smith 1999, J. Bagnall-Smith, Votive Objects and Objects of Votive Significance from Great Walsingham. *Britannia* 30, 21-56.

Bonnamour and Dumont 1994, L. Bonnamour, and A. Dumont, Les armes romaines de la Saône: état des découvertes et données récentes de fouilles. In: C. van Driel-Murray (ed.) *Military Equipment in Context. Proceedings of the Ninth International Roman Military Equipment Conference, Leiden, 1994* Journal of Roman Military Equipment Studies Vol. 5, 141-154.

Bradley 2000, R. Bradley, *An Archaeology of Natural Places.* London: Routledge

Braund 1996, D. Braund, *Ruling Roman Britain. Kings, Queens, Governors and Emperors from Julius Caesar to Agricola.* Routledge: London and New York.

Brickstock 2008, R. Brickstock, The Coins. In: D. Mason and H. Cool (eds.) *Roman Piercebridge: Excavations by D W Harding and Peter Scott 1969-1981.* Durham: Architectural and Archaeological Society of Durham & Northumberland Research Reports, 159-167.

Buttrey 1972, T.V. Buttrey, Halved coins, the Augustan reform and Horace, Odes I.3. *American Journal of Archaeology* Vol. 76, No. 1, 31-48.

Casey 1989, J. Casey, A votive deposit from the River Tees at Piercebridge. *Durham Archaeological Journal* 5, 37-42.

Chapman 2000, J. Chapman, *Fragmentation in Archaeology: People, Places and Broken Objects in the Prehistory of South Eastern Europe.* Routledge: London and New York.

Collingwood, Wright and Tomlin 1995, R. G. Collingwood, R. P. Wright and R. S. O Tomlin (eds) (new edition): The *Roman Inscriptions of Britain. Volume I: Inscriptions on Stone,* Stroud: Alan Sutton. <https://romaninscriptionsofbritain.org>

Cool and Mason 2008, H. E. M. Cool, and D. Mason, *Roman Piercebridge: Excavations by D. W. Harding and P. Scott 1969 - 1981* Durham: Architectural and Archaeological Society of Durham and Northumberland Research Report 7.

Croom 1995, A. Croom, A hoard of Roman military equipment from South Shields. *The Arbeia Journal,* Vol. IV, 45-53.

Croxford 2003, B. Croxford, Iconoclasm in Roman Britain? *Britannia* 34, 81-96.

Cüppers 1969, H. Cüppers, *Trier Romerbrücken.* Trierer Grabungen und Forschungen, 5. Trier: Rheinisches Landesmuseum Trier.

Derks 1988, T. Derks, *Gods, Temples and Ritual Practices: The Transformation of Religious Ideas and Values in Roman Gaul.* Amsterdam University Press: Amsterdam.

Derks 1995, T. Derks, The Ritual of the Vow in Gallo-Roman Religion, in J. Metzler et al. (eds), *Integration in the Early Roman West: The Role of Culture and Ideology.* Luxembourg: Dossier d'archéologie du Musée National d'Histoire et d'Art 4, 111–127.

Eckardt and Walton 2021, H. Eckardt, and P. J. Walton, *Bridge Over Troubled Water: The Roman Finds from the River Tees at Piercebridge in Context.* Roman Society: Britannia Monograph Vol. 34.

Fitzpatrick and Scott 1999, A. P. Fitzpatrick and P. R. Scott, The Roman Bridge at Piercebridge, North Yorkshire-County Durham. *Britannia* 30, 111-132.

Franconi 2014, T. Franconi, Provincial Cults of Mars in the Roman Empire. In: L.R. Brody and G.L. Hoffman (eds.) *Roman in the Provinces: Art on the Periphery of Empire.* McMullen Museum of Art: Chestnut Hill, 145-154.

Frier and Parker 1970, B. W. Frier, and A. Parker, Roman coins from the River Liri. *Numismatic Chronicle* 10, 89-109.

Gerrard 2013, J. Gerrard, Pottery report on the Piercebridge river material. Unpublished.

Gerrard, J., Mills, J.M. and Hudák 2021 ‚Chapter 16: The Pottery Assemblage' in H. Eckardt and P.J. Walton eds. *Bridge Over Troubled Water: The Roman Finds from the River Tees at Piercebridge in Context*, Britannia Monograph Series No. 34, 190-214.

Gilles and Wiesser 2007, K.-J. Gilles and B. Wiesser, Antike Münzen aus Philippopolis und Perinth aus der Mosel bei Trier. *Trierer Zeitschrift* 69/70 (2006/07),127-136.

Guest 2008, P. Guest, Coins. In: P. Booth, A-M. Bingham and S. Lawrence (eds.) *The Roman Roadside Settlement at Westhawk Farm, Ashford, Kent, Excavations 1998-9.* Oxford: Oxford Archaeology Monograph Series, 135-139.

Gurney 1986, D. Gurney, Leylands Farm, Hockwold-cum-Wilton; excavations by Charles Green, 1957. In: *Settlement, Religion and Industry on the Roman Fen-edge, Norfolk.* EAA Report No. 31, 49-92.

Hassall and Tomlin 1989, M. W. C. Hassall, and R. S. O. Tomlin, Roman Britain in 1988. II. Inscriptions. *Britannia* 20, 327-345.

Haynes 1997, I. Haynes, Religion in the Roman army: unifying aspects and regional trends.' In: H. Cancik and J. Rüpke (ed.) *Römische Reichsreligion und Provinzialreligion.* Tübingen: Mohr Siebeck, 113-126.

Henig 1993, M. Henig, Chapter 8: Votive objects: weapons, miniatures, tokens, and fired clay accessories. In: A. Woodward (ed.) *The Uley Shrines : Excavation of a ritual complex on West Hill, Uley, Gloucestershire, 1977-1979.* London: English Heritage, 131-147.

Henig, Brown, Baatz, Sunter and Allason-Jones 1988, M. Henig, D. Brown, D. Baatz, N. Sunter and L. Allason-Jones, Objects from the Sacred Spring in B. Cunliffe (ed.) *The Temple of Sulis Minerva at Bath Volume II: The Finds from the Sacred Spring.* Oxford: Oxford University Committee for Archaeology, 5-57.

Hingley 2006, R. Hingley, The Deposition of Iron Objects in Britain during the Later Prehistoric and Roman Periods: Contextual Analysis and the Significance of Iron. *Britannia* 37, 213–257.

Hobley 1998, A. S. Hobley, *An Examination of Roman Bronze Coin Distribution in the Western Empire AD 81-192.* BAR International Series 688. Oxford: Archaeopress.

Hoss 2011, S. Hoss, The Roman Military Belt. In: M.-L. Nosch (ed.) *Wearing the Cloak. Dressing the Soldier in Roman Times.* Ancient Textiles Series vol. 10, Oxford, 29-44.

Hoss 2013, S. Hoss, A theoretical approach to Roman military belts. In: M. Sanader, A. Rendić-Miočević, D. Tončinić and I. Radman-Livaja (eds) *Weapons and military equipment in a funerary context.* Proceedings of the XVII Roman Military Equipment Conference, Zagreb: Filozofski Fakultet, 317-326.

Houghtalin 1885, L. Houghtalin, Roman coins from the River Liri III. *Numismatic Chronicle .* 145, 67-81.

Kelleher 2011, R. Kelleher, Interpreting single finds in medieval England – the secondary lives of coins. In. N. Holmes (ed.) *Proceedings of XIVth International Numismatic Congress Glasgow 2009 II.* Glasgow, 1492-1499.

Kiernan 2001, P. Kiernan, The Ritual Mutilation of Coins on Romano-British Sites. *British Numismatic Journal* 71, 18-33.

King 2007, A. King, Characterising Assemblages of Votive Offerings at Romano-Celtic Temples in Britain, in M. Hainzmann (ed.), *Auf den Spuren keltisher Gotterverehrung*, Vienna: Verlag der Osterreich. Akademie der Wissenschaften, 183–196.

Mackreth 2002, D. F. Mackreth, Brooches from Catterick. In: P. R. Wilson (ed.) *Cataractonium: Roman Catterick and its hinterland. Excavation and research, 1958-1997.* CBA Research Report 129. York: Council for British Archaeology, 149-163.

Manning 1976, W. H. Manning, *Catalogue of Romano-British Ironwork in the Museum of Antiquities, Newcastle-upon-Tyne.* Newcastle-upon-Tyne: Department of Archaeology.

Marchant 1990, D. Marchant, Roman weapons in Great Britain, a case study: spearheads, problems in dating and typology. *Journal of Roman Military Equipment Studies* (JRMES) Vol. 1, 1-6.

McIntosh 2019, F. McIntosh, *The Clayton Collection; an archaeological appraisal of a 19th century collection of Roman Artefacts from Hadrian's Wall.* BAR Brit.ser.646, 2019.

Moorhead 2001, T. S. N. Moorhead, Roman coin finds from Wiltshire. In: P. Ellis (ed.) *Roman Wiltshire and After. Papers in honour of Ken Annable.* Devizes: Wiltshire Archaeological and Natural History Society, 85-105.

Metcalf 1974, W. E. Metcalf, Roman coins from the River Liri II. *Numismatic Chronicle* 14, 42-53.

Mould 2002, Q. Mould, 'Iron objects from Catterick Bypass.' In: P. Wilson (ed.) *Cataractonium. Roman Catterick and it Hinterland: Excavations and Research 1958-1997 Part II* CBA Research Report 129 (2002), 82-106.

Niblett 2001, R. Niblett, *Verulamium: The Roman City of St Albans.* Tempus Publishing: Stroud.

Nicolay 2007, J. Nicolay, *Armed Batavians: Use and Significance of Weaponry and Horse Gear from Non-Military Contexts in the Rhine Delta (50 BC to AD 450).* Amsterdam: Amsterdam University Press.

Parker-Pearson and Richards (eds) 1994, M. Parker-Pearson and C. Richards (eds), *Architecture and order: Approaches of social space.* Routledge: London

Robertson 2000, A. S. Robertson, *An Inventory of Romano-British Coin Hoards. Edited by Richard Hobbs and T.V. Buttrey.* Royal Numismatic Society Special Publication 20. London.

Rhodes 1991, M. Rhodes, The Roman coinage from London Bridge and the development of the City and Southwark. *Britannia* 22, 179-90

Rouvier-Jeanlin 1972, M. Rouvier-Jeanlin, *Les Figurines Gallo-Romaines en Terre Cuite au Musée des Antiquités Nationales.* Gallia Supplement XXIV. CNRS: Paris.

Roymans 1993, N. Roymans, Romanisation and the transformation of a martial elite-ideology in a frontier province. In: *Frontières d'empire. Actes de la Table Ronde International de Nemours 1992.* Mémoires du Musée de Préhistoire d'Ile-de-France 5, 33-50.

Sauer 2005, E. Sauer, *Coins, cult and cultural identity: Augustan coins, hot springs and the early Roman baths at Bourbonne-les-Bains.* Leicester: University of Leicester.

Smith 2016, A. T. Smith, Ritual deposition. In: M. Millett, L. Revell and A. Moore (eds) *The Oxford Handbook of Roman Britain.* Oxford University Press (accessed online).

Smith and Brookes 2001, A. T. Smith and A. Brookes, Holy Ground: Theoretical issues relating to the landscape and material culture of ritual space. In: A. T. Smith and A. Brookes (eds) *Holy Ground: Theoretical Issues Relating to the Landscape and Material Culture of Ritual Space Objects. Papers from a session held at the Theoretical Archaeology Group Conference, Cardiff 1999.* BAR Int. Series 956, 5-8

Tomlin, Wright and Hassall 2009, R. S. O. Tomlin, R. P. Wright and M. W. C. Hassall, *The Roman Inscriptions of Britain III. Inscriptions on Stone found or notified between 1 January 1955 and 31 December 2006.* Oxbow Books for the Haverfield Bequest, Oxford.

Walker 1988, D. R. Walker, The Roman Coins in B. Cunliffe (ed.) *The Temple of Sulis Minerva at Bath Volume II: The Finds from the Sacred Spring*

Walton 2008, P. J. Walton, The finds from the river in H. E. M. Cool and D. Mason (eds) *Roman Piercebridge: Excavations by D. W. Harding and P. Scott,* 286-93.

Walton 2012, P. J. Walton, *Rethinking Roman Britain: Coinage and Archaeology* (Moneta Monograph No.137).Wetteren: Moneta.

Walton 2016, P. J. Walton, Was the Piercebridge assemblage a military votive deposit? In: X.P. Jensen and T. Crane (eds.) *Imitation and Inspiration. Proceedings of the 18th International Roman Military Equipment Conference held in Copenhagen, Denmark, 9-14th June 2013.* Journal of Roman Military Equipment Studies (JRMES) 17, 191-194.

Walton, P.J., Humphreys, O. and Tomlin, R.S.N 2021 'Objects associated with writing and communication' in H. Eckardt and P.J. Walton eds. *Bridge Over Troubled Water: The Roman Finds from the River Tees at Piercebridge in Context*, Britannia Monograph Series No. 34, 108-125.

Wessex Archaeology 2010, *Piercebridge, County Durham. Archaeological Evaluation and Assessment of Results.* Unpublished report by Wessex Archaeology produced for Videotext Communications Ltd.

Woodward and Leach 1993, A. Woodward and P. Leach, *The Uley Shrines: Excavation of a Ritual Complex on West Hill, Uley, Gloucestershire 1977-9*

Worrell and Pearce 2012, S. Worrell and J. Pearce, Roman Britain in 2011 II. Finds Reported Under the Portable Antiquities Scheme' *Britannia* 43, 355-392.

Wright 1967, R.P. Wright, Roman Britain in 1966: Inscriptions. *Journal of Roman Studies* 57, 203-210.

Zehnacker 1986, H. Zehnacker, Un trésor de monnaies défigurées de l'époque augustéenne. *Bull. De la Sociéte Nationale des Antiquaires de France*, 51-54.

Water and Liminality in Pre-Roman Gaul

Aaron Irvin

It is the purpose of this chapter to combine two fields of inquiry that have approached pre-Roman Gaul from distinctly different angles: ancient religion and the development of pre-Roman Gallic societies. Archaeologists have traditionally examined the development of Gallic communities through the developmental complexity of Gallic settlements. In these cases, complexity is quantified through a process that compares these pre-Roman Gallic sites with Mediterranean urban centers, noting the growth of the sites as reflective of a more complex social structure due to contact and influences from Mediterranean societies. Instead, this article will focus on recent scholarship on the nature of cult communities and orthopraxy in the context of polytheistic societies, and the implication that this approach has in analyzing the results of orthopraxic rituals in the archaeological record, specifically the deposition of goods and votive offerings in watery sites and streams. In doing so, this chapter will argue that Gallic communities developed first as cult communities tied through ritual to certain sites within Gaul, and that it was this common underlying cultic membership and cultic connection with specific *topoi* that defined Gallic identity. Ritual water depositions thus emerge as the first connection between individual, community, and place, serving to delineate the boundaries between differing communities beyond the standard central-place model common within the Mediterranean world.

Iron Age settlement patterns: models, interpretations, and shortcomings

As Nico Roymans succinctly points out, sedentary agricultural regimes increase a region's archaeological profile, as they demand greater landscape management and intensify the regional differentiation as the population adapts the natural environment to itself.[1] The ability to archaeologically trace the development and growth of complexity within a community is predicated on the existence and discovery of artifacts that reflect this complexity.[2] Thus, as Lindner states, 'Historians dislike nomads'.[3] Archaeologists note the emergence in the Late Bronze Age (pre-1200 BCE) in Europe of a common material culture referred to as the Urnfield tradition, building off of bronze trade into Europe from southwest Asia and the Mediterranean.[4] With the 1200 BCE collapse, the Urnfield culture in Europe gave way to a new material culture broadly referred to as the Hallstatt culture and seen by many archaeologists as the beginnings of the Celtic populations throughout Europe.[5]

The pattern of early Iron Age Hallstatt (ca. pre-500 BCE) settlement in the Gallic region is seen in isolated, rural farmsteads that were rarely concentrated and, if so, were only unified

---

[1] Roymans 1996, 49-50
[2] Crumley 1974a, 254
[3] Lindner 1982, 689
[4] Kristiansen 1998; Kristiansen and Larsson 2005
[5] Cunliffe 1997, 43-44; Kristiansen 1998, 62-64

for brief periods of time.[6] Indeed, while the Iron Age was a period of rapid development and evolution, it was a period that began with extreme localisation and a breakdown of outside contacts and trade, necessitating the transition from foreign-supplied bronze alloy to locally sourced iron.[7] Thus, Collis's division between Hallstatt C and Hallstatt D settlements, with the primary differentiation being trade and contact with the Mediterranean. However, in Collis' own formulation, the difference in contacts with the Mediterranean, as evidenced by the trade goods present within burials, does not change the decentralised nature of the community.[8]

With the emergence of the early La Tène period (ca. 500 BCE), these loosely aligned Hallstatt farmsteads are replaced for what are termed 'Celtic fields', a more complex level of spatial arrangement that integrates pastoral and low-intensity agriculture.[9] With Celtic fields, the area of habitation and exploitation varied throughout the year; homesteads only lasted about 30-50 years within a community of seldom more than 5 family units.[10] A central, cleared rural village area existed, but was lacking in specialised structures such as animal shelters, and it likewise might move within the shared range of territory as the settlements themselves were reorganised.[11]

By the middle La Tène period (ca. 450-100 BCE) Gallic sites expanded and included evidence of ironworks, coinage, food storage, and weaving, as well as specialised wares made of bone, metal, and glass.[12] Campanian ware imports reached the interior in this period, in particular along major rivers which acted as lines of trade and communication.[13] The middle La Tène period also saw the emergence of what might best be described as a semi-nomadic, de-nucleated settlement pattern, a kind of ranged pastoralism. Separate from settlement patterns, there was in this period an increasing standardisation of water depositions and sites throughout the region, as items became restricted to unfinished blades, 'currency bars', coins, or models of weapons.[14] Several deposition sites were abandoned, such as those along the Seine around Paris, while others such as Neuchâtel include more weaponry and spoils from warfare.[15] Weapon deposits were bent or broken before placement in deep water, rendering them unusable or inaccessible, while deposits likewise came to include horses and horse-riding equipment.[16] Votive offerings, statues, even objects shaped like human body parts, became regularised and identifiable, while deposits of agricultural produce and human and animal remains revealed the increasing value of sedentary agriculture.[17] Inscriptions appear at several sites, identifying the deity to be invoked at the location, further formalizing the process begun in earlier periods.[18]

---

[6]   Audouze and Büchenschütz 1992, 217

[7]   Bradley 1998, 155-156; cf. Woudhuizen and van Binsbergen 2011

[8]   Collis 1995, 75

[9]   Audouze and Büchenschütz 1992, 160-162; Brun 1995, 123

[10]   Derks 1998, 57; Audouze and Büchenschütz 1992, 162-164

[11]   Audouze and Büchenschütz 1992, 164

[12]   Audouze and Büchenschütz 1992, 231-232; Collis 1984, 171

[13]   Audouze and Büchenschütz 1992, 232; Brun 1995, 123

[14]   Bradley 1998, 171-173

[15]   Bourgeois 1992, 198; Cunliffe 1997, 194-195

[16]   Bradley 2000, 58; Brunaux 1988, 94-95, 126-127

[17]   Bradley 1998, 164, 171; Cunliffe 1997, 196-197, 204

[18]   Bourgeois 1992, 193

It is in the latter portion of the La Tène period then (ca. 150-50 BCE) that archaeologists note the emergence of the Gallic *oppida*; extensive, fortified urban-like sites situated throughout the Gallic interior. In broad terms, the emergence of urbanism in the Gallic interior is presented as having been brought about through increased trade and contact with the urban societies of the Mediterranean such as the Greeks, Romans, and Etruscans.[19] The general perception is that these sites are primarily defensive in nature and situated along major river routes and trade lines.[20] The *oppida* likewise might have served as market centers, allowing for ease of access but developed away from the area of agricultural produce as per the Mediterranean model. The effect was the creation of an area of crafting and redistribution coordinating between productive zones; the general assumption is that these large, fortified, proto-urban centers emerged to control trade and contact with the emergence of a centralised control and command structure.[21]

The interaction between the *oppida* and trade remains unclear, especially as regards rivers. Collis notes there is an assumption that rivers formed easy boundaries between Gallic polities before Rome, yet the placement of *oppida* do not allow for this to be universally the case.[22] The combination of defensive structure and market center into a single site is counter-intuitive, requiring the *oppida* to be simultaneously accessible and inaccessible, to be open to trade and travel while also restricted to outside contact and assault.[23] Nor is the analysis that the *oppida* were inherently defensive structures universally viable: significant areas within the *oppida* were essentially empty space, while settlements outside the walls persisted into the Roman period.[24] The size and stone facings of the *oppida*, held loosely by iron clamps and providing little defensive value, indicate a preference for aesthetics over effectiveness.[25] With the practicality of the walls set aside, the effect then is to physically separate space. Imposing a monumental wall complete with elaborate gateways on the land itself reshaped and altered the way the geography functioned, as well as creating an ideological statement that those in power had the ability to identify and exclude outsiders and potential threats.[26]

As Collis states as regards the transition to *oppida*:

> The evidence so far suggests that the processes of social change, for instance the appearance of a social elite, that the foundation of the *oppida* implies had already commenced before their foundation. The necessary political organization of a primitive state may equally have been developed. If so, these were primitive states which lacked what for many archaeologists is a prerequisite of state organization – urban centers.[27]

---

[19] Brun 1995, 122-123
[20] Collis 1984, 167; Hawkes 1931, 60-97
[21] Collis 1984, 174-175; Grant 1986; Cunliffe 1991, Ralston 2006
[22] Collis 1984, 176; Hamilton and Manley 2001, 7-42
[23] Audouze and Büchenschütz 1992, 235
[24] Collis 1984, 179
[25] Brun 1995, 123-124; Audouze and Büchenschütz 1992, 235
[26] Brun 1995, 124-125; Crumley 1974a, 255-259; Roymans 1996 57; Hamilton and Manley 2001, 34
[27] Collis 1995, 80

In the same volume, Haselgrove likewise echoes Collis's statements that the sudden changes in the later Iron Age must have some precursor not seen in the settlement remains.[28] Thus the work of Fitzpatrick and Oswald in particular, seeking to re-examine and re-evaluate the development of middle La Tène sites, in particular with an eye towards their development as an outgrowth of local religious traditions and activities.[29] The *oppida* thus becomes an ideological construct, a common statement of power and purpose amongst the Gallic elite rather than an attempt to mirror Mediterranean urbanisation. In short, *oppida* and urbanisation in pre-Roman Gaul exist as a series of paradoxes: isolated market centers, open defensive structures, impractically practical in their layout and construction, the sometimes blank and open centerpieces of a society perhaps beginning to create urban centers like those of the Mediterranean, but utterly unlike that society in every way.

Water, ritual, and the significance of place

Central organisation and standardisation during the middle La Tène period is seen in the ritualised water deposits of the period, not in the urban-like settlement patterns. Standard central-place theory and models dependent on Mediterranean style urbanisation have been found lacking in their application to settlement patterns within Iron Age Gaul. Bradley has argued for a 'process of ritualization' emerging from everyday activities and objects, arguing that the previous divisions between the sacred and practical do not exist within the pre-modern world.[30] This analysis has likewise been taken up by Gosden, examining the concept of the 'agency of objects', as well as by Nongbri, who argues that the concept of religion itself as a separate sphere of inquiry and activity is a Christian and modern concept that has little usefulness in analyzing the ancient world.[31]

In the ancient world, religion served as the explanation for the unexplainable, providing the cause and effect for both natural and seemingly unnatural phenomena. Paired with this view of the world is the means by which human beings might interact with those unseen forces that govern the universe, thereby achieving some sense of control over the uncontrollable. As Rüpke states, polytheism served as a means of interpreting reality and establishing lines of communication between the constituent elements of that reality.[32] Religion was primarily pragmatic in its outlook and application; the gods were served in order to gain specific rewards, or to avoid punishments, and offerings were made in order to placate and encourage divine favor and action.[33] From this basic system of what we might consider 'economic exchange', complex systems of exchange, performance, and ritual emerged.

Ritual activities, and not dogmatic belief, were fundamental to the relationship between communities and those divine entities that represented the abstract mechanisms that governed the unexplainable and uncontrollable natural world.[34] Likewise, as Connerton outlines, ritual

---

[28] Haselgrove 1995, 85-87
[29] Oswald 1997, 87-95; Fitzpatrick 1997, 73-86; Hill 1989, 19-20
[30] Bradley 2003, 12
[31] Gosden 2005, 193-211; Nongbri 2008, 440-460
[32] Rüpke 2014, 171, 175
[33] Rüpke 2007, 149-150; Poux 2006, 117-134
[34] Brunaux 1988, 66-67; Derks 1998, 22, 94; Feeney 1998

activities were significant in the life of the community in expressing the shared values of the group and thereby reducing internal dissent.[35] Ritual and religion were external and communal, concerned not with correct, dogmatic identification, belief, and internalisation of the nature of the gods, but *orthopraxis*, the correct performance of rites, rituals, vows, sacrifices, and festivals that incorporated whole communities of worshippers and actors and thereby displayed externally the adherence to internal community values and ethos.[36] Ritual thus served to establish a simple binary connected to personal and group identity; one either performed correctly and thus proved one's adherence to the communal order, or one did not.[37] The community thus reproduced itself through the extension of a shared religious identity and narrative produced through the intersection of ritual, community, and place.[38]

In an orthopraxic context, significance is to be found in the continuation of ritual activities, the external expression of religion tied to specific location, and modes of behavior. Watson notes the continuity of numerous Gallic cults, gods, and religious practices from the pre-conquest Iron Age period well into the second century CE.[39] While he does not use the specific term, Brunaux places Gallic religious activity firmly within the context of orthopraxis, with Gallic religious life consisting of constant movement between places of settlement and places of sacred ritual and deposition of offerings, and all activities beginning and ending with a performance of ritual. All Gallic existence was marked by rituals which themselves set the 'rhythm of life' in movements to and from sanctuaries and sacred places; these sacred sites of ritual deposit thus formed the boundaries and contours of communities and communal interaction.[40] Settlements were not defined based on economic, defensive, or practical aspects of the landscape; as the discussion of the relevant scholarship above has shown, this inconsistency is itself acknowledged within the field. Water deposits marked the boundaries of participation and religious activity within a broader, more nebulous landscape that extended beyond the standard central-place model imposed upon the *oppida*.

Religious rites and traditions were held and performed at the local level, with individuals, families, villages, and cities part of a religious collective that allowed for variations in practice and belief at all levels.[41] Rituals were dynamic and specific to their location, requiring knowledge of how to act in a local, rather than universal, setting and creating a shared, communal experience of interacting with the gods as a unit, rather than a sense of shared belief.[42] It is thus telling that evidence indicates the regulation and standardisation of religious rites at watery deposition sites in the period *before* the emergence of *oppida*. These rituals, tied to specific sites of ritual water deposition, marked the contours of communities, determining those to be counted as insiders and outsiders.[43] The lack of specific or universal orthodoxy allowed variations in myth and practice at the local level, but these variations still existed within the bounds of established orthopraxic themes and activities that could be played out

---

[35] Connerton 1989, 45, 49

[36] Derks 1998, 22-24, Connerton 1989, 50; Scheid 2003, 18

[37] Connerton 1989, 59-60

[38] Beard, North, and Price 1998, 42-54; Lovell 2010, 105-106; Scheid and De Polignac 2010, 428-429

[39] Watson 2007, 89, 92, 94-96, 183-184, 224

[40] Brunaux 1988, 8, 48-49

[41] Scheid 1999, 383-384

[42] Connerton 1989, 45, 49-50; Revell 2007, 226

[43] Scheid 1995, 15-31

at common sacred locales, both within and between communities; as Connerton emphasises, ritual created an economy of performance through formalisation and restricted vocabulary, rhythm, and intonation, demanding either compliance or variation within the realm of performative action versus variable ways of telling or saying.[44] Deposition sites did not act as a liminal border or boundary in and of themselves, rather through the actions that took place there and through participation, they established membership in the communities that utilised these places. In this way, participation at deposition sites created abstract boundaries and borders between the otherwise nebulous groups within the region, creating the first connections between person, place, and community within the region.

As religion was external, membership within the cult community was easily verified through proper behavior, thus identifying those who were to be considered insiders and safe members of the community, and those who were outsiders and potential threats. Within Gaul prior to Roman conquest, it was the *pagus* that had served as the center of cult in Gallic communities, maintaining its own rituals, sacred sites, cult functionaries, and even its own pantheon of gods.[45] As Derks elaborates extensively these cult communities could extend from the private and individual level, to public places maintained by the collective community, to religious *foci* for a variety of different types of kinship groups or co-residents or even those engaged in a common trade or craft.[46] Finally, Derks takes special note of open air sanctuaries at the location of natural phenomena such as the sources of rivers, brooks, or springs, that were communally accessible, but were used primarily by individuals as sites of ritual deposition.[47]

Ritual and the creation of community

The developments of the late La Tène period, with the emergence of *oppida* and a variety of urban-like agglomerations, exist as an expression and outgrowth of a pre-existing Gallic community that had come to define itself through ritual connection to the land in the middle La Tène period. The emergence of *oppida* thus served as an extension of a pre-existing pattern of settlement and occupation, rather than its transformation by an urban typology drawn from settlements along the Mediterranean coast.

In their seminal 1997 work, Kolb and Snead identify three 'irreducible elements' of human communities within a spatially defined locus of human activity: social reproduction, subsistence production, and self-identification.[48] It is this intersection between the individual and the community, through place and ritual, and its reproduction over time, which concerns this chapter and its focus on the meaning and significance of ritual water depositions in pre-Roman Gaul. As Bradley argues, a deposited object is itself connected to the meaning attached to the location of its deposition which, by extension, connects the individual performing the ritual with the nature of the community and its history.[49] These ritual deposits occurred away from settlements, and included a restricted range of goods that were allowed to be rendered

---

[44] Revell 2007, 226; Brunaux 1988, 11, 60; Connerton 1989, 59-61 *passim*

[45] Derks 1998, 96, 123; Roymans 1990, 20, 50-51

[46] Derks 1998, 185-190

[47] Derks 1998, 138, 187

[48] Kolb and Snead 1997, 611

[49] Bradley 2000, 27-28, 48

unrecoverable or destroyed as a part of the deposition.[50] The place of deposition determined the suitability of the objects to be deposited, and presumably the reasons for deposition as well, allowing only certain objects and activities at particular locations, creating a complex sacred geography across a landscape.[51]

For the most part, these sites were sacred in and of themselves rather than as an extension of their natural features, such as a hot spring or mineral spring. Likewise, these sites served as areas of central cultic activity, not as an extension of any pre-existing urban cultic agglomeration.[52] Localised traditions dictated the nature of each site, the depositions allowed, and those allowed to participate in the rituals. For example, at the sources of the Seine the construction of an elaborate shrine on the site, while no shrine was constructed at the source of the Roches, while the shrines of Glanum and Nîmes were monumentalised and incorporated into the urban center.[53] While local variations occurred between deposition sites, there existed an overall logic and organisation behind the act of deposition itself, including distinctions between deposits in wet versus dry locations, the creation of specialised structures and even goods specifically for deposition.[54] As Burke discusses in examining the archaeology of mixed settlement patterns:

> Identity is... best understood as a constellation of markers attributed to or claimed by a given group and, therefore, various sub-affiliations may be collectively identified by a single label, which is otherwise inadequate to explain either similarities or differences among subgroups.[55]

The act of deposition likewise necessitates a connection between the individual and the site of deposition in order to be effective in an orthopraxic system; differentiation might occur in the types of offerings made, or where and how the offerings are made, but what remains consistent is the intersection between individual, place, and community, all of which is made manifest in the moment the ritual is performed and the items are deposited.

Centralisation and competition

As indicated in the review of scholarship above, previous dichotomies between nomadic and sedentary, urban and rural, and centralised and decentralised are increasingly found to be inapplicable to the nature of the archaeological remains of Iron Age Gaul. Previous models predicated on central-place theory, developed from an analysis derived from Mediterranean city-states among the Greeks, Etruscans, and Phoenicians, do not seem immediately applicable to Iron Age sites stretching from Poland and Scandinavia all the way to the Iberian interior and British Isles. Indeed, simply based on sheer volume, it would seem that the city-state models of the Mediterranean world stand as outliers rather than the standard data set to which other sites should be compared. This model ignores broader concepts of ethnic affiliation and political identity, and fails to fully identify more complex social models that

---

[50] Bradley 1998, 10
[51] Bradley 1998, 14, 178; Bradley 2000, 48-49
[52] Bourgeois 1994, 15; Scheid and De Polignac 429-430, 432-433
[53] Bradley 1998, 51-53; Bourgeois, 1994, 16-19
[54] Bradley 2000, 52-53; Bourgeois 1994, 20; Deyts 1983, 197-203
[55] Burke 2016, 4

endure over distance and allow for the exposure and integration of foreign ideas without the loss of internal cohesion.[56]

Crumley's analysis of the Gallic elite as a heterarchical group must likewise be taken into account, requiring a reassessment of traditional chieftain and central-place archaeological models and their application to pre-Roman Gaul. As Earle has argued, the manipulation of the landscape itself in the creation of settlements, boundaries, and irrigation served a symbolic as well as practical purpose, emphasizing the dominant role of the chieftain and creating the hierarchy over which he held dominance.[57] Similarly, Lillios has argued chieftains were necessarily vulnerable; thus, beyond control of necessary resources or labour, chieftains sought to create a displayed, ideological difference between themselves and highlight the degree to which their position could only be filled by one such as themselves.[58] However, these expressions require the existence of an established settlement and developed economic connection to the land; in the case of a nomadic or semi-nomadic settlement pattern as seen through the middle La Tène period, Lindner discusses the significance of genealogy, with the caveat that,

> Genealogy may serve as an idiom or charter that nomads use to explain their history and politics. Thus, the rule of a particular chief finds its *ex post facto* justification: as the tribal genealogy is rearranged, his lineage is 'discovered' to be the senior lineage.[59]

Yet, within Gallic society, as Crumley has extensively outlined, there was not a singular hierarchy but at least three differing bases of authority, linked together through kin relationships, economic ties, and social bonds of patronage and clientage.[60] This is not to argue that Earle's models are inapplicable, but rather that they apply to a more diverse group of potential leaders than previous theories based on centralisation and central place might allow; Gallic society presents not a single, centralised ruler, but multiple potential rulers who in particular circumstances may exercise greater authority than their peers.

> In this regard, much work has been done in analyzing the native settlements of the Rhône valley, and the influence of Greek colonies such as Massilia. As Dyson states,
>
> Far from losing their cultural vitality in the face of Greek influence, these Celts, Iberians, and Ligurians developed a dynamic social system that used Greek elements to articulate and develop native forms. Greek architecture graced native shrines. Greek letters expressed native language. Moreover ... there was among the Celts... [some] sense of ethnic identity.[61]

In Dyson's statement, there is a dichotomy drawn between the Celts and the Greeks, those elements that are native to Gaul and those that are Greek and 'foreign'. Yet the picture painted

---

[56] Crumley 1974a, 254; Burke 2014, 396, 403
[57] Earle 2002, 330
[58] Lillios 1999, 236
[59] Lindner 1982, 696-697
[60] Crumley 1974b; Crumley 1995
[61] Dyson 1985, 141

by the archaeological remains of the region is far more complex and dynamic; it was not simply a matter of native versus foreign. As Dietler states:

> As late as the end of the second century BCE, five hundred years after the foundation of the Greek colony [Massalia], the inhabitants of Entremont, a mere twenty-six kilometers to the north, were cooking their meals in pots that had changed little since the Bronze Age, were affixing human skulls to the walls of a sanctuary in a practice the Greeks found repugnant, and were engaged in a violent struggle with Massalia that threatened its very existence. Clearly, Entremont had not been transported to Greece; nor did its citizens have any desire to be like Greeks.[62]

Mediterranean contacts provided the Gallic populations with a diverse 'cultural tool set'; a range of styles, types, and technologies that expanded the ability of the Gauls to express themselves. As outlined by Crumley, different regions responded and reacted to this toolset in different ways, yet even the northernmost groups, those most distant from direct Mediterranean influence, showed similar degrees of monumentalisation and centralisation in the same period; the deciding factor in developments of the late La Tène period was not Roman trade, but elements of the Gallic elite who found new ways of expressing their authority.[63] Thus, in the case of the Rhône valley, the setting for the earliest Gallic urban spaces, the key factor in their growth and development was not emulation of the Greek city-state of Massalia, but rather competition among both the insiders and outsiders of Gallic society.[64]

The significance of water deposition sites in terms of ritual, community, and identity have been discussed above. Scheid and De Polignac likewise argue for the power of cult place to act as central-places.[65] In Scheid's and De Polignac's model, cult places emerge as areas of economic centralisation through the gathering, deposition, and potential redistribution of offerings; over time, the most economically successful cult places emerge creating a level of religious centralisation in the rural landscape.[66] In a heterarchical model, these deposition sites likewise serve as a conduit for competition between spheres of authority within Gallic society, allowing the expression and display of competitive advantage, but then removing those displays so as to ease tensions between competing spheres and allow cooperation once again.

The moment of deposition itself serves to display the victories and therefore the suitability of the party depositing for leadership and authority within the system, such as the deposit of weapons and war booty, or specialised prestige goods created specifically to be deposited, or rare items from foreign trade, or the remains of a successful hunt or harvest. The act itself allows the victor a moment of display, of pomp and circumstance regarding their achievement, before dedicating the objects of power to the sacred site, rendering then unusable and unrecoverable. The physical nature of water itself speaks to its suitably as a repository of these memories, as it both reveals and occludes, it is necessary yet potentially deadly to the living, always present yet constantly in movement; it is in the available range

---

[62] Dietler 2010, 333
[63] Crumley 1974a, 255-259; Roymans 1996, 54-57; DeWitt 1940, 608-609; Février 1973, 1-28; Arselin 1992, 13-27
[64] cf. Dietler 2010; Irvin 2012, 29-31
[65] Scheid and De Polignac 2010, 428
[66] Scheid and De Polignac 2010, 429-433

of potential metaphors and meanings that might have been ascribed to the same watery deposition site that water finds its utility, not because it contained a single meaning but because of the flexibility of paradoxical meanings that could have been ascribed to it. The moment of success was acknowledged, as was the dedicator's competitive advantage over their heterarchical rivals, and then just as the moment of tension between differing elites was created, it was released by its being rendered no longer an active element of the community, but rather a memory, one as fluid and flexible as the potentiality of metaphorical meanings attached to the substance in which the memory was deposited. The cycle of triumph, revelry, and deposition likewise serves to benefit the community itself in not allowing any single element of heterarchical leadership to depend on a single victory, a single accomplishment, or a single benefit to society. Key to Crumley's analysis of heterarchy in Gallic society is its cyclical nature, that the favor of the commons could only be captured for a moment before greater deeds and greater accomplishments became necessary to justify authority in the face of heterarchical competition.[67]

Conclusions

In drawing then from more fluid social models than a strictly centralised model, it is possible that a more cohesive and explanatory model for settlement pattern and development might emerge. Rather than strictly economic or materialist models of settlement, water depositions allow for the development of a more abstract, substantivist analysis of Gallic communities, but the value and importance invested in these sites by the Gallic population must necessarily be recognised. As Osborne notes, despite the work of Bradley and others there is still much to be done in recognizing the significance of deposits and seeing these deposits as more than a collection of objects.[68]

Water depositions mark in many cases the first direct link between a population and a specific location; they are the beginning of a process that ultimately culminates in the permanent settlements discussed previously. These deposits, if seen as gifts, mark a degree of self-identity and reciprocity between the dedicators and those powers the object is dedicated to. That this exchange is communicated through a direct interaction with the landscape makes it all the more noteworthy. The location itself becomes tied to the individuals dedicating the object, and vice-versa, allowing the orthopraxic ritual to affect and impact the person and community. Finally, the nature of deposition itself, presenting through ritual a prize and accomplishment for a brief moment before removing that symbolic object from everyday existence, reveals further elements of the highly competitive internal structure of Gallic elite society and leadership, elements of internal competition and complexity that scholars have already noted in the development of complex Gallic sites.

We return then to Roymans' remarks from the beginning, that sedentary agricultural regimes increase a region's archaeological profile by revealing how the population adapted the natural environment to suit its own needs.[69] Water depositions allow the analysis of the earliest stages of this process, specifically how human populations first adapted themselves to the region's

---

[67] Crumley 1974b, 19-23

[68] Osborne 2004, 3

[69] Roymans 1996, 49-50

environment, and how they incorporated that most central and most important of resources, water, into their growing identity, community, and connection to a specific land and location.

Bibliography

Arselin 1992, P. Arselin, Salles, hypostyles, portqiues et espaces cultuels d'Entremont et de Saint-Blaise, *Documents d'archéologie méridionale*, No. 15, 13-27.

Audouze and Büchsenschütz 1992, F. Audouze and O. Büchsenschütz, *Towns, Villages and Countryside of Celtic Europe*. Indiana: Indiana University Press.

Bourgeois 1992, C. Bourgeois, *Divona I: Archaeologie du Culte Gallo-Romain De L'Eau* , Paris: De Boccard.

Bourgeois 1994 , C. Bourgeois, *Divona II. Monuments et Sanctuaires du Culte Gallo-Romain de L'Eau*, Paris: De Boccard.

Beard, North and Price 1998, M. Beard, J. North and S. Price, *Religions of Rome: A History*, Vol. 1, Cambridge: Cambridge University Press.

Bradley 1998, R. Bradley, *The Passage of Arms: An Archaeological Analysis of Prehistoric Hoards and Votive Deposits* ,Oxford: Oxbow Books.

Bradley 2000, R. Bradley, *An Archaeology of Natural Places* , London: Routledge.

Bradley 2003, R. Bradley, A Life Less Ordinary: The ritualization of the domestic sphere in later prehistoric Europe, *Cambridge Archaeological Journal*, 13, No. 1 (April 2003), 5-23.

Brun 1995, P. Brun, Oppida and Social 'complexification' in France. In J. D. Hill and C. G. Cumberpatch (eds.), *Different Iron Ages: Studies on the Iron Age in Temperate Europe*, Oxford:BAR International Series 602, 121-128.

Brunaux 1988, J. L. Brunaux, *The Celtic Gauls: Gods, rites and sanctuaries*, translated by D. Nash (London: B.A. Seaby Ltd.

Burke 2014, A. Burke, Entanglement, the Amorite *Koiné,* and Amorite Cultures in the Levant. *Aram* 26, Nos. 1&2 , 391-409.

Burke 2016, A. Burke, Amorites, Climate Change and the Negotiation of Identity at the End of the Third Millenium BC. In F. Höflmayer (ed.), *The Early/Middle Bronze Age Transition in the Ancient Near East: Chronology, C14 and Climate Change*, Chicago: Oriental Institute Seminars 10, 261-307.

Collis 1984, J. Collis, *Oppida: Earliest Towns North of the Alps*, J. R. Collis Publications.

Collis 1995, J. Collis, States without centers? The Middle La Tène period in temperate Europe'. In B. Arnold and D. Blair Gibson (eds), *Celtic Chiefdom, Celtic State* , Cambridge: Cambridge University Press, 75-80.

Connerton 1989, P. Connerton, *How Societies Remember*. Cambridge: Cambridge University Press.

Crumley 1974a, C. Crumley, The Paleoethnographic Recognition of Early States: A Celtic Example, *Arctic Anthropology* 11, 254-260.

Crumley 1974b, C. Crumley, *Celtic Social Structure*, Ann Arbor: The University of Michigan.

Crumley 1995, C. Crumley, Heterarchy and the analysis of complex societies. In R. M. Ehrenreich, C. Crumley, and J. E. Levy (eds), *Heterarchy and the Analysis of Complex Societies*, Washington, DC: American Anthropological Association, Archaeological Papers No. 6, 1-5.

Cunliffe 1991, B. Cunliffe, *Iron Age Communities in Britain*, London: Routledge.

Cunliffe 1997, B. Cunliffe, *The Ancient Celts*, Oxford: Oxford University Press.

Derks 1998, T. Derks, *Gods, Temples, and Ritual Practices: The Transformation of Religious Ideas and Values in Roman Gaul* , Amsterdam: Amsterdam University Press.

De Witt 1940, N. DeWitt, Massilia and Rome. *Transactions and Proceedings of the American Philological Association* 71, 605-615.

Deyts 1983, S. Deyts, *Les Bois Sculptés des Sources de la Seine: XLIIe supplement à <<Gallia>>* Paris: Éditions du Centre National de la Recherche Scientifique.

Dietler 2010, M. Dietler, *Archaeologies of Colonialism: Consumption, Entanglement, and Violence in Ancient Mediterranean France*, Berkeley and Los Angeles: University of California Press.

Dyson 1985, S. Dyson, *The Creation of the Roman Frontier* , Princeton: Princeton University Press.

Earle 2002, T. Earle, Property Rights and the Evolution of Chiefdoms. In T. Earle (ed.), *Bronze Age Economics: The Beginnings of Political Economies* ,Boulder, CO: Westview Press, 325-347.

Feeney 1998, D. Feeney, *Literature and Religion at Rome: Cultures, Contexts, and Beliefs*, Cambridge: Cambridge University Press.

Février 1973, P. A. Février, The Origin and Growth of the Cities of Southern Gaul to the Third Century AD: An Assessment of the Most Recent Archaeological Discoveries, *Journal of Roman Studies* 63, 1-28.

Fitzpatrick 1997, A. P. Fitzpatrick, Everyday life in Iron Age Wessex. In A. Gwilt and C. Haselgrove (eds), *Reconstructing Iron Age Societies* , Oxford: Oxbow Publishing, 73-86.

Gosden 2005, C. Gosden, What Do Objects Want?, *Journal of Archaeological Method and Theory*, 12, No. 3 (September 2005), 193-211.

Grant 1986, E. Grant (ed.), *Central Places, Archaeology, and History*, Sheffield: University of Sheffield.

Hamilton and Manley 2001, S. Hamilton and J. Manley, Hillforts, Monumentality, and Place: A Chronological and Topographic Review of First Millenium Hillforts of South-East England, *European Journal of Archaeology*, 4, No. 1 (April 2001), 7-42.

Haselgrove 1995, C. Haselgrove, Late Iron Age Society in Britain and north-east Europe. In B. Arnold and D. Blair Gibson (eds), *Celtic Chiefdom, Celtic State* , Cambridge: Cambridge University Press, 81-87.

Hawkes 1931, C. Hawkes, Hill-Forts, *Antiquity* 5, Issue 17 (March 1931), 60-97.

Hill 1989, J. D. Hill, Re-thinking the Iron Age, *Scottish Archaeological Review* 6, 16-23.

Irvin 2012, A. Irvin, Romanization and the Creation of an Imperial Culture. PhD Dissertation, University of California Los Angeles.

Kristiansen 1998, K. Kristiansen, *Europe Before History*, Cambridge: Cambridge University Press.

Kristiansen and Larsson 2005, K. Kristiansen and T. Larsson, *The Rise of Bronze Age Society: Travels, Transmissions, and Transformations*, Cambridge: Cambridge University Press.

Lillios 1999, K. Lillios, Objects of Memory: The Ethnography and Archaeology of Hierlooms, *Journal of Archaeological Method and Theory* 6, No. 3 (Sep. 1999), 235-262.

Lindner 1982, R. P. Lindner, What Was a Nomadic Tribe?, *Comparative Studies in Society and History*, 24, No. 4 (October, 1982), 689-711.

Lovell 2010, J. Lovell, Community is Cult, Cult is Community: Weaving the Web of Meanings for the Chalcolithic, *Paléorient* 36, No. 1 (2010), 103-122.

Nongbri 2008, B. Nongbri, Dislodging 'Embedded' Religion: A Brief Note on a Scholarly Trope, *Numen* 55, No. 4, 440-460

Osborne 2004, R. Osborne, Hoards, Votives, Offerings: The Archaeology of the Dedicated Object, *World Archaeology* 36, No. 1 (Mar. 2004), 1-10.

Oswald 1997, A. Oswald, A doorway on the past: Practical and mystic concerns in the orientation of roundhouse doorways. In A. Gwilt and C. Haselgrove, *Reconstructing Iron Age Societies*, Oxford: Oxbow Publishing, 87-95.

Poux 2006, M. Poux, Religion et Société: La sanctuaire arverne de Corent. In C. Goudineau (ed.), *Religion et Société en Gaule* ,Paris: Editions Errance, 117-134.

Ralston 2006, I. Ralston, *Celtic Fortifications*, Stroud: Tempus Publishing.

Revell 2007, L. Revell, Religion and Ritual in the Western Provinces, *Greece and Rome* 54, No. 2 (2007), 210-228.

Roymans 1990, N. Roymans, *Tribal Societies in Northern Gaul*, Amsterdam: Albert Egges van Giffen Instituut voor Prae- en Protohistorie.

Roymans 1996, N. Roymans, The sword or the plow. Regional dynamics in the Romanization of Belgic Gaul and the Rhineland area. In N. Roymans (ed.), *From the Sword to the Plow: Three Studies on the Earliest Romanization of Northern Gaul*, Amsterdam: Amsterdam University Press, 9-126.

Rüpke 2007, J. Rüpke, *Religion of the Romans*, Cambridge: Polity Press.

Scheid 1995, J. Scheid, Graecu Ritu: A Typically Roman Way of Honoring the Gods, *Harvard Studies in Classical Philology: Greece in Rome: Influence, Integration, Resistance* 97, 15-31.

Scheid 1999, J. Scheid, Aspects Religieux de la Municipalisation. In M. Dondin-Payre and M.-T. Raepsaet-Charlier (eds.), *Cités, Municipes, Colonies*, Paris: Publications de la Sorbonne, 381-424.

Scheid 2003 J. Scheid, *An Introduction to Roman Religion*, Bloomington, IN: Indiana University Press.

Scheid and De Polignac 2010, J. Scheid and F. De Polignac. Qu'est-ce qu'un <<paysage religieux>>? Redprésentations cultuelles de l'espace dans les sociétés anciennes, *Revue de l'histoire des religions* 227, No. 4 (October-December 2010), 427-434.

Watson 2007, A. Watson, *Religious Acculturation and Assimilation in Belgic Gaul and Aquitania from the Roman Conquest until the End of the Second Century CE*, Oxford: Archaeopress.

Woudhuizen and van Binsbergen 2011, F. Woudhuizen and W. van Binsbergen, *Ethnicity in Mediterranean Protohistory*, Oxford: British Archaeological Reports.

Worship of the Nymphs at *Aquae Iasae* (Roman Pannonia Superior): Cognition, Ritual, and Sacred Space

Blanka Misic

The territory of the Iasi tribe, located between the rivers Sava and Drava in southern Pannonia, became prominent in the Roman period due to its naturally occurring hot springs, the most significant of which was located at *Aquae Iasae* (modern-day Varaždinske Toplice, Croatia). Gradually built and renovated from the early first to the fourth century AD, the site of *Aquae Iasae* initially developed around the thermal spring and grew to include a religious complex, a bathing complex, a forum, a basilica, and commercial and residential areas. Visitors to the site came to seek the help of the healing divinities of the hot spring, the most popular of which were the Nymphs.[1]

Although the site of *Aquae Iasae* has been systematically excavated since 1953, studying the nature of its religious rituals has proved problematic since many finds from the site have remained unpublished until recently.[2] Thus, in light of recently-published finds,[3] a re-examination of material evidence is needed in order to ascertain the range of ritual activities which could have occurred in the worship of the Nymphs at *Aquae Iasae*.[4] This examination will also offer an insight into how the religious space and sacred objects at *Aquae Iasae* may have been perceived and used by the worshippers at the site.

It has been acknowledged within the field of cognitive science that material culture is a physical expression of human cognitive framework(s).[5] In light of this, the present paper will argue that the organisation of the sacred space and the nature of material culture at *Aquae Iasae* played a defining role in the way religious rituals were understood, practiced, and transmitted. This study will demonstrate that ritual practices can be transferred not only from one person to another, but also from inanimate objects to human beings. In this way, the organisation of the sacred space can act as a 'religious roadmap', tacitly informing the worshippers of proper movement within the sacred space and of expected, proper ritual actions.[6]

---

[1] Rendić-Miočević 1992, 69; Schejbal 2003, 394-395, 403, 405; Lučić 2014, 195; Rendić-Miočević 2014, 189; Kušen and Kušen Tomljanović 2015, 73; and Kušan Špalj 2017, 270, 302.

[2] Kušan Špalj 2017, 256. For an overview of archaeological excavations see Kušan Špalj and Nemeth-Ehrlich 2012, 107-129.

[3] For the most comprehensive publication of previously unpublished finds see Pirnat-Spahić 2014/2015.

[4] The present paper will focus primarily on the development of the religious complex and the forum, from the first to the third centuries AD, where most of the archaeological evidence attesting the worship of the Nymphs is concentrated. Since there is (of yet) scant archaeological evidence of religious ritual for the Nymphs in the bathing complex and the commercial and residential areas, these areas are excluded from the present paper.

[5] Donald 1998, 182; and Misic 2015, 32.

[6] Petsalis-Diomidis (2007, 185) touches upon this idea when she claims: 'It is a reading both of the physical layout of the sanctuary – the architectural remains – and of an inscribed set of ritual rules which directed the movement and

When it comes to explaining the transmission of religious practices, Harvey Whitehouse's 'modes of religiosity' theory has garnered much interest within the field of cognitive science of religion. Whitehouse puts forth two modes of religious transmission: one named the doctrinal mode, and the other which he describes as the imagistic mode. In the doctrinal mode, religious knowledge and rituals are transmitted widely, often in oral and textual form. Doctrinal religious practices elicit low emotional arousal due to their more 'routine' nature, but they tend to be more socially inclusive. According to the doctrinal mode, repetition enables ritual practices to be encoded in the semantic memory of the worshippers. In the imagistic mode, religious notions are transferred visually and through participation in emotionally arousing rituals. Although each worshipper's experience of the ritual is highly personal, due to their shared ritual participation worshippers come to form a close-knit group. Imagistic religious practices often lack a centralized religious authority and are therefore more versatile. Combined with emotional arousal, the infrequent performance of these rituals encodes them in the episodic memory.[7] As our evidence from *Aquae Iasae* will come to show, religious rituals were transmitted through a combination of emotionality and repetition, merging aspects of both the doctrinal and the imagistic modes.

Topography

The fact that the organisation of the sacred space played a defining role in the nature and transmission of religious rituals at *Aquae Iasae* can be seen first through the chosen location and delineation of the sacred site.[8] Great care was taken by the Roman builders to preserve, incorporate, and accentuate the natural features of the site, including the thermal spring, into the architectural design of the public-religious-bathing complex.[9] Located on top of an elevated plateau, the site was built around the thermal spring.[10] In order to access the site, the worshipper would have had to undertake an ascending trek which itself may have served as a form of preparation ritual – building emotional anticipation while cognitively signalling to the worshipper that they were about to enter a sacred area, and reminding them of proper, expected religious behaviours.

Once at the top, the worshipper's senses would have been engaged by the features of the thermal spring – the sound of water bubbling up from the ground, the sight of the steam rising, the heat emanating from the water's surface, and the pungent smell of sulphur – all would have demarcated the spring as an otherworldly, sacred phenomenon.[11] The combination of these unusual sensory cues paired with the numinous quality of the spring may have invoked a heightened emotional response, forming an imagistic imprint on the worshipper. It is in this

---

religious observances of pilgrims.'

[7]   Whitehouse 2000, 124, 130; Whitehouse 2002, 293-294, 304, 309; Whitehouse 2004a, 216; Whitehouse 2004b, 4, 8; Whitehouse 2009, 5-6; and Whitehouse 2013, 77.

[8]   Petsalis-Diomidis (2007, 184) stresses that '...there is an emphasis on the role of location in facilitating contact with the divine.'

[9]   Kušan Špalj and Nemeth-Ehrlich 2012, 111; Kušan Špalj 2014/2015b, 115; and Kušan Špalj 2017, 257.

[10]   Kušan Špalj and Nemeth-Ehrlich 2012, 111-112; and Rendić-Miočević 2015, 43. Springs feature as the focal point of many spas and bathing complexes throughout the Roman world, exemplified by the architecture of the sites which are predominantly built *around* the spring (as, for example, at Alange, Caldas de Malavella, Ameliès-les-Bains, and Bath, among others). Gonzáles Soutelo 2014a, 213-214.

[11]   According to Croon (1967, 246): '...hot springs were products of awesome supernatural chthonic powers.' See also Gonzáles Soutelo 2012, 80; and 2014a, 206.

heightened emotional state that subsequently performed rituals would have been encoded in the worshippers' episodic memory.

Thermal pool

The importance of the spring as the focal point of religious activity is also testified by its architectural enclosure. Archaeological evidence from the first century AD indicates that initially a wall was built around the thermal spring, delineating it as a sacred place.[12] In the second century AD renovations took place and the thermal water was collected into a pool of rectangular shape measuring approximately 8m x 13.5m. A fence was built around the pool, enclosing the thermal waters further.[13] Deposits discovered in the thermal pool, consisting of coins and small personal objects such as jewellery and *fibulae*,[14] indicate that it was likely that this was the most popular form of ritual practice at *Aquae Iasae*.[15] Over 17 000 coins were found in the thermal pool, dating from the first to the fourth centuries AD.[16] Although we must be careful not to attribute *all* of the coin deposits to the Nymphs, as other divinities were also venerated at *Aquae Iasae*, it is possible that a good proportion of coins from the thermal pool were intended for the Nymphs as these goddesses were specifically associated with water.[17]

This predominance of coins and small personal objects seems to point to primarily individual, rather than communal, worship.[18] The continued deposition of these objects for centuries attests to the healing powers of the thermal waters as well as to the fact that the thermal pool played a vital role in the learning and transmission of ritual practices, tacitly informing worshippers of expected ritual behaviour. Namely, when worshippers approached the thermal pool they may have noticed coins and other small personal objects deposited in the water by worshippers before them. They would have quickly realized that this was the expected and appropriate manner of worshipping the divinities of the thermal spring, without necessarily needing a religious official[19] or a fellow worshipper to explain or perform the ritual action in front of them. Moreover, the more deposited objects a worshipper saw, the more he or

---

[12] Kušan Špalj 2014/2015b, 114; and Kušan Špalj 2017, 265-267.

[13] Kušan Špalj and Nemeth-Ehrlich 2012, 109, 111; Nemeth-Ehrlich and Kušan Špalj 2014, 137; Ehrlich Nemeth and Kušan Špalj 2014/2015, 41, 46; Kušan Špalj 2014/2015b, 115; and Kušan Špalj 2017, 258-259, 267-268.

[14] Pirnat-Spahić 2014/2015, 170-171 #90-#92 (beads); 171-172 #93-#96 (belt buckles); 172 #97 (*fibula*); 173-177 #98-#112 (rings); and 178 #113-#114 (bracelets). Kušan Špalj 2017, 260.

[15] As with many religious sites throughout the ancient world, we have no clear idea of how many worshippers may have visited the site. While our evidence of ritual worship is varied (ranging from small deposits such as coins, to large gifts of stone monuments), we must be careful not to assume that everyone would have performed only one ritual action. Certain individuals may have dedicated several objects or performed several ritual actions, as is the case of Hermadion, who dedicates an altar and a *phiala* to the Nymphs (*AE* 1985, 714).

[16] Ninety-four bronze coins were discovered in 2006, and approximately another 17 000 bronze, silver, and gold coins were discovered during excavations in 2011-2012. Kušan Špalj and Nemeth-Ehrlich 2012, 109; and Ehrlich Nemeth and Kušan Špalj 2014/2015, 42.

[17] Kušan Špalj 2017, 260. The deposition of coins in association with the worship of the Nymphs is well-attested throughout the Roman world, such as at Caldas de Cuntis in Pontevedra, Spain. Diez de Velasco 1992, 134-135.

[18] Kušan Špalj 2017, 300.

[19] We have no explicit evidence which indicates that the cult of the Nymphs at *Aquae Iasae* may have been supervised by a religious official or had a priestly structure. One dedication to the Nymphs seems to point to a lack of religious authority figures within this cult. A mid-second century AD inscription (Pirnat-Spahić 2014/2015, 165 #80), dedicated to the Nymphs by a slave of a customs service official, bears a carving of an ear in the last line of the dedication. According to Kušan Špalj, the representation of an ear may symbolize the 'hearing ears' – indicating that worshippers' pleas can reach the divine ear without the intervention of a religious official. Kušan Špalj 2014/2015a, 86.

she would have been convinced of the efficacy of the ritual, consequently reinforcing the doctrinal repetition of this ritual behaviour.[20] On the other hand, depositing personal objects, such as jewellery and *fibulae*, may have denoted an emotional bond between the worshipper and the divinity, as the worshipper 'gave up' something from his or her personal belongings that had come to constitute a part of the votary's individual identity. Thus, in an imagistic fashion, this ritual act of depositing a cherished, personal object would have made a strong emotional imprint on the worshipper.[21]

Another way that objects might communicate expected ritual practices to humans is through their positioning within the sacred site and their relationship with other objects. In addition to depositing coins in the thermal pool, money was also placed in a *thesaurus* (ritual collection box) located by the northern wall of the thermal pool and dedicated to the Nymphs.[22] In use from the first to the third centuries AD, the *thesaurus* most likely served to collect monies for the operation of the religious site. This box would have reminded the visitor that they had entered a sacred space and that the divinities of the thermal waters required their due, reinforcing the ritual practice of depositing coins. The *thesaurus* thus attests to the continued use of a specific religious ritual at this site: the act of placing offerings in monetary form. According to the doctrinal mode, this repetition of a specific ritual practice served to encode it into the semantic memory of the worshippers.

Other types of ritual practices, which did not leave traces in material culture, possibly also took place in or around the thermal pool. In the first century AD at least, before the pool was enclosed, worshippers were able not only to stand, sit, or pray by the water,[23] but could have also come in direct contact with it – collecting and using it for washing[24] and purification[25] during various rituals. This may be evidenced by two large pieces of a stone bowl which bear a damaged dedication likely to the Nymphs (*[N]ymp(his)*), found near the northern wall of the thermal pool.[26] Thus, like the *thesaurus*, the sight of the ritual bowl would have cognitively signalled to the worshipper expected ritual behaviour. The architectural organisation of the

---

[20]   Petsalis-Diomidis (2007, 187, 206) discusses this visual reinforcement at the *Asklepieion* in Pergamon: '...the viewing of thank-offerings...seems to have been of particular importance in *Asklepieia* where the efficacy of the god in curing sickness was central to his prestige and worship.'

[21]   We must also consider the possibility that personal objects may have been deposited *in lieu* of coinage – that is, by individuals or groups who had no access to coinage and/or operated outside the monetary economy (gratitude to Dr. Jason Lundock for this remark, see also: Walton and Moorehead 2014 and Walton 2015). While it is possible that certain visitors to *Aquae Iasae* may have functioned outside the monetary economy, the present author finds it hard to believe that they would have been unable to procure coinage to deposit, replacing it instead with personal objects. *Aquae Iasae* belonged to the territory of Poetovio, a major administrative centre of Pannonia Superior, and was linked by roads to several nearby cities, including the *coloniae* of Siscia and Mursa. A pilgrim who wished to travel to *Aquae Iasae* would have likely passed through at least one of these cities, where they would have had ample opportunity to acquire coinage. This leads the present author to believe that deposited personal objects, such as jewellery or *fibulae*, rather reflected an emotional bond on the part of the worshipper.

[22]   The lid of the *thesaurus* bears the inscription *SAC(rum) NYMP(his)*. Pirnat-Spahić 2014/2015, 166 #81; Kušan Špalj 2014/2015a, 91-92; and Kušan Špalj 2014/2015b, 117.

[23]   Kušan Špalj 2014/2015b, 115; and Kušan Špalj 2017, 267.

[24]   González Soutelo 2014a, 207; and Kušan Špalj 2017, 267.

[25]   Ritual purification was a key aspect of Greek and Roman religion. McMullen (2013, 5670) states: 'The practice of hand-washing or sprinkling oneself with water (*chernips*) before pouring libations and sacrificing was a staple requirement of Greek cult.' Other forms of religious purification include fasting, sexual abstinence, fumigation, and *lustratio* (encircling procession). See also: Moitrieux 1992, 72; and Bradley 2013, 5672-5673.

[26]   Kušan Špalj and Nemeth-Ehrlich 2012, 110.

sacred site at *Aquae Iasae* would have also influenced the types of rituals being performed. Namely, rituals involving direct contact with the thermal water (washing, purification etc.) were possible because worshippers had easy access to the thermal water.

The thermal waters at *Aquae Iasae* may also have held oracular power. Ginouvès notes that in certain parts of the Greek world the Nymphs were attributed with prophetic gifts.[27] Incubation rituals may have taken place at *Aquae Iasae* as of the second or third century AD, when in addition to the Nymphs, healing gods such as Asklepios,[28] Apollo,[29] Isis and Serapis[30] were introduced. A portico was also constructed around the thermal pool at this period.[31] This space may have been used by visitors for rest,[32] for therapeutic treatment,[33] or perhaps for incubation.[34] Due to the sulfuric nature of the waters visitors may have experienced vivid dreams or hallucinations, especially if they were exposed to the toxic gases of the thermal spring for an extended period of time, such as during incubation.[35] One visitor to the site erected a votive inscription to Diana as a result of a divine command, implying contact with the divine through perhaps an altered mind-state.[36] Individuals who came to partake in the thermal waters of *Aquae Iasae* possibly suffered from specific illnesses or ailments, and may have been therefore more cognitively receptive to believing in divine intervention in their healing. From an imagistic perspective, heightened emotional states produced as a result of exposure to the unusual sensory stimuli of the thermal spring and/or as a result of exceptional rituals such as incubation would have facilitated the encoding of performed ritual proceedings.

Nymphaeum

A rectangular structure – a Nymphaeum – was built in the first century AD on the north side of the thermal pool.[37] Although originally presumed to be a small sanctuary for the Nymphs, recent excavations and interpretations put forth the idea that it could have been

---

[27] Ginouvès 1962, 365. Mentions of Nymphs in association with oracular power can be found in Pausanias (8.37.11; and 9.3.9), Plutarch (*Aristides*, 11), and Rendić-Miočević 2015, 45.

[28] Croon 1967, 243, footnote #3; Petsalis-Diomidis 2007, 198-203; Pirnat-Spahić 2014/2015, 156-157 #69; Kušan Špalj 2017, 302.

[29] Pirnat-Spahić 2014/2015, 158 #71; Kušan Špalj 2014/2015a, 83; Kušan Špalj 2017, 282, 302.

[30] Pirnat-Spahić 2014/2015, 159 #73. Strabo (17.1.17) and Diodorus Siculus (1.25.5) point to the healing powers of both Isis and Serapis. Isis, in particular, is associated with incubation. Pachis 2014, 55.

[31] Kušan Špalj 2014/2015b, 115-116, and Kušan Špalj 2017, 267-268.

[32] González Soutelo 2012, 81.

[33] Treatments may have included massages and/or the application of medicinal mud found at the site. Such practices are recorded by Aelius Aristides (*Sacred Tales*, 2. 74-76), as well as by the doctors Galen and Hippocrates. Vlahović 2012a, 100.

[34] For a comprehensive examination of incubation in the Graeco-Roman world see Renberg 2017. Although it appears that incubation was practiced primarily in Greece and the East, this does not necessarily mean that incubation could not have occurred at *Aquae Iasae*. After the Marcomannic Wars, Pannonia received immigrants from Syria and North Africa who certainly brought their divinities and customs with them. If they contributed to the spread of gods such as Isis and Serapis into Pannonia, does it not follow then that they would have also introduced accompanying rituals and practices, such as incubation?

[35] Toxic gasses include carbon monoxide and hydrogen sulphide. Ehrlich Nemeth and Kušan Špalj 2014/2015, 42; and Kušan Špalj 2014/2015a, 83. For the chemical composition of the thermal waters see Vlahović 2012b, 310-311.

[36] *AIJ* 1938, 459.

[37] Nemeth-Ehrlich and Kušan Špalj 2014, 137; Rendić-Miočević 2014, 193; Rendić-Miočević and Šegvić 2014, 237; Ehrlich Nemeth and Kušan Špalj 2014/2015, 46; and Kušan Špalj 2017, 265-267, 269.

a fountain.[38] The monument and the area around it were decorated with relief mythological scenes evoking water elements and depictions of heroes/warriors.[39] Votive inscriptions found at the site indicate that its earliest Roman users (and probable builders) were soldiers of *Legio XIII Gemina*, stationed in the neighbouring colony of Poetovio.[40] It is they who first begin to equate the divinities of the thermal spring with the Nymphs.[41] Only three inscriptions survive from the first century AD, while there are still no relief depictions or statues of the goddesses from this period.[42] Two of the three inscriptions, explicitly dedicated to the Nymphs, were set up by legates (*legatus Augusti legionis XIII Geminae*) Marcus Fabius Fabullus and Marcus Rutilius Lupus.[43] The third inscription was set up by a freedman of Quintus Gavius Fronto, who is either a *primus pilus* or a centurion of the *XIII Gemina*.[44] These dedications suggest that the ritual of setting up inscribed stone votives was a preferred form of worship among high-ranking officers who frequented *Aquae Iasae* in the first century AD, serving both as a display of socio-economic status (due to the cost of setting up a large stone votive) and a display of identity (highlighting citizenship, education/literacy, military affiliation, and professional achievement/rank). Since this act of setting up inscribed dedications in stone was practiced by a select group of military officers, it would have promoted the creation of tight-knit in-group ties, thereby facilitating the transmission and learning of ritual practices according to the imagistic mode. On the other hand, ordinary soldiers who may not have been able to afford a large stone votive likely deposited smaller offerings such as coins, *fibulae*/jewellery, and perhaps military equipment.[45] Since these smaller offerings predominate in the first century AD, they may indicate that at this time the site of *Aquae Iasae* was visited, for the most part, by ordinary soldiers who sought the healing help of the thermal waters and their divine incarnations, the Nymphs.[46]

Much like small votives deposited in the thermal spring, stone votive inscriptions also served to transmit expected ritual behaviours to worshippers. By being displayed in a public space and by becoming a permanent fixture of the site, inscribed dedications transmitted not only the cultural *habitus* of setting up epigraphic votives, but also conveyed the appropriate manner of worship to site visitors.[47] Thus, those unfamiliar with the ritual of setting up a votive altar would have been able to learn, simply by looking at the object, what shape it was supposed to take, where the decorations and the inscription field were supposed to be placed, what type of invocatory *formulae* were appropriate for addressing the Nymphs etc. Since votive

---

[38] Rendić-Miočević 2014, 193; and Rendić-Miočević 2015, 43-44, and 47-48.

[39] Vikić-Belančić 1996, 19; Rendić-Miočević 2014, 193, 200-202, 210 and 212; and Rendić-Miočević 2015, 49-50, figs. 6, 7 and 8.

[40] Galić and Radman-Livaja 2006, 173-174; Lučić 2014, 187; and Misic 2019, 211.

[41] Kušan Špalj 2014/2015b, 115; and Rendić-Miočević 1975, 43.

[42] Relief depictions of the Nymphs at *Aquae Iasae* become popular in the second and the third centuries AD. Kušan Špalj 2014/2015a, 89.

[43] *CIL* III 4118 = *AIJ* 1938, 463 = *ILS* 996 (approx. AD 46-69) and *CIL* III 10893 = *AIJ* 1938, 462 = *ILS* 3865 (approx. AD 41-68)

[44] Pirnat-Spahić 2014/2015, 152 #64 (approx. mid to late first century AD) identifies him as a *primus pilus* while HD075016 identifies him as a centurion.

[45] Remains of a military belt were found within the thermal bathing complex. It is unclear whether the belt was a ritual offering or if it was lost or intentionally discarded. Galić and Radman-Livaja 2006, 166, 168-169, 173.

[46] Rendić-Miočević 1992, 74; Galić and Radman-Livaja 2006, 174; Lučić 2014, 201; and Kušan Špalj 2017, 302. The thermal waters at Aquae Iasae and the mud derived from them are still today used to treat ailments of the bones, ligaments, and muscle tissue - all injuries which would have been common among soldiers. Schejbal 2003, 402, footnote #36; Vlahović 2012b, 310, and 312; and Kušen and Kušen Tomljanović 2015, 79.

[47] Revell 2007, 219-220.

altars, by and large, tended to look similar, seeing multiple, repetitive examples of inscribed stone dedications would have encoded this ritual practice into the semantic memory of the worshippers, conforming to the doctrinal mode. We can see this transmission of ritual knowledge as civilian worshippers (imperial administrative officials[48], customs officials[49], and city officials[50]) begin to frequent *Aquae Iasae* in the second and the third century AD. Some of these worshippers adopt the same invocatory epithets given to the Nymphs by the military officers in the first century AD.[51] Therefore, repeated exposure to stone votives bearing similar shape and invocatory *formulae* serves not only to encode this ritual practice in the memory of the worshippers, but also aids in its spread to a wider worshipper base. In this respect, objects such as stone votive altars communicate and help to transfer ritual knowledge from object to individual in a doctrinal manner.

The perception and personification of the thermal spring as multiple female divinities enabled the Nymphs to develop a versatile character, appealing to a wider variety of worshippers as of the second century AD, characteristic of the doctrinal mode. At *Aquae Iasae* the Nymphs are invoked as *Salutares*,[52] *Augustae*,[53] *Sanctae*,[54] and *Iasae*,[55] by worshippers of military and various civilian backgrounds. The thermal waters may even have been worshipped under the personification of the goddesses Silvanae, who are mentioned on two dedications from *Aquae Iasae*.[56] This versatility likely allowed their worshippers to engage with them on multiple levels, resulting in a variety of ritual activities.[57] At the same time, it is interesting to see the emphasis on the local character of these divinities in the second and the third centuries AD. The Nymphs come to be worshipped not only with the epithet *Iasae*, but also with the local variations of the spelling of their names (*Nifeis* and *Nyfris/Nyfeis*[58]),[59] as well as by the use of Norico-Pannonian decorative volutes on their dedications[60] - all of which point to a localised version of the cult of the Nymphs, characteristic of the imagistic mode. On the other hand, the repetition of water-themed motifs on reliefs dedicated to the Nymphs (e.g. flowing drapery reminiscent of water, jugs, dolphins, fish, seashells etc.)[61] would have encoded

---

[48] *CIL* III 4117 = *AIJ* 1938, 461 (approx. AD 162-166).

[49] *AE* 1985, 714 (approx. AD 150-250); and Pirnat-Spahić 2014/2015, 165 #80 (approx. AD 161-168).

[50] *CIL* III 10891 = *AIJ* 1938, 464 (approx. AD 151-250).

[51] *Nymphas Salutares*: *CIL* III 10893 = *AIJ* 1938, 462 = *ILS* 3865 (first century AD military dedicator); *Nymphis Salutaribus*: *CIL* III 10891 = *AIJ* 1938, 464 (mid second to mid third century AD civilian city official); and *Nymphis Salutaribus*: Kušan Špalj 2017, 292-294 (mid to late second century AD civilian).

[52] *CIL* III 10893 = *AIJ* 1938, 462 = *ILS* 3865; *CIL* III 10891 = *AIJ* 1938, 464; and Kušan Špalj 2017, 292-294 (joint dedication to Serapis and the Nymphs).

[53] *CIL* III 10891 = *AIJ* 1938, 464; *CIL* III 4119 = *AIJ* 1938, 465; *CIL* III 4117 = *AIJ* 1938, 461; *CIL* III 10892; and Pirnat-Spahić 2014/2015, 167 #83.

[54] EDCS-68100093.

[55] *AE* 1985, 714; and *ILJug*-02, 1170.

[56] *AIJ* 1938, 467; *AIJ* 1938, 468 and Rendić-Miočević and Šegvić 2014, 237.

[57] Revell 2007, 221.

[58] Pirnat-Spahić 2014/2015, 167 #83; and Pirnat-Spahić 2014/2015, 169 #88.

[59] Diez de Velasco (1992, 142-143) notes that localised spelling variations in Spain – *Nimphis* (Baños de Molagas); *Nymfis* (Baños de Bande); and *Nimpis/Nympis* (Baños de Montemayor) – occur on dedications set up, in most cases, by autochthonous dedicators, whereas the standard spelling (*Nymphis*) belongs largely to dedicators bearing the *tria nomina*, or to those with non-autochthonous names. Kušan Špalj (2014/2015a, 89) does not believe that the variation in the spelling of the name of the Nymphs at *Aquae Iasae* is an error but that it represents a local characteristic.

[60] Rendić-Miočević 2014, 193; and Pirnat-Spahić 2014/2015, 163 #78; and 165 #80.

[61] Rendić-Miočević 1992, 69; Kušan Špalj and Nemeth-Ehrlich 2012, 110, images #22 and #23; Vlahović 2012b; and

elements of their cult and rituals in the doctrinal manner. This combination of visual and textual elements found on votive dedications may have facilitated the transmission of ritual knowledge from object to individual. Evidence suggests that individuals in the ancient world simultaneously absorbed both the image and the text in their reading of monuments.[62] In this respect, inscribed and relief stone monuments reached both those who were fully literate as well as those with limited or no literacy, transferring religious information through visual (seeing the image and the text), auditory (inscriptions were meant to be read out aloud) and even tactile (touching/manipulating the object during ritual use) manner. This combination of image and text on inscribed and relief dedications would have served as a 'learning aid' in the understanding of elements of ritual practice, especially if religious authority figures were absent.[63] Thus, ritual actions, such as the setting up of inscribed altars and reliefs, were learned and transmitted from object to worshipper through elements of both the doctrinal and the imagistic modes.

Forum

The open area around the thermal pool, measuring 26m x 23m, was paved in the early second century AD, becoming the forum.[64] Since this area could accommodate approximately a hundred individuals,[65] group ritual activities could have taken place. In the second century the thermal pool and forum also became enclosed with porticoes.[66] According to Kušan Špalj, the construction of these high, covered colonnades around the pool created an even smaller space in which the thermal water could evaporate, making the vapours and sulfuric smells denser, thereby creating 'an even more mystical atmosphere.'[67] This imagistic imprint created on the worshipper may have been even more intense depending on the weather conditions. Adverse or peculiar weather would have affected the religious experience of the worshipper,[68] likely rendering the ritual events even more memorable. This additional enclosing of the thermal spring and change in architectural design possibly precipitated changes in ritual, which due to more restricted space, now became more imagistic. These changes in the organisation of the sacred space affected not only the nature of religious rituals but would also have influenced ritual movement within the sacred complex, indicating again that religious objects and architecture could convey expected ritual practices to human minds.

Pirnat-Spahić 2014/2015, 133 #2; 162 #77; 163 #78 and 166 #82.

[62] Upon seeing the statue of Hadrian, Arrian (*Periplus Ponti Euxini*, 1) notes both the image and the text. Petsalis-Diomidis 2007, 207, footnote #45.

[63] Diez de Velasco (2008, 459) believes that rituals performed at thermal water sites may not have needed to be conducted under the auspices of a religious official, as he considers the worship largely of individual, rather than communal nature, and believes that worshippers would have readily made the connection between the thermal waters and instances of healing. Although we have no clear evidence of religious officials serving at *Aquae Iasae*, it is possible that as of the second and third centuries AD, once differing deities are introduced, a greater variety of religious rituals would have followed, and therefore religious officials may have been needed to inform visitors of the particularities of worship for each divinity.

[64] Vikić-Belančić 1996, 18-19; Kušan Špalj and Nemeth-Ehrlich 2012, 111. Rendić-Miočević (2015, 48) questions whether the area around the thermal pool should be called a forum since it is not located on the *cardo* and *decumanus*.

[65] This figure is obtained by calculating the size of the open space around the thermal spring, where rituals would have been performed, while keeping in mind that in a standing position each person, on average, takes up a space of approximately 60cm x 60cm.

[66] Vikić-Belančić 1996, 18-19.

[67] Kušan Špalj 2014/2015b, 115; and Kušan Špalj 2017, 268.

[68] My gratitude to Adam Parker for this observation.

The enclosing of the sacred space possibly intended to cut off the thermal spring from its natural environment, and to 'urbanise' the religious complex through the addition of extra buildings. This may be evidenced by the fact that the Nymphs become supplanted by the rising popularity of 'civic' divinities at *Aquae Iasae*. A temple complex, believed to have housed the cults of the Capitoline deities (Jupiter, Juno and Minerva), was constructed to the north of the thermal pool in the second century AD.[69] The three temples were accessed from the forum by a monumental staircase. On the eastern and western side of the Capitoline temples, two smaller rooms were added. It is believed that the western room, close to the temple of Minerva, housed the imperial cult; while the eastern room, close to Juno's temple, may have become the Nymphaeum.[70]

These extensive architectural additions could be attributed to Poetovio gaining the status of *colonia* under Trajan, and the incorporation of *Aquae Iasae* into its territory. Votive inscriptions reveal that although military worshippers continue to be attested, as of the second century AD civilian worshippers of various backgrounds become more numerous at *Aquae Iasae*.[71] Many visitors to *Aquae Iasae* probably came from neighbouring towns, including Poetovio.[72] Such was the case of Gaius Valerius Priscus[73] and Gaius Valerius Posphorus[74], who both held the post of Augustalis in Poetovio.[75] Two members of the Illyrian customs service are also attested, Verus[76] and Flavius Hermadion,[77] both seemingly stationed at Poetovio.[78]

It may be no coincidence then that, as of the second century AD, we begin to see at *Aquae Iasae* the introduction of some of the same divinities which are found at Poetovio – Juno,[79]

---

[69] Most scholars believe that the three temples should be attributed to the Capitoline deities although no inscribed dedications to Jupiter have been found yet. Kušan Špalj and Nemeth-Ehrlich 2012 111; Lučić 2014, 190; Rendić-Miočević and Šegvić 2014, 234; Rendić-Miočević 2015, 43; and Kušan Špalj 2017, 300-301.

[70] Vikić-Belančić 1996, 19-20; and Kušan Špalj 2017, 301.

[71] Kušan Špalj 2017, 267.

[72] *CIL* III 4117 = *AIJ* 1938, 461; and *ILJug-02*, 1168. González Soutelo (2012, 84) shows that most visitors to thermal/ religious complexes in Spain came from neighbouring major cities.

[73] Pirnat-Spahić 2014/2015, 159 #73 = *RICIS-03*, 613/1001.

[74] Pirnat-Spahić 2014/2015, 164 #79.

[75] Kušan Špalj 2014/2015a, 88, 94; and Kušan Špalj 2017, 291.

[76] Pirnat-Spahić 2014/2015, 165 #80.

[77] *AE* 1985, 714.

[78] Kušan Špalj 2017, 289.

[79] *ILJug-02*, 1168 (joint dedication to Juno Regina and Fortuna by the people of Poetovio) and Kušan Špalj 2017, 287-288 (joint dedication to Juno Regina, Minerva, Apollo and the Nymphs).

Minerva,[80] Fortuna,[81] Diana/Luna,[82] Isis and Serapis,[83] Sol/Apollo,[84] Pollux,[85] and Hercules.[86] This reorganization of the sacred space and introduction of more varied cults likely went hand-in-hand with the shift in worshippers, as new visitors brought with them such divinities as Hercules, Pollux, Isis and Serapis, and Sol Apollo.[87] However, we must also take into consideration that certain divinities, such as Hercules and Pollux, were popular among members of the Roman army and may have served to express loyalty to the imperial house, especially from the reign of Commodus onwards.[88] While it is true that the late second and early third centuries AD saw a rise in popularity of Graeco-Eastern divinities in general under the imperial encouragement of the Severans,[89] it should also be noted that after the Marcomannic Wars (AD 166-180) Pannonia received an influx of immigrants from North Africa and Syria, who probably also aided in the spread and popularity of Graeco-Eastern cults at *Aquae Iasae* as well as within Pannonia in general.[90]

In addition to visitors from Poetovio, prominent worshippers from other parts of Pannonia are also attested at *Aquae Iasae*. This is the case of Lucius Claudius Moderatus, the decurion of Savaria;[91] Lucius Alfenus Avitianus, the legate of *X Gemina* (stationed in Vindobona) and governor of Pannonia Inferior;[92] as well as the *speculator* Lucius Arrius Florentinus[93] and *primus pilus* Lucius Larius Celer, both with the *Legio XIIII Gemina* (stationed in Carnuntum).[94] A further inscription attests Titus Flavius Domitius Valerianus, a centurion of *Legio XIIII Gemina*, who

---

[80] Pirnat-Spahić 2014/2015, 153 #65, 154 #66, 154-155 #67, and 155 #68; and Kušan Špalj 2017, 287-288.

[81] There are four dedications to Fortuna attested at *Aquae Iasae*: *ILJug*-02, 1167; *ILJug*-02, 1168; *AE* 1976, 540; and Pirnat-Spahić 2014/2015, 161 #76 (joint dedication to Fortuna Iasoniana, the healing Nymphs and other (unnamed) gods and goddesses). This is a curious occurrence as dedications to Fortuna are relatively rare in this part of Pannonia. Rendić-Miočević 1975, 45. However, the presence of Fortuna can perhaps be explained by her frequent worship at thermal water sites in the western Empire, or by the ancient belief that illnesses can be attributed to fickle fortune. Pachis 2014, 57.

[82] *AIJ* 1938, 460 = *AE* 1938, 156 (joint dedication to Diana and the Nymphs); *AIJ* 1938, 459; *ILJug*-02, 1166; and Pirnat-Spahić 2014/2015, 158 #72.

[83] Pirnat-Spahić 2014/2015, 159 #73 and Kušan Špalj 2017, 290-292 (joint dedication to Isis and Serapis); and Kušan Špalj 2017, 292-294 (joint dedication to Serapis and the Nymphs).

[84] *AE* 1994, 1386 = *AE* 1998, 1044; Pirnat-Spahić 2014/2015, 158 #71; and Kušan Špalj 2017, 280-282.

[85] *CIL* III 4120 = *AIJ* 1938, 466.

[86] *CIL* III 10890 = *AIJ* 1938, 458. According to Croon (1967, 230, 236, 239, 242, and 244) Herakles (and perhaps by association, his half-brother Pollux), as well as Artemis (Diana), and Apollo are all well-attested as patrons of thermal waters in Greece and Asia Minor. In the western Roman Empire, for example in Spain and Portugal, Juno Regina (Alange, Spain), Apollo (Caldes de Montbui/Barcelona and Caldes de Malavella/Gerona, Spain), Minerva (Caldes de Malavella, Spain), Fortuna (Fuente de la Mortera/Asturias, Spain), Isis (Aquae Flaviae / Chaves, Portugal), and Serapis and the Nymphs (Caldas de Cuntis, Orense, Baños de Molgas, Baños de Bande, Chaves, Caldelas, Bem-Saude and Baños de Montemayor, among others) are all popularly associated with healing and/or thermal springs. Diez de Velasco 1992, and Peréx *et al.* 2008, 351. The presence of these divinities at *Aquae Iasae* thus, is not surprising.

[87] Kušan Špalj 2017, 269-270.

[88] Rendić-Miočević and Šegvić 2014, 236. See the dedication to Aesculapius, Hygieia and Telesphorus erected for the health/well-being and victory of Caracalla by Lucius Alfenus Avitianus, legate of *X Gemina* (Pirnat-Spahić 2014/2015, 156-157 #69). Kušan Špalj 2017, 271-280, 300.

[89] Kušan Špalj 2014/2015a, 97; and Kušan Špalj 2017, 289, 300.

[90] Dzino and Domić Kunić 2012, 102; and Rendić-Miočević and Šegvić 2014, 239.

[91] Vikić-Belančić 1996, 21-22; and *ILJug*-02, 1169 = *AE* 1983, 774 = Pirnat-Spahić 2014/2015, 153 #65.

[92] Kušan Špalj 2017, 275-277.

[93] Kušan Špalj 2017, 285-287.

[94] *ILJug*-02, 1172.

originates from Oescus in Moesia Superior.[95] These inscriptions suggest that some visitors undertook a significant pilgrimage to the site in order to be healed by the thermal waters at *Aquae Iasae*. The fact that *Aquae Iasae* attracted visitors from near and far indicates that the location and natural features of this sacred site played a key role in worship.[96] Certain individuals made the pilgrimage in person, possibly accompanied by family members who would have tended to them during the voyage and helped them complete the rituals required. Such is the case perhaps of Flavius Hermadion and his wife who jointly with their two sons dedicated an altar and a silver bowl to the Nymphs.[97] Other individuals would have made the pilgrimage on behalf of a loved one, who may have been too ill to travel. Such may be the case of Titus Iulius Ianuarius who dedicates an altar to the Nymphs on behalf of his son.[98] Dedicating with, or on behalf of, a loved one would have made an emotional impact on the worshipper, fostering, in an imagistic fashion, close-knit bonds between the participants. Ritual proceedings, therefore, would have been learned and transmitted within this tight-knit group, being passed down from parent to child, as in the case of Hermadion and the sons who accompanied him. Moreover, in preparation for the ritual and in order to ensure its proper execution, the worshipper may have mentally rehearsed the ritual actions to be performed, perhaps for several days prior. This repeated mental rehearsal would have built up emotional anticipation in addition to reinforcing the learning (and remembering) of ritual proceedings.[99]

While it may appear that religious rituals performed at *Aquae Iasae* would have become more repetitive and doctrinal due to the introduction of new deities and higher frequency of ritual performance; the introduction of very different deities (Roman, Greek, Egyptian etc.) would probably have resulted also in the introduction of more varied rituals.[100] Although certain rituals remained similar across cults (e.g. coin deposition), in the second and the third century AD greater variety is demonstrated by the presence of new types of votive objects, such as a phallus-shaped pendant[101] and a verse inscription mentioning an abdomen,[102] pointing towards the adoption of new ritual practices. It is likely that with the paving of the forum in the second century AD public religious events in the form of processions, sacrifices, and feasts became more popular at *Aquae Iasae*. Some of these group ritual proceedings, such as communal meals and processions, may have been introduced as early as the first century AD by the soldiers of *Legio XIII Gemina* . Public religious festivals were not only traditionally ingrained in Roman culture, but Roman soldiers would have been well-accustomed to group processions and communal meals, which formed important aspects of their profession. Considering that the worship of nature and healing divinities formed a key aspect of religious life at *Aquae Iasae*, it is likely that ritual activities were centred on natural elements. Perhaps these festivities were comparable to the festival and feast of *Floralia*, usually celebrated in late April/early May

---

[95]   *AE* 1976, 540.

[96]   Petsalis-Diomidis (2007, 186) states that 'The decision to make a pilgrimage to the god at a particular, perhaps more distant, sanctuary must have been partly based on a deeply held sense of location of the god in *that place*.'

[97]   *AE* 1985, 714.

[98]   *AIJ* 1938, 465 = *CIL* III 4119.

[99]   Gratitude to Dr. Stephen Adams for his insights on the connection between mental rehearsal and learning/memory. See also: Paivio 1985 and Hale *et al.* 2005.

[100]   Gratitude to Dr. Josipa Lulić for her insight and suggestions regarding this paper and this argument in particular.

[101]   Pirnat-Spahić 2014/2015, 141 #27.

[102]   *AIJ* 1938, 470.

in the Roman world, including in the Pannonian city of Aquincum which was famous for its mineral springs. According to Póczy, the *Floralia* at Aquincum was celebrated with a sacrifice in the forum, followed by a procession leading out of the city and towards the aqueducts where sacrifices were made to water divinities. Every *collegium* would have participated, and the festivities ended with public entertainments.[103] Inscriptions and archaeological evidence from another Pannonian settlement – Brigetio – also point to a religious space featuring sacred waters and a portico where public festivals and communal feasts took place.[104]

An inscribed relief fragment found at *Aquae Iasae* may be evidence of similar public rituals. The fragment inscription records the celebration of a religious festival in June of AD 192. The relief depicts half-naked seated goddesses, identified as the Nymphs, accompanied by Venus, Amor, and a standing Isis Fortuna.[105] Isis Fortuna holds a *patera*, making an offering over a burning altar. In addition to featuring the act of sacrifice/libation, the religious festival recorded on the relief may have also included a procession and a communal meal, as at Aquincum and Brigetio. Several fragments of cups, bowls, plates, and other various vessels,[106] dating from the first to the fourth century AD, and made of *terra sigillata*, ceramic, and glass, have been found in and around the thermal pool and in the bathing complex/basilica. Some of these may have been used and/or deposited as part of ritual festivities. It is likely that public rituals and festivals performed in the religious space at *Aquae Iasae* were imprinted imagistically onto the worshippers/participants. The 'mystical' atmosphere of the site, created due to the sulfuric smells and vapours of the spring, would have contributed to enhancing memory formation and consolidation of the already attention-grabbing ritual proceedings. The architectural enclosure of the forum space may have also created a relatively intimate ambiance where the worshippers would have been able to experience the public festivities at a close range and, most likely, in considerable detail. Coupled with the usual pomp and visually-arousing elements of festivals, as well as with the ever-greater shift towards relief and sculptural depictions of divinities at *Aquae Iasae* as of the second century AD, it is likely that the transmission of religious ritual became more characteristically imagistic. On the other hand, repeated imagery of water elements, featured on decorative reliefs throughout the site and/or during ritual proceedings, would have reminded the ritual participants of the waters' sacred power, reinforcing in a doctrinal manner the ritual experience and religious knowledge of the worshippers. The religious space at *Aquae Iasae*, therefore, would have played a crucial role in the transmission and remembrance of ritual proceedings. The way the worshippers experienced the religious site and its divinities would have been altered alongside architectural modifications; creating, negotiating, and re-negotiating ritual practices and the local religious character of *Aquae Iasae*.[107]

In the fourth century AD, the religious complex sustained further renovations due to ravages of a fire.[108] Among several changes to the architecture of the site we find the addition of a Christian basilica.[109] During these renovations, many altars and reliefs dedicated to the

---

[103] Póczy 1998, 33.

[104] Póczy 1998, 34.

[105] Pirnat-Spahić 2014/2015, 160 #74; and Kušan Špalj 2017, 294-297.

[106] Pirnat-Spahić 2014/2015, 135 #9, 136 #10 and #11, 137 #15 and #16, 138 #17, 143 #35, 178 #115 and #116.

[107] Petsalis-Diomidis 2007, 204.

[108] *CIL* III 4121 = *AIJ* 1938, 469 = *ILS* 704; and Kušan Špalj 2017, 302.

[109] Rendić-Miočević 2015, 44; and Kušan Špalj 2017, 303.

Nymphs and other Graeco-Roman divinities worshipped at the site were reused as building material,[110] indicating that the old gods were gradually abandoned as the site became increasingly frequented by Christians. However, old rituals were not entirely forgotten. The practice of depositing coins and small personal objects into the thermal spring continued in the fourth century AD, as is evidenced by small finds including coins of Constantine and Constans,[111] various pieces of jewellery,[112] *fibulae*[113] and belt buckles,[114] as well as by rings bearing Christogram designs.[115] In terms of public gatherings, an inscription recording the renovation of *Aquae Iasae* during Constantine's reign indicates that fairs were established on the day of Sol (*die Solis*),[116] and a fragmentary monumental verse inscription affixed on the walls of the temple complex in the fourth century AD[117] may have been erected to commemorate an important public event such as a religious festival. Parts of plates and glass vessels found in the thermal pool[118] may also indicate that feasting rituals continued to be practiced, probably in a festival context. Additionally, the cult statue of Minerva, discovered well-preserved *in situ* in her temple, indicates that her worship continued after the reign of Constantine,[119] syncretised perhaps under the guise of a healing Virgin. This evidence points to the fact that the thermal waters at *Aquae Iasae* continued to attract worshippers of various backgrounds, Christian and polytheist alike into the fourth century AD. The syncretisation of divinities that we begin to see in the second and third centuries possibly continued into the fourth century AD, with some polytheistic rituals being preserved and/or renegotiated (e.g. deposition in the thermal spring, festivals/processions, feasting, worship of Minerva etc.) alongside the introduction of Christian ritual practices.

Conclusions

The nature and organisation of sacred space at *Aquae Iasae* played a defining role in the types of religious rituals performed and in their transmission. Although religious spaces were designed, replicated, and reshaped throughout the Roman world in order to meet specific religious, social, political, and civic needs of the population; the particular topography and natural properties of the sacred space at *Aquae Iasae* dictated the perseverance of specific types of ritual practices which could not be divorced from this location (e.g. deposition of offerings into the thermal spring).[120] As the focus of religious and healing activity throughout the centuries, the thermal spring at *Aquae Iasae* shaped how ritual practices were experienced, encoded and transmitted. On the other hand, the changing architecture around the thermal spring enabled the performance of new ritual activities and the creation of new ritual experiences. As this work has argued, when we examine the transmission of religious notions and rituals we should not only think about how they can be transferred from individual to

---

[110] Rendić-Miočević 2015, 45; and Kušan Špalj 2017, 259, 264.

[111] Pirnat-Spahić 2014/2015, 186-187 #142-#145.

[112] Pirnat-Spahić 2014/2015, 173-175 #98-#106 and 176-178 #109-#114.

[113] Pirnat-Spahić 2014/2015, 172 #97.

[114] Pirnat-Spahić 2014/2015, 171-172 #93-#96.

[115] Pirnat-Spahić 2014/2015, 176 #107 and #108; and Kušan Špalj 2017, 303.

[116] *CIL* III 4121 = *AIJ* 1938, 469 = *ILS* 704; and Rendić-Miočević 2015, 44.

[117] Kuntić-Makvić *et al.* 2012, 285-286.

[118] Pirnat-Spahić 2014/2015, 178 #115 and #116.

[119] Kušan Špalj 2017, 303.

[120] Diez de Velasco 2008, 458.

individual, but also how material culture, consisting of consciously-created objects, can tacitly communicate with the worshipper, influencing their behaviour and experience within a sacred space. Thus, minds can be truly shaped through matter.

Bibliography

Ancient and epigraphic sources

AE, R. Cagnat, *L'Année Épigraphique (AE)*. Paris: Presses Universitaires de France, 1889-
Aelius Aristides, *Sacred Tales*, 2.74-76.
AIJ, V. Hoffiler and B. Saria, *Antike Inschriften aus Jugoslavien (AIJ)*. Zagreb: St. Kugli, 1938.
Arrian, *Periplus Ponti Euxini*, 1.
CIL, Th. Mommsen, *Corpus Inscriptionum Latinarum (CIL)*. Berlin: Reimer, 1873.
Diodorus Siculus, *Library of History*, 1.25.5.
EDCS, Epigraphik-Datenbank Clauss / Slaby (EDCS) http://www.manfredclauss.de/
HD, Epigraphic Database Heidelberg (HD) https://edh-www.adw.uni-heidelberg.de/home
HEp, Hispania Epigraphica (HEp). Vol. X. Madrid: Publicaciones Universidad Complutense de Madrid, 2004.
ILJug 02, A. Šašel and J. Šašel, *Inscriptiones latinae quae in Iugoslavia inter annos MCMLX et MCMLXX repertae et editae sunt (ILJug 02)*. Ljubljana: Narodni Muzej, 1978.
ILS, H. Dessau, *Inscriptiones Latinae Selectae (ILS)* 2(1). Berlin, 1902.
Pausanias, *Description of Greece*, 8.37.11 and 9.3.9.
Plutarch, *Aristides*, 11.
RICIS, L. Bricault and R. Veymiers, *Receuil des inscriptions concernant les cultes isiaques (RICIS) supplément III, Bibliotheca Isiaca 3*, Bordeaux, 2014.
Strabo, *Geography*, 17.1.17.

Modern sources

Bradley 2013. M. Bradley, Purification, Roman, in R.S. Bagnall, K. Brodersen, C.B. Champion, A. Erskine, and S.R. Huebner, *The Encyclopedia of Ancient History Vol.10* (Wiley-Blackwell, Malden, MA), 5672-5673.
Croon 1967. J.H. Croon, Hot Springs and Healing Gods, *Mnemosyne* 20(3), 225-246.
Diez de Velasco 1992. F. Diez de Velasco, Divinités des eaux thermales dans le nord-ouest de la prouincia Tarraconensis et dans le nord de la prouincia Lusitania: Une approche au phénomène du thermalisme romain dans l'occident des provinces Ibériques, in R. Chevallier, *Les eaux thermales et les cultes des eaux en Gaule et dans les provinces voisines. Actes du colloque 28-30 septembre 1990. Aix-les-Bains* (Antropologia Alpina, Turin), 133-149.
Diez de Velasco 2008. F. Diez de Velasco, Mutation et perduration de l'espace sacré: l'exemple du culte des eaux thermales dans la Pénisule Ibérique jusqu'à la romanisation, in X. Dupré Raventós, S. Ribichini and S. Verger, *Saturnia Tellus: Definizioni dello spazio consacrato in ambiente Etrusco, Italico, Fenicio-Punico, Iberico e Celtico. Atti del convegno internazionale svoltosi a Roma dal 10 al 12 novembre 2004* (Consiglio Nazionale delle Ricerche, Roma), 457-469.
Donald 1998. M. Donald, Material Culture and Cognition: Concluding Thoughts, in C. Renfrew and C. Scarre, *Cognition and Material Culture: the Archaeology of Symbolic Storage* (The McDonald Institute for Archaeological Research, Cambridge, U.K.), 181-187.

Dzino and Domić Kunić 2012. D. Dzino and A. Domić Kunić, Pannonians: Identity-Perceptions from the Late Iron Age to Later Antiquity, in B. Migotti, *The Archaeology of Roman Southern Pannonia: The state of research and selected problems in the Croatian part of the Roman province of Pannonia* (Archaeopress, Oxford, U.K.), 93-115.

Ehrlich Nemeth and Kušan Špalj 2014/2015. D. Ehrlich Nemeth and D. Kušan Špalj, The Roman Settlement Aquae Iasae – Findings of Archaeological Excavations in the Area of the Varaždinske Toplice Municipal Park, in N. Pirnat-Spahić, *Aquae Iasae - Recent Discoveries of Roman Remains in the Region of Varaždinske Toplice* (Cankarjev Dom, Ljubljana/Zagreb), 36-54.

Galić and Radman-Livaja 2006. M. Galić and I. Radman-Livaja, VTERE FELIX – Pojasna garnitura iz Varaždinskih Toplica, *Vjesnik Arheološkog Muzeja u Zagrebu (VAMZ)* 39(1), 165-186.

Ginouvès 1962,.R. Ginouvès, *Balaneutike: recherches sur le bain dans l'antiquité grecque* (Éditions E. de Boccard, Paris).

González Soutelo 2012. S. González Soutelo, Thermal Spas in the Roman Age: An Approximation to the Architectonic Configuration of Baths with Mineral-Medicinal Water in Hispania, in R. Kreiner and W. Letzner, *Spa Sanitas Per Aquam. Proceedings of the International Frontinus-Symposium on the Technical and Cultural History of Ancient Baths. Aachen, March 18-22, 2009* (Peeters, Leuven), 79-86.

González Soutelo 2014a. S. González Soutelo, Medicine and Spas in the Roman Period: The Role of Doctors in Establishments with Mineral-Medicinal Waters, in D. Michaelides, *Medicine and Healing in the Ancient Mediterranean World* (Oxbow Books, Oxford), 206-216.

González Soutelo 2014., S. González Soutelo, Systems for Collecting Mineral Waters in Roman Healing Spas: A Proposal of Characterization from Hispania's Best Documented Examples, in J.M. Álvarez Martínez, T. Nogales Basarrate, and I. Rodà de Llanza, *Proceedings of the XVIIIth International Congress of Classical Archaeology (CIAC). Centre and Periphery in the Ancient World. Vol.1* (Museo Nacional de Arte Romano, Mérida), 289-292.

Hale *et al.* 2005. B.D. Hale, L. Seiser, E.J. McGuire and E. Weinrich, Mental imagery, in J. Taylor, and G.S. Wilson, *Applying Sport Psychology: Four Perspectives* (Human Kinetics, Champaign, IL), 117-135.

Jouffroy 1992. H. Jouffroy, Les *Aquae* Africaines, in R. Chevallier, *Les eaux thermales et les cultes des eaux en Gaule et dans les provinces voisines. Actes du colloque 28-30 septembre 1990. Aix-les-Bains* (Antropologia Alpina, Turin), 87-99.

Kuntić-Makvić *et al.* 2012. B. Kuntić-Makvić, A. Rendić-Miočević, M. Šegvić and I. Krajcar, Integracija i Vizualna Prezentacija Ulomaka Monumentalnog Metričkog Natpisa iz Varaždinskih Toplica, in J. Balen and M. Šimek, *Arheologija Varaždinskog Kraja i Srednjeg Podravlja* (Izdanja Hrvatskog Arheološkog Društva, Zagreb), 285-295.

Kušan Špalj 2014/2015a. D. Kušan Špalj, Aquae Iasae – A Centre of Health, Cult and Oracle. Cults at the Sanctuary in the Period Between the 1st and 4th Centuries, in N. Pirnat-Spahić, *Aquae Iasae – Recent Discoveries of Roman Remains in the Region of Varaždinske Toplice* (Cankarjev Dom, Ljubljana/Zagreb), 82-102.

Kušan Špalj 2014/2015b. D. Kušan Špalj, Reconstruction of the Area around the Natural Thermal Spring – Rituals and Utilization, in N. Pirnat-Spahić, *Aquae Iasae – Recent Discoveries of Roman Remains in the Region of Varaždinske Toplice* (Cankarjev Dom, Ljubljana/Zagreb), 114-119.

Kušan Špalj 2017. D. Kušan Špalj, Aquae Iasae – nova otkrića u rimskom svetištu – s posebnim osvrtom na kultove Apolona, Eskulapa i Serapisa, *Vjesnik Arheološkog Muzeja u Zagrebu (VAMZ)* 50(1), 255-308.

Kušan Špalj and Nemeth-Ehrlich 2012. D. Kušan Špalj and D. Nemeth-Ehrlich, Aquae Iasae – Varaždinske Toplice. Arheološka Istraživanja Rimskog Izvorišnog Bazena i Okolnog Prostora, *Izdanja Hrvatskog Arheološkog Društva* 28, 107-129.

Kušen and Kušen Tomljanović 2015. E. Kušen and N. Kušen Tomljanović, Aquae Iasae na Razmeđu Zdravstvenog i Kulturnog Turizma, *Radovi Zavoda za znanstveni rad Varaždin* 26, 73-92.

Lučić 2014. L. Lučić, Rimski Natpisi iz Varaždinskih Toplica, *Vjesnik Arheološkog Muzeja u Zagrebu (VAMZ)* 46(1), 185-255.

McMullen 2013. P.I. McMullen, Purification, Greek, in R.S. Bagnall, K. Brodersen, C.B. Champion, A. Erskine and S.R. Huebner, *The Encyclopedia of Ancient History, Vol.10* (Wiley-Blackwell, Malden, MA), 5669-5670.

Misic 2015. B. Misic, Cognitive Theory and Religious Integration: The Case of the Poetovian Mithraea, in T. Brindle, M. Allen, E. Durham and A. Smith, *TRAC 2014: Proceedings of the Twenty-Fourth Annual Theoretical Roman Archaeology Conference* (Oxbow Books, Oxford), 31-40.

Misic 2019. B. Misic, Cognitive Aspects of Funerary Commemoration of Soldiers and Veterans in Roman Poetovio, in M. Giangiulio, E. Franchi and G. Proietti, *Commemorating War and War Dead: Ancient and Modern* (Franz Steiner Verlag, Stuttgart), 207-218.

Moitrieux 1992. G. Moitrieux, Hercule et le culte des sources en Lorraine : Les exemples de Thil, Dugny et Deneuve, in R. Chevallier, *Les eaux thermales et les cultes des eaux en Gaule et dans les provinces voisines. Actes du colloque 28-30 septembre 1990. Aix-les-Bains* (Antropologia Alpina, Turin), 67-76.

Nemeth-Ehrlich and Kušan Špalj 2014. D. Nemeth-Ehrlich and D. Kušan Špalj, Aquae Iasae – Varaždinske Toplice, in D. Marković and M. Šegvić, *Klasični Rim na Tlu Hrvatske: Arhitektura, Urbanizam, Skulptura* (Galerija Klovićevi Dvori, Zagreb), 133-140.

Pachis 2014. P. Pachis, Data From Dead Minds? Dream and Healing in the Isis/Serapis Cult During the Graeco-Roman Age, *Journal of Cognitive Historiography* 1(1), 52-71.

Paivio 1985. A. Paivio, Cognitive and motivational functions of imagery in human performance, *Canadian Journal of Applied Sport Sciences. Journal canadien des sciences appliquées au sport* 10(4), 22S-28S.

Paunier 1992. D. Paunier, Eaux thermales et cultes des eaux en Suisse à l'époque romaine, in R. Chevallier, *Les eaux thermales et les cultes des eaux en Gaule et dans les provinces voisines. Actes du colloque 28-30 septembre 1990. Aix-les-Bains* (Antropologia Alpina, Turin), 385-401.

Peréx et al. 2008. M.J. Peréx, J. Cabrero, J. Andreu, C. Miró, C.M. Escorza, H. Frade and A. Hernando, The Use of Water for Health Purposes in Roman Hispania, in C. Ohlig, *Cura Aquarum in Jordanien, Schriften der DWhG, Band 12* (Herstellung und Verlag, Siegburg), 349-352.

Petsalis-Diomidis 2007. A. Petsalis-Diomidis, The Body in Space: Visual Dynamics in Graeco-Roman Healing Pilgrimage, in I. Rutherford and J. Elsner, *Pilgrimage in Graeco-Roman and Early Christian Antiquity: Seeing the Gods* (Oxford University Press, Oxford), 183-218.

Pirnat-Spahić 2014/2015. N. Pirnat-Spahić, *Aquae Iasae – Recent Discoveries of Roman Remains in the Region of Varaždinske Toplice* (Cankarjev Dom, Ljubljana/Zagreb).

Póczy 1998. K. Póczy, Healing Deities, in J. Fitz, *Religions and Cults in Pannonia* (Fejér Megyei Múzeumok Igazgatósága Székesfehérvár), 33-36.

Renberg 2017. G. H. Renberg, *Where Dreams May Come: Incubation Sanctuaries in the Graeco-Roman World. Volume I and Volume II* (Brill, Leiden).

Rendić-Miočević 2014. A. Rendić-Miočević, Rimsko Kiparstvo Sjevernog Ilirika (Hrvatskog Dijela Provincije Panonije), in M. Šegvić and D. Marković, *Klasični Rim na Tlu Hrvatske: Arhitektura, Urbanizam, Skulptura* (Galerija Klovićevi Dvori, Zagreb), 183-213.

Rendić-Miočević 2015. A. Rendić-Miočević, A Reconstruction of the Central Part of the Nymphaeum (Fountain) at Varaždinke Toplice (*Aquae Iasae*) with a Relief Depiction of Nymphs, in C-G. Alexandrescu, *Cult and Votive Monuments in the Roman Provinces. Proceedings of the 13th International Colloquium on Roman Provincial Art* (Mega Publishing House, Cluj-Napoca), 43-54.

Rendić-Miočević and Šegvić 2014. A. Rendić-Miočević and M. Šegvić, Religija i Kultovi u Južnim Panonskim Krajevima, in M. Šegvić and D. Marković, *Klasični Rim na Tlu Hrvatske: Arhitektura, Urbanizam, Skulptura* (Galerija Klovićevi Dvori, Zagreb), 233-242.

Rendić-Miočević 1975. D. Rendić-Miočević, Jedan novi legionarski spomenik iz Varaždinskih Toplica, *Vjesnik Arheološkog Muzeja u Zagrebu (VAMZ)* 9(1), 37-49.

Rendić-Miočević 1992. D. Rendić-Miočević, O Akvejasejskoj Epigrafskoj Baštini i o Posebnostima Njenih Kultnih Dedikacija, *Vjesnik Arheološkog Muzeja u Zagrebu (VAMZ)* 24-25, 67-76.

Revell 2007. L. Revell, Religion and Ritual in the Western Provinces, *Greece & Rome* 54(2), 210-228.

Schejbal 2003. B. Schejbal, Nova Razmatranja o Aquae Balissae i Narodu Jaza: Pejzaž – Vode – Etimologija – Kultovi – Mitologija, Pitanje Atribucije i Kontinuiteta, *Opuscula Archaeologica* 27(1), 393-416.

Vikić-Belančić 1996. B. Vikić-Belančić, Rezultati Arheoloških Istraživanja Lokaliteta u Varaždinskim Toplicama, *Radovi Zavoda za Znanstveni Rad HAZU Varaždin* 8-9, 11-34.

Vikić-Belančić and Gorenc 1958. B. Vikić-Belančić and M. Gorenc, Arheološka Istraživanja Antiknog Kupališta u Varaždinskim Toplicama od 1953.-1955. Godine, *Vjesnik Arheološkog Muzeja u Zagrebu (VAMZ)* 1(1), 75-127.

Vlahović 2012a. S. Vlahović, Povijest antičke masaže i prikaz projekta revitalizacije i rekonstrukcije iste za potrebe antičkog scenskog prikaza: 'Iz života rimskih terma' naselja Aquae Iasae u Varaždinskim Toplicama, *Historia Varasdiensis Časopis za Varaždinsku povijesnicu* 2, 99-111.

Vlahović 2012b. S. Vlahović, Prikaz Konzervatorsko-Restauratorskih Radova na Novootkrivenom Rimskom Reljefu s Motivom Tri Nimfe iz Varaždinskih Toplica, *Radovi Zavoda za Znanstveni Rad HAZU Varaždin* 23, 301-319.

Walton 2015. P. Walton, From Barbarism to Civilization? Rethinking the Monetisation of Roman Britain, *Revue Belge de Numismatique et de Sigillographie* 161, 105-120.

Walton and Moorehead 2014. P. Walton and S. Moorehead, Coinage and the Economy, in M. Millett, L. Revell, and A. Moore, *The Oxford Handbook of Roman Britain* (Oxford University Press, Oxford), 834-849.

Whitehouse 2000. H. Whitehouse, *Arguments and Icons: Divergent Modes of Religiosity* (Oxford University Press, Oxford).

Whitehouse 2002. H. Whitehouse, Modes of Religiosity: Towards a Cognitive Explanation of the Socio-Political Dynamics of Religion, *Method & Theory in the Study of Religion* 14(3), 293-315.

Whitehouse 2004a. H. Whitehouse, Theorizing Religions Past, in H. Whitehouse and L.H. Martin, *Theorizing Religions Past: Archaeology, History and Cognition* (Alta Mira Press, Walnut Creek, CA), 216-232.

Whitehouse 2004b. H. Whitehouse, *Modes of Religiosity: A Cognitive Theory of Religious Transmission* (Alta Mira Press, Walnut Creek, California).

Whitehouse 2009. H. Whitehouse, Graeco-Roman Religions and the Cognitive Science of Religion, in L.H. Martin and P. Pachis, *Imagistic Traditions in the Graeco-Roman World: A Cognitive Modeling of History of Religious Research. Acts of the Panel Held During the XIX Congress of the International Association of History of Religions (IAHR), Tokyo, Japan, March 2005* (Vanias Editions, Thessaloniki), 1-13.

Whitehouse 2013. H. Whitehouse, Immortality, Creation and Regulation: Updating Durkheim's Theory of the Sacred, in D. Xygalatas and W.W. McCorkle Jr., *Mental Culture: Classical Social Theory and the Cognitive Science of Religion* (Acumen, Durham), 66-79.

An Empire Written on Water: A Personal View

Martin Henig

I remember, quite vividly, being told as a child that the Romans, in contrast to the Greeks, were frightened of the sea. This entirely incorrect information derives from a misunderstanding of the way in which the Romans understood geography. The landmass of Europe, Asia and (North) Africa together with the Mediterranean, which encompassed for them the entire inhabited world was surrounded by the mysterious Ocean. Few Greeks, with the exception of Pytheas, the remarkable fourth century BC Massiliot adventurer,[1] had explored the mysterious shores of Ocean, and indeed Socrates stated that 'we who dwell between the Pillars of Hercules and the river Phasis ...live about the [Mediterranean] sea, like ants or frogs about a pond'.[2] However, when the Roman Empire expanded to the shores of the Atlantic, they were confronted with the mysteries and terrors of Ocean, a world beyond. For example, in AD16 Germanicus' fleet was overcome by storms in the North Sea, some ships being swept over to Britain, being returned from thence by the client kings. Tacitus, possibly drawing on a contemporary poem by Pedo Albinovanus, records that 'not a man returned ...without his tale of marvels – furious whirlwinds, unheard-of birds, enigmatic shapes half-human and half-bestial: things seen, or things believed in a moment of terror'.[3] This was an enduring *topos* through the Roman period and beyond, which continued to treat Britain as liminal, situated between Ocean and the inhabited world (the *oikoumene*, to employ the Greek term). Claudius' invasion of Britain in AD 43 was lauded as a victory over Ocean,[4] and triumph over Ocean is implicit in monuments connected with Britain including the Arch of Claudius in Rome and the pediment of the Temple of Sulis Minerva at Bath, with its central Oceanus mask, and tritons in the spandrels (Figure 1). Thus Claudian, in his poem on Stilicho's Consulate in AD 400, figures Britannia herself, clad in the skin of a Caledonian bear, her cheeks tattooed and 'her sea-blue cloak sweeping over her feet like the surge of Ocean'. As late as the sixth century Procopius writes of souls being carried over to *Thanatos* in Britain; in Greek the word signifies the place of the dead, and the author is surely punning on the place name Thanet in Kent, although, in any case, Thanet and Britain itself is still conceived as lying on the other side of Ocean.[5]

Within the Mediterranean world, the Roman fleets were as successful at sea over many centuries as were her legions on land, from at least the time of the first Punic War onwards, though even before that the orators' platform in the Forum was embellished with the rams of ships seized from Antium by Caius Maenius in 338 BC during Rome's wars against the Latins, and hence the name, Rostra, given to the structure.[6] Caius Duilius' column in the Roman Forum,[7]

---

[1] Cunliffe 2001
[2] Plato, *Phaedo* 109
[3] Tacitus, Annals II,24.trans. J. Jackson
[4] Suetonius, Claudius 17
[5] Procopius, *de Bello Gothico* I.iv.20; and see Rivet and Smith 1979, 468-9
[6] Dudley 1967,92-93
[7] Dudley 1967, 93-94

Figure 1. The Pediment of the Temple of Sulis Minerva at Bath. Photo: Penny Coombe

adorned with a ship's prow (*rostra*), commemorated his great victory over the Carthaginians at Mylae in 260 BC, while the site of Rome's triumph at the Battle of the Aegidian islands on the 10th of March 241 BC has recently been located, and the rams of war- galleys from prows of vessels of both fleets, sunk in this very costly conflict, have quite recently been recovered from the sea.[8] Most famous amongst Rome's naval victories, of course, is Octavian's triumph over the fleets of Cleopatra and Antony at Actium in 31BC. Antony had, indeed, issued a famous series of coins, all depicting a war galley on the obverse and the eagle and standards of his legions on the reverse,[9] but to no avail as many of the prows of his ships ended up in the victory monument in the sanctuary of Apollo which Octavian erected on the site of his headquarters during the engagement, near Nikopolis, the city he founded to commemorate that event.[10] Thereafter the Navy, like the Legions, came to be organised on a regular basis throughout the Empire.[11] Claudius' invasion of Britain in AD43 would only have been possible with the aid of a fleet brought together at Boulogne (*Bononia*), the port in north-west Gaul which was to become the headquarters of the *Classis Britannica*,[12] and under the Empire such fleets were stationed at key maritime ports and on major waterways throughout the Empire, for example on the Danube and on the Rhine. Remains of ships including a war galley of the

8   Prag 2014
9   Mattingly 1960, pl.XX nos.17-19
10   Chrysostomou and Kefallonitou 2001, 6-10
11   Starr 1960
12   Mason 2003

Rhine fleet are preserved in a designated ship-museum at Mainz.[13] Warships with their crews are familiar in art and one, for example, is depicted on a late first or early second-century jasper intaglio from the Walbrook, London, and may figure a galley of the *Classis Britannica*.[14] It is now considered possible that the barge which sank in the River Thames off Blackfriars with a cargo of Kentish ragstone probably intended for the building of the land wall of *Londinium* was a vessel from the same fleet.[15] At a later period in the history of the province, we might note the warships that the usurper Allectus (AD 293-6/7) displayed on his coins as well as the similar vessel that was depicted on a gold medallion struck in Trier depicting the victorious Caesar Constantius, having overthrown Allectus, entering a 'liberated' London.[16] A similar late third or early fourth-century warship is depicted on a cornelian intaglio from a ring found in the Thames at Southwark.[17] It is possible that the third-fourth century County Hall Ship, though evidently not a galley, was none-the-less a naval vessel attached to a fleet detachment stationed on the south bank of the Thames.[18]

Ocean was always treated by the Romans with respect and awe as demarcating the edge of the unknown. There was a temple near Cadiz that marked that limit of the world, the limit of Empire, and very probably another was a focus for 'religious tourism' in North Britain near Carlisle, if a remarkable series of enamelled handled pans, many of them inscribed with names of the western forts on Hadrian's Wall, may be regarded as productions of a workshop from the area of this particular *Limes*, here the very limit of Roman power and of civilized humanity.[19] Nevertheless, Roman propaganda allowed Emperors to claim Ocean as their comrade, not least the late third-century British usurpers, Carausius (AD 286-293) and Allectus (AD 293-6/7), each of whom struck coins depicting Oceanus as *Comes Aug(usti)*.[20] There is plenty of evidence for voyaging from the Roman Empire out into the Atlantic, well beyond the supposed limits of the *oikoumene* and into the regions of chaos and night, to the Western Isles, to the Orkney Isles and beyond, while, in the East, trade links ran down the Indian Ocean to Muziris on the Malabar coast of India and even beyond to Malaysia, the sources of precious gems, pepper and other rare spices and ivory, luxuries craved by the Roman elite.[21] Pepper even reached Britain, as attested by four silver pepper pots (*piperatoria*) in the Late Roman treasure from Hoxne, Suffolk.[22]

There were great sea-ports to service trade both between the provinces of the Empire and beyond, amongst them that of Alexandria with its famous Pharos (light-house) going back to Hellenistic times, and spectacularly Portus, the great harbour that fed Rome, originally of Claudian date but supplemented with Trajan's remarkable second harbour of hexagonal form, while nearby was the port-city of Ostia.[23] Around the Mediterranean and on the Atlantic

---

[13] Pferdehirt 1995
[14] Henig 2007, 161 and pl. XVII no. 535
[15] Marsden 1967; Marsden 1994, 33-95; Barker, Hayward and Coombe 2021
[16] Casey 1994; Henig 2015
[17] Henig and Ross 1998; Mason 2003, col. pl. 4
[18] Marsden 1994, 109-129
[19] Henig 2010/2011
[20] Henig 2015, 6
[21] Miller 1969; Mathew 2017; Kunnappilly 2018
[22] Johns 2010, 74-92
[23] Meiggs 1973; Keay 2013

Figure 2. Red Jasper intaglio from Caesarea
Maritima, Israel depicting the Tyche of the Port.
12.1mm by 8.9mm, Photo: courtesy of Shay Hendler

coast of Europe there were other important sea-ports, for example at Piraeus, Caesarea Maritima, Lepcis Magna, Carthage, Marseilles, Bordeaux and Dover. As with many other aspects of Roman infrastructure, for example the aqueducts and bridges discussed later, much was owed to developments in Roman technology, notably concrete technology in a marine environment, especially for harbour works but also for marine fish tanks.[24] Of course there were also riverine ports inland, amongst them those at Cologne and Mainz on the south bank of the Rhine, Lyons at the confluence of the Rhône and Saône and London on the north bank of the Thames.[25] Ports, then as later, had their own distinctive, cosmopolitan societies of mariners and merchants as well as those who were native to these lively communities and serviced their needs, as shopkeepers or those who serviced public amenities.[26] Port scenes are familiar tropes in art, though representations are perhaps best viewed, in the majority of instances, as more generic than as true representations of specific harbours, such as those of Alexandria or Lepcis Magna.[27]

In that regard, it is also instructive to study figures on intaglios depicting city-goddesses, *Tyche*, of sea ports which perhaps supports this idea of generic types. One gem, a red jasper, excavated at the *Classis Britannica* fort at Dover depicts a Tyche holding a bust of Serapis in one hand and with one foot resting on a river or marine deity. Serapis suggests that the marine who wore it came from an Eastern port, perhaps Alexandria, and he might, as I previously proposed, have been a sailor in the *Classis Augusta Alexandrina* (Henig 2012), in which case the

[24] Brandon, Hohlfelder, Jackson and Oleson 2014
[25] Milne 1985; Marsden 1994, 15-32 and 105-108
[26] Arnaud and Keay 2020
[27] Ugolini 2020

water god was perhaps the Nile but, more probably, the harbour. Very similar is a gem from Caesarea (Figure 2), again with Tyche holding a bust of Serapis, but here resting her foot on a ship's prow, though a small figure at her feet probably again represents the harbour.[28] Another red jasper intaglio from Caesarea (no. 69) bears a similar motif, but here the figure holds a head of an Emperor, perhaps intended for Divus Augustus, as on a gem from Sidi-Daoud, Cap Bon in Tunisia, and it too was perhaps recognised by the wearer as the Tyche of a Mediterranean port, possibly here that of Carthage. Such a Tyche holding a bust is certainly depicted on coins of Caesarea dating down to the third century.[29] It may be noted that the stance of Tyche, with one foot on the prow, is similar to that of Oceanus on coin issues of Carausius and Allectus mentioned above,[30] though there the god of Ocean has his other foot resting on a dolphin rather than, as is the case for Tyche, on a river or harbour god.

Merchant vessels criss-crossed the Mediterranean bearing cargoes of wine amphorae and grain (the grain fleet sailing each year from Alexandria to Portus fed the plebs of Rome and was regarded as important by the State to prevent dangerous riots). Marbles and other stone, timber and metals (in the form of ingots), as well as exotic wild animals for the amphitheatre (depicted, for example, in mosaic at Piazza Armerina in Sicily) were also carried to Rome and the west from the southern and eastern Mediterranean shores by large sea-going vessels.[31] In Ostia, the double colonnade known as the Piazzale delle Corporazione housed over sixty officers of shipping corporations with monochrome mosaics, inscribed with the names of the firms: 'stat(io) Sabratensium' , '[navic]ulari Syllecti[ni]', 'navicul(ari) et negotiantes Karalitani' for example, mostly, like these, North African and carrying grain but also oil and in the case of Sabratha (employing the image of an elephant), ivory. There were also firms of shippers from Sardinia and from Narbo and Arles in Narbonensis.[32] Wine, olive oil and fish-sauce in Spanish amphorae were all brought north to British ports on vessels which hazarded the storms of Biscay and the Atlantic coast. Some merchants made the dangerous run in the other direction; thus, for example, Marcus Aurelius Lunaris, who was a sevir Augustalis in both York and Lincoln, set up an altar of millstone grit in Bordeaux following a successful voyage, probably to purchase wine.[33] Other trade was simply across the Channel or North Sea, as was the case for the Rouen merchant Lucius Viducius Placidus, who set up an arch in York and was probably the same merchant who earlier set up an altar to Nehalennia at the mouth of the East Scheldt.[34] The same site has yielded altars dedicated by two merchants trading with Britain, one of them a 'negotiator cretarius Britannicianus' in pottery.[35] Of course, the coastal and inland waterways were traversed by boats of all sorts, from barges like the Blackfriars ship from London mentioned above[36] to smaller vessels like the first-century Sea of Galilee boat on Lake Tiberias in Israel,[37] the New Guys House boat from London[38] or the early fourth-century

[28] Amorai-Stark and Hershkovitz 2016, 92-5, no. 68
[29] Amorai-Stark and Hershkovitz 2016, 94-5, pl. Ia
[30] Henig 2015
[31] D'Arms and Kopff 1980; White 1984, 143-155
[32] Meiggs 1973, 283-288, pl. XXIVb; Dunbabin 1999, 62 and 65, fig.64; and see Rice 2016, especially 106-7, fig.4.4
[33] Tomlin 2018, 308-9 no. 11.39
[34] Tomlin 2018, 306-7 nos 11.37 and 11.36
[35] Tomlin 2018, 305, nos 11.34 and 11.35
[36] Marsden 1994, 33-95
[37] Wachsmann 1990
[38] Marsden 1994, 97-104

Barland's Farm boat excavated in the Severn Estuary near Magor, Monmouthshire in Wales,[39] all of which could have been used as fishing boats or else have transported light goods along or across waterways.

Lighthouses aided navigation, by helping ships either to avoid dangerous shoals or to guide them into port, and the famous Alexandrian *Pharos* has already been mentioned.[40] There are surviving examples of lighthouses, notably the Tower of Hercules at La Coruña in Galicia in Spain, which still stands to the height of thirty four metres; it was built by Sevius Lupus from *Aeminium* (Coimba). The Classis Britannica headquarters at *Gesoriacum* (Boulogne) had another majestic lighthouse, the *Tour d'Ordre*, until the sixteenth century when it was demolished; its other major base at *Dubris* (Dover) originally had two, on the Western and Eastern heights one each side of the harbour, the latter of which is a remarkable survival.[41] One of my favourite intaglios, a cornelian from Caistor St Edmund, just south of Norwich, depicts a merchant ship with its mainsail and foresail raised while beyond it is a friendly lighthouse with its beacon blazing.[42] In this volume Federico Ugolini writes of lighthouses depicted in art often in port scenes and suggests that though these are generically based on those of Alexandria and Portus, they are symbolic of Roman power 'across the Mediterranean waters and beyond' and are suggestive of 'Roman supremacy over waters and territories, commerce and trade'.

However, despite all precautions, the mariner's life was always extremely dangerous as literary texts as various as Petronius's *Satyricon* mentioning Trimalchio's early losses of cargoes at sea, Luke's gripping narrative detailing St Paul's voyage to Rome in the *Acts of the Apostles*[43] – both of the mid-late first century – and, in the late fourth century, Synesius of Cyrene's account of a voyage from Alexandria[44] all testify. The perils of sea voyaging have been archaeologically confirmed by the discovery of numerous shipwrecks with cargoes of stone statues, amphorae of wine and olive oil and much else, not only in the Mediterranean[45] but even well beyond the Pillars of Hercules and out into the Atlantic Ocean. St Paul's voyage – whether it is a strictly historical account or based on an account or accounts of other voyages does not matter in this context – was surely based on the actual experience and ship logs of navigators and is of immense importance in preserving a rare account of the complex issues involved in voyaging, especially out of season when regular navigation was closed and storms were far more frequent. This voyage was beset by incident and the famous shipwreck in Malta, traditionally in St Paul's Bay, is paralleled by a rather later disaster of a ship laded with a cargo of mortars grounding in Mellieha Bay, the next bay on the south-east coast.[46] The risks in the Atlantic were even greater, and the *negotiatores* who carried cargoes in merchant ships from western Gaul and the mouth of the Rhine to Britain were in constant need of divine aid, as is emphasised by altars set up by mariners near the mouth of the River Scheldt in the Netherlands to a goddess called Dea Nehalennia (see above). She is depicted resting her foot on a prow in one relief carved upon a votive altar and was clearly concerned with navigation

---

[39] Nayling and McGrail 2004

[40] White 1984, 105-106

[41] Mason 2003, 109-11, fig.45, col.pls 2 and 15

[42] Henig 2007,161 and pl. XVII no.538; Mason 2003, col. pl. 5

[43] Henig 2017/2018

[44] Ep. 4, cited by White 1984, 155-6

[45] see Wilson 2014, 111

[46] Frost 1969

in the southern North Sea as well as up and down the Rhine.[47] One ship from a continental port, laden with samian pottery, came to grief with its cargo off the coast of Kent on what became known as Pudding Pan rock.[48] On the opposite, western, side of Britain at Bowness-on-Solway in Cumbria, a mariner called Antonianus made a vow in hexameter verse to the Mother goddesses, offering to gild the letters if he returns safely;[49] presumably he was trading with Ireland. But the dangers of disaster were horribly present, as is shown by a tombstone from Chester of a young legionary, an *optio*, about to be promoted to be a centurion *qui naufragio perit*, 'who died by shipwreck'; most probably he was on a naval patrol from the Fortress's port on the River Dee. Most poignantly his body was never recovered because the 'H' of *hic situs est*, 'here he lies', was never carved so the stone is merely a cenotaph.[50] Another loss at sea in the Atlantic is attested by a pottery vessel dredged up 150 miles off the west coast of Ireland from the Porcupine Bank.[51] On its base is a graffito showing an otter with an apparent *tria nomina*, Gai Pisci Fagi- probably a pun for Gaius the Fish-eater, who, with his ship-mate, had presumably been lost far out to sea, beyond any hope of rescue.

However, the Roman interest in water ranged beyond naval dominance and maritime trade. The rivers of the Empire, the Nile, the Rhine, the Moselle, the Rhone and the Danube among them, were likewise arteries of trade, with countless barges conveying heavy goods, including building stone, corn, wine, oil and much else along them, attested in inscriptions, sculpture and the physical remains of such commerce. Sometimes river and sea navigation were, of necessity, combined as when wine from the Rhine and Moselle region was shipped across in barrels across the sea to London and other ports in Britain.

The seas, rivers and lakes were rich in fish, a favourite food in Roman times both fresh and as the prized fish sauce, *garum*, essential in so many recipes.[52] Additionally, shell fish were gathered in vast numbers for the table, but in the case of the murex for valuable purple dye.[53] While salt fish was a staple food, fresh fish was always a luxury.[54] On the whole fishermen (*piscatores*) were of low status, though in famous examples from the Levant we get the impression that Jesus of Nazareth's fishermen disciples, Simon and Andrew and James and John, were reasonably prosperous boat owners with hired staff,[55] and at Ostia there were even *collegia* of fishermen. The Gospels, of course, provide memorable accounts of fishing in Lake Tiberias, Galilee in the first century; and in a different and later, fourth-century context, Ausonius describes fishing on one of the great rivers of north west Europe in his *Mosella*.[56] Fishing was a favourite activity both commercially and as a leisure activity in the sea, as on the bay of Naples, and inland in streams and rivers and on lakes. Lake Balaton in Hungary provides one example, if the name (*Pelso*) inscribed on the fourth-century hunting plate from the Sevso Treasure above a frieze of fish indeed refers to that lake; the picnickers depicted

---

[47] Kooijmans, Stuart, Bogaers and Burger 1971

[48] Walsh 2017

[49] Collingwood and Wright 1965, 630-631 no. 2059

[50] Collingwood and Wright 1965, 181 no. 544; Henig 2004, 20 no. 55

[51] Frere and Tomlin 1995, 101 no. 2503.379

[52] Grainger 2021

[53] Marzano 2013

[54] Marzano 2018

[55] e.g. Mark 1:16-20

[56] Ausonius, *Mosella* 240-282

on the plate are about to consume a large fish on a dish in front of them.[57] While commercial fisheries would rely on nets, the elite enjoyed the excitement and skills of angling, with bait or artificial flies.[58] Along the Mediterranean littoral there was large-scale commercial fish farming employing large tanks fed with water from the sea.[59] Fish were also probably farmed in ponds and lakes inland; this has been suggested at villas in northern Europe as may have been the case at Shakenoak, Oxfordshire.[60]

A piscatorial interest is, of course, very well reflected in art, especially in mosaics: both combinations of fish swimming in the sea as in an especially graphic representation of numerous varieties of fish on an *emblema* from Pompeii[61] and scenes of fishing as on an exedra from Piazza Armerina in Sicily depicting fishing cupids.[62] There are bronzes like the line fisherman, a fountain head from a house in Pompeii,[63] and smaller items such as engraved gems, on which fishing with rod and line is quite a common theme . Examples from Britain include red jasper intaglios from Charterhouse-on-Mendip, Somerset, and Caerleon, Monmouthshire, depicting in one case a cupid, in the other a youth both in the act of landing a fish.[64] A charming cornelian intaglio in the collection of the Hermitage Museum, St Petersburg, emphasises the popularity of fishing as a leisure activity, for it depicts the columned portico of a villa as it were facing the sea; below it is figured a man seated on a rock fishing with rod and line, while below him, in the lowest register of the field, is a fleet of three fishing boats; this gem was surely the signet of a man, probably a villa owner, with a passion for fishing.[65]

Seas, rivers and lakes were also venues for other pleasurable leisure activities by the elite, including boating and swimming . In the mid first century BC, the poet Catullus enjoyed boating on Lake Garda (*Benacus*) from his little country house on the shore at the southern end of the lake at Sirmio (modern Sirmione), as he describes so movingly in his poems on the vessel he brought back from a tour of duty in Bithynia,[66] as well as on his home on the Sirmio peninsula (*Paene īnsulārum, Sirmiō*) itself:

> Salve, o venusta Sirmio, atque ero gaude
> gaudente; vosque, o Lydiae lacus undae,
> ridete quidquid est dome cachinnorum.

> 'Greetings, beautiful Sirmio, and share my happiness. And rejoice also, you waves of the Lydian lake, and may all the joyfulness of my home bring laughter!'[67]

---

[57] Mundell Mango 1994, 55-97, figs 1.29, 1.11 and 1.37
[58] Aelian, On the Nature of Animals XV,1
[59] Higginbotham 1997; Farrar 1998, 64-66
[60] Brodribb, Hands and Walker 2005, 420-423 and 553
[61] Roberts 2019, 139, pl. 145
[62] Dunbabin 1999, 141, fig. 144
[63] Roberts 2019, 114-116
[64] Henig 2007, 107, pl. IV no. 125 and 256-7, pl. XVI no. 506
[65] Neverov 1976,76 no.125
[66] Catullus, Carmen 4
[67] Catullus, Carmen 31

The poetic description of the lake as Lydian recalls the Trojan origins of the Etruscans, real or supposed. In any case, Catullus' own modest house was much later replaced during the Imperial period by a lavish villa of palatial size which occupied much of the peninsular jutting out into the lake.[68] A personal description of a lavish maritime villa on the coast near Rome is provided by Pliny the Younger with his enthusiastic and detailed account of his own Laurentine villa[69] though, in the same letter, he mentions that villas were spread along the Latium coast, so as to produce the effect on the eye of a series of towns. The same situation was to be found equally around the Bay of Naples, a region which included Imperial villas with amenities including seaside grottos, like Tiberius' grotto at his Sperlonga villa, a maritime banqueting hall furnished with baroque-style statuary depicting scenes from Greek epic. Tiberius spent the last years of his life mainly on Capri (also well endowed with sea caves such as the Blue Grotto). On the island, Tiberius' most famous residence was the Villa Iovis high on the cliffs, commanding superb views over the bay.[70] His successor as Emperor, Gaius (Caligula), took luxury onto the water and had large barges constructed for his leisure on Lake Nemi.[71] Maritime and lakeside villas were erected elsewhere on the shores of the Mediterranean and even far beyond, as was the case with the 'palace' at Fishbourne and other smaller villas situated on the Sussex coast in Southern England, which equally express a love of looking out at the sea, a taste which chimes with more modern attitudes to the seaside.[72] Even the banks of favoured rivers such as the Moselle were chosen as the loci of strings of villas along their banks as Ausonius reveals in his poem *Mosella*. Then, as now, people enjoyed swimming both in the sea and also in rivers, for which there is rather more evidence, as well as in specially constructed swimming pools in baths complexes.[73] Pliny describes boys racing each other and swimming out to sea at Hippo in North Africa.[74] And the young, as now, indulged in seaside games too. Minucius Felix describes boys skimming potsherds along the waves,[75] the same game that children enjoy today. For older people, as both Pliny and Felix testify, there was also the chance for a gentle stroll along the beach.

The management of water necessitated technological advances in hydraulics. It impinged on urban planning, on law regarding conflicting water rights and even on politics, certainly when it came to major infrastructure projects.[76] A basic, universal need of all the inhabitants of the Empire was the availability of water for drinking, cooking and washing as well as for many aspects of craft and manufacture. If water was not directly obtainable from streams and rivers or could be piped from these sources, it would often have been sourced by sinking wells, frequently to great depth. Such wells would have been a central feature of life for individuals and communities in towns, villages and the countryside throughout the Empire and they were usually simply accessed by letting down a rope with a bucket attached to its end, perhaps operated by turning a handle attached to a capstan. As James Gerrard reminds us in his contribution, citing the gospel narrative of the Samaritan woman who Jesus encountered at the

---

[68] McKay 1975, 132-133, fig. 51

[69] Pliny the Younger, Ep.II.17

[70] D'Arms 1970; McKay 1975, 121-128

[71] Barrett 1989, 201-2

[72] Cunliffe 1998; Rudling 1998, 43-46

[73] see Harris 1972, 116-8 and especially Amphaeris and Henig in this volume

[74] Pliny the Younger, Ep. IX,33

[75] Minucius Felix, *Octavius* III,2-6

[76] Irby 2021

well,[77] this was often women's work. Sometimes, however, a semi-mechanical system might be employed for major projects, as was demonstrated in London when four massive plank-lined wells together with lifting gear and bucket chains were excavated on a site in Gresham Street; the latter were presumably powered by a tread-wheel or capstan, and provided a constant supply of water for the nearby Cheapside Baths and perhaps other users.[78]

The vast population of Roman cities, including especially Rome, had an increasing need for pure water, for hygiene (drinking and bathing) as well as for industry, which wells and natural water courses (often in any case polluted) could not hope to supply; this necessitated the building of aqueducts[79] at vast expense, and hence the provision of water often devolved on wealthy patrons, entire communities and in significant examples on the Emperor and the State, for instance the *Aqua Claudia* bringing water to Rome, which was begun by Caligula but brought to completion by Claudius. Sextus Iulius Frontinus, who had been a successful governor of Roman Britain between AD 74 and 77, subsequently serving in Germany under Domitian and then as proconsul of Asia in the 80s, before, in 97, becoming Curator of Aqueducts. With the knowledge so obtained, he wrote a book on the subject, surveying the history and management of the aqueducts of Rome, which is still extant (*de aquae ductu*) and thus provides a remarkable contemporary source for these constructions. The most ambitious of these artificial water channels ran for miles and, in the most dramatic examples, such as the

Figure 3. The Pont du Gard, near Nimes. Photo: Tony King

[77] John 4
[78] Blair, Spain, Swift, Taylor and Goodburn 2006
[79] Dudley 1967, 38-42; White 1984, 162-8; Jackson 1988, 43-46

Figure 4. The castellum divisiorum at Nimes. Photo: Tony King

Aqua Claudia supplying Rome, the Segovia aqueduct in Tarraconensis[80] and Nîmes (*Nemausus*) aqueduct, the water was, wherever necessary, carried over gorges or low ground to the city on arches. When aqueducts needed to be constructed above ground they were a dominating feature of the landscape and were monuments testifying to the might of the Empire; the last stretch of the 18 kilometre long Segovia aqueduct was carried into the city on no less than 119 arches. In the case of the Nîmes aqueduct, the most famous section is of course the Pont du Gard (Figure 3), the aqueduct-bridge carrying water over the river Gard to Nîmes , where the water fed into the *castellum aquae* or *castellum divisiorum* (distribution tower) (Figure 4).[81] Sections of an aqueduct have been revealed in Britain at the *Colonia* of Lincoln (*Lindum*), consisting of a buried pipeline encased in waterproof concrete, as well as remains of the *castellum divisiorum*, which at least supplied the nearby public baths, both of which, together with the sewer system, were very probably conceived at the same time as a co-ordinated campaign of public works.[82]

Apart from urban amenities, drinking water, baths and fountains, aqueducts had industrial value too, for example feeding water-mills, amongst them the grain mills at Barbegal near

---

[80] Keay 1988, 137-138 and col. pl. op. P.160
[81] Rivet 1988, 165-7; King 1990, 78-80
[82] Jones 2002, 57-8; 96-98

Arles,[83] and, of course, the public baths, as well as fountains and gardens. Water management also involved the building of dams, especially in arid regions: Spain, Syria and North Africa, where conservation of water for irrigation as well as mitigating seasonal flooding were important. The Cornalvo and Proserpina dams near Mérida (*Emerita Augusta*) in western Spain are impressive examples.[84] Equally vital, in areas where there was no shortage of water, was the digging of channels for drainage and for navigation, as we are reminded by Stijn Heeren and Mark Driessen in their paper on the major engineering projects undertaken to shape the Lower Rhine waterscape in the first century of our era. Impressive works, comparable in terms of man-hours to the construction of the great defensive and customs barrier ditch, the *Vallum* immediately south of Hadrian's Wall, may also be discerned across the North Sea, in the digging of channels for drainage and perhaps for navigation that are still in parts visible in Eastern Britain, notably in the impressive system of dykes along the Fen edge in Cambridgeshire and Lincolnshire known as the Car Dyke, though this does not seem to have been a continuous canal as was once thought.[85] The Foss Dyke canal further north in Lincolnshire may, however, have originated as a Roman construction connecting the River Trent at Torksey to Lincoln. Nero's project to have a canal dug across the Isthmus of Corinth was launched with great ceremony by the Emperor himself in AD 67, and despite the labour of 6,000 prisoners from the Judaean war, it was left uncompleted by the time of his death;[86] nevertheless it must count as a monument to Roman engineering endeavour. The younger Pliny wanted to obtain the Emperor Trajan's approval for a canal from a lake near Nicomedia in Bithynia to the sea to aid transport of marble and other heavy goods, though this ambitious plan likewise failed to materialise.[87]

Bridges were another aspect of the taming of the environment, allowing places separated by rivers to be joined up, and facilitating transport both within and between provinces.[88] The bridges of Rome, such as the *pons Sublicius*, the *pons Aemilius* and the *pons Fabricius*, allowed the city to function on both sides of the Tiber and also embrace the *Isola Tiberina*. Bridges over the Mosel at Trier[89] and over the Thames at London[90] brought life to these cities. Some bridges were stupendous works of engineering, both beautiful and imposing. The Pont du Gard has already been mentioned, a bridge of course, as well as an aqueduct, but of equal majesty is the bridge over the rive Tagus at Alcántara built by Caius Iulius Lacer and dedicated to Trajan in AD 106.[91] Almost contemporary with this (AD 105) was the bridge, 1,135 metres in length, built by Trajan over the Danube east of the Iron Gates, between what is now Drobeta-Turnu Severin in Romania and Kladovo in Serbia, by Apollodorus of Damascus.[92] It was constructed in the context of the Dacian wars, indicative of the political and strategic element in such infrastructure projects.

---

[83] White 1984, 55-56 and 196-199
[84] White 1984, 102-104
[85] Upex 2008, 184-9
[86] Suetonius, *Nero* 19.1; Josephus, *Bell. Jud.* 3.532; see Opper 2021, 252
[87] Pliny the Younger, *Ep.* 10.41
[88] Adam 1994, 284-288
[89] Wightman 1970, 78-79, pl. 4b
[90] Milne 1985, 44-54
[91] Keay 1988, 137 and col. pl. opposite p. 80
[92] Serban 2009

All these were the amenities of Roman civilization that were later bequeathed by Rome to Byzantium, to the Arabs and eventually back to us in the Medieval West. Tacitus, in writing about Agricola's governorship in Britain singles out in a series of *topoi* baths and banquets as luxurious vices introduced to the Britons.[93] At banquets, an important ritual before dining and between courses was the washing of the diner's hands, generally employing a jug and a handled pan (*trulleum*), as is for example figured on a dining scene from the Late Roman Vergilius Romanus.[94] Other more elaborate vessels for ablutions were employed in later antiquity including fluted dishes.[95] A type of vessel perhaps developed from these shallow basins and also designed for ablutions was the hanging bowl, which could be raised and lowered by a servant holding a chain .There is an early example of the type in bronze , perhaps late fourth- or early fifth- century in date, from the Draper's Gardens cache in the City of London,[96] but hanging bowls were further elaborated with intricate enamelling in Britain in the centuries following the end of Roman political control, and one from Sutton Hoo, Suffolk, even sports at its centre a figurine of a fish on column which allowed it to swivel in the water in the bowl.[97] These bowls reflect a continuation of one of the major conventions of civilised life, personal cleanliness, a concomitant of that polite dining detailed by Tacitus,[98] even if by then that other great institution, the baths, had fallen into disuse. These vessels, including the fourth century silver Water Newton hanging bowl, wrongly described as a lamp,[99] were also, it seems, employed in priestly – Christian – ablutions prior to celebrating the Eucharist.[100]

At Roman feasts, wine was served in cups of silver or fine glass, but it was always mixed with water, which was often kept in a bucket-shaped *situla*; the water might either be iced or else heated in a samovar known as an *authepsa* to produce mulled-wine, and then the wine would be distributed to guests in special bag-shaped vessels known as *askoi*, generally carried by servants in pairs.[101] A particularly fine silvered bronze *askos* handle of rare elaboration, incorporating the mask of a young satyr at the base of the handle, and best paralleled at Boscoreale, was found in excavations at the palatial Fishbourne villa in Sussex.[102] Thus even water might become a luxury item for the most wealthy members of society.[103]

Wherever there was provision of a constant water supply, lavatories could be flushed through sewers, of which examples have been recorded under streets and at the bath complexes of major cities such as at Ostia in Italy or Vaison in Narbonensis.[104] In Britain, as noted above, only the *Colonia* of Lincoln seems to have possessed a sewer system, and other towns here and throughout the Empire – even major ones – often lacked such civic provision. Even where there was a supply of water from an aqueduct, people still dug wells for drinking water, and, as

---

[93] Tacitus, *Agricola* 21
[94] Harris and Henig 2010, 28-29, fig. 2
[95] Hobbs 2016, 178-194; Harris and Henig 2010, 30, fig. 3
[96] Gerrard 2009, 168-171, fig. 5.1
[97] Harris and Henig 2010, 32, fig. 4
[98] Tacitus, *Agricola* 21
[99] Painter 1999, 9-10, pl. IIa
[100] Harris and Henig 2010, 30-31
[101] Roberts 2019, 154-5
[102] Down and Henig 1988
[103] Roberts 2019, 147-155
[104] Jackson 1988, 50; Rivet 1988, 289

at Pompeii, the house sewer simply led to an individual cesspit. Thus, in private houses, even those most richly appointed, standards of hygiene were often very poor; indeed latrines were often situated in the kitchens, where food preparation also took place.[105]

Latrines and sewers have also been found in many fortresses and forts, for instance the legionary fortress at York and the auxiliary fort at Housesteads, Northumberland, in Britain.[106] Here at least, where the health of soldiers was of paramount importance for the Empire, there was incentive to maintain a high level of hygiene; thus the availability of a good quality water supply for the bath-houses and latrines was of paramount importance.[107]

Fountains, both modest and elaborate, graced the streets and squares of towns, for instance in Pompeii, where people – especially women – congregated, as in villages they would tend to congregate around a well. The more elaborate fountains (especially in the Eastern provinces) were embellished with statuary and might have possessed an additional religious function, perhaps dedicated to the local nymphs. The Trajanic nymphaeum at Miletus[108] and the Peirene fountain in Corinth as reconstructed in the early second century are splendid examples of such opulent urban fountains.[109] Like other public works, these buildings would often have been financed by wealthy patrons, in the case of Corinth by the immensely wealthy Herodes Atticus. Even legionary fortresses possessed significant water features: the *natatio*, the pool in front of the Fortress Baths at Caerleon (*Isca*), which evidently served as a swimming pool,[110] doubtless also possessed a more formal, quasi-religious function in addition, as implied by a statue of Venus or a nymph beside a water-spout in the form of a dolphin at one end, though only the dolphin water-spout now remains;[111] and a figure of Venus or a nymph with an urn was almost certainly a fountain ornament in the first-century Fortress at Wroxeter (*Viroconium*), Shropshire, demolished in the Hadrianic period when a great new planned city for the Cornovii, the local tribe, replaced it.[112] It has been conjectured that the statue may have originally come from the Legionary legate's private garden, rather than any public space like the Caerleon *natatio*. One wonders at what might have been the original setting of a statue of Venus excavated at Dover and perhaps later re-used in the quay wall.[113] Ornamental ponds graced luxurious villas as well as the larger town houses.[114] On the largest scale, the Canopus and other water features in Hadrian's villa at Tivoli were fed by aqueducts and would have provided a watery setting for both contemplation and feasting, for here Hadrian and his guests could be soothed by the sound of the waters and watch the fish that swam in these artificial ponds.[115] Water features, complete with fountains,[116] were important features of the gardens of the wealthy throughout the Empire, from urban Pompeii to rural Britain, where

---

[105] Hobson, Molesworth and Trusler 2009; Roberts 2019, 173-177

[106] Jackson 1988, 51-52; Crow 1995, 38-42, col. pl. 4

[107] Webster 1969, 198-9; 203

[108] Lyttelton 1974, 266-7, pl. 190

[109] Lyttelton 1974, 278-9, pl. 204

[110] see the paper on swimming by Amphaeris and Henig in this volume

[111] Zienkiewicz 1986, 277-280

[112] M. Henig and G. Webster in Webster and Chadderton 2002, 135-136

[113] Coombe, Grew, Hayward and Henig 2015, 38-39, no. 64

[114] Farrar 1998, 64-84

[115] Macdonald and Pinto 1995, 170-182

[116] Kapossy 1969

Figure 5. A fish-spout fountain head, Tockenham, Wiltshire. 650mm by 290mm. Photo: Martin Henig
[from Heir photo archive, School of Archaeology, Oxford]

statuary might provide a decorative source from which water debouched into the pool.[117] Two especially interesting examples, one from southern Europe and another from the north, are the bronze fisherman from a house in Pompeii mentioned above[118] and a river fish (Figure 5) with gaping mouth carved in Cotswold oolitic limestone which came from a pond in a luxurious villa in the British countryside at Tockenham, Wiltshire.[119]

Baths were an essential amenity to leisured life in rich villas everywhere, but the grandest were the public baths of cities, towns and forts, where people would come to cleanse themselves by passing through a suite of cold, tepid and hot rooms, provided with plunge baths. Provision for swimming (as at the baths, notably the Great Bath attached to the Temple of Sulis Minerva at Bath)[120] was rarer, but at Bath there was, of course, a specifically religious aspect to the complex with its important hot springs and temple apart from any 'secular' secular use. All baths were provided with courtyards or specific halls for exercise, and sometimes lecture halls too. The provision of water, though essential, was not the sole reason for the existence of these great structures. The large Imperial *thermae* at Rome, provided for the populace by the emperors Titus, Trajan, Caracalla and Diocletian were especially luxurious in their décor and housed expensive statues and other works of art often brought from Greece, Egypt and

---

[117] Farrar 1998, 85-96
[118] Roberts 2019, 114-116
[119] Henig 1997
[120] Cunliffe 1969, 94-147

elsewhere. In Britain, the remains of the civic baths of Leicester and Wroxeter, both with a wall of the basilica of the bath complexes surviving to near full height, provide some idea of the importance of public baths in even the furthest provinces.[121] The Barbarathermen at Trier were even larger,[122] while in the early fourth century, when the city was elevated to Imperial capital, the Kaiserthermen was one of the new structures advertising its civic status.[123] These great *thermae* symbolised the power of Rome throughout its Empire. Every major city would have had the amenity of major suits of baths to which citizens were able to resort, for bathing and for general recreation. The legionary fortresses with their large citizen population of legionaries were provided with lavish baths modelled on the Imperial baths of Rome; for example, the massive baths at the fortress of *Legio II Augusta* at *Isca* (Caerleon) in south-east Wales[124] were almost equally luxurious in decor to the major bath suite of a city.

Often, such amenities as baths and fountains have been excavated as adjuncts to religious sanctuaries, and the case of *Aquae Sulis* (Bath) has already been mentioned. Something similar probably existed at Buxton, Derbyshire, *Aquae Arnemetiae,* in which the name of the spring goddess contains the word *nemet*, a sacred grove (Rivet and Smith 1979, 254-5), and she seems to be attested by an altar from Brough-on-Noe as *Dea Arnomecta*.[125] The great spa at Aachen, *Aquae Granni*, in Germany[126] was dedicated to the healing deity Apollo Grannus who is often paired with a goddess called Sirona or Thirona, a deity likewise generally associated with regional healing sanctuaries with associated springs. Both were especially venerated in the Moselle valley.[127] Sirona recalls the Greek goddess Hygeia (Roman Salus) and like her is often portrayed with a serpent. All major sanctuaries and many minor ones would have possessed bath suites as water was required both for the ritual purification of worshippers and where relevant for healing purposes, for example at the sanctuary of Mars Nodens at Lydney in the Forest of Dean.[128] Nodens presumably presided over the iron-rich waters of the local spring, but may also have exercised power over the river Severn below with its celebrated bore. In any case, all water courses, natural or artificial, would have been dedicated as sacred either to Neptune, to individual river gods or goddesses or to the nymphs who appear under a variety of names. Whether or not there was a flowing stream of living water, an invariable aspect of religious ritual was the liturgical washing of hands, with a flagon and *trulleum* employed for the purpose, a practice which, as we have seen, also featured in secular feasting. The set is very commonly figured in relief on the sides of altars.[129]

Classical authors write of sacred rivers and the beauty of beloved riverine landscapes; thus in the Roman period the younger Pliny describes the temple and smaller shrines along the banks of the River Clitumnus in Umbria,[130] while Horace describes the Bandusian spring, its waters

---

[121] Wacher 1995, 346-50; 368-9

[122] Wightman 1970, 82-85

[123] Wightman 1970, 98-102, pl. 9

[124] Zienkiewicz 1986

[125] Collingwood and Wright 1965, p.95 no. 281

[126] Cüppers 1982

[127] Woolf 2003

[128] Jackson 1988, 166-168, fig. 45

[129] Harris and Henig 2010, 28-30; Henig 2004, 5-6 no. 12 from Chester and 9 no. 21 from Heronbridge near Chester; Coombe, Grew, Hayward and Henig 2015, 67-8, no.117 from Springhead, Kent

[130] Pliny the Younger, *Ep*, VIII, 8

clear as glass and deserving of wine and flowers, but then goes on to describe the sacrifice of a kid to the goddess,[131] a reminder that though his sensitive response to the natural beauty of a tranquil well-watered landscape might be one we share it was always combined with veneration for local deities and demanded the sacrifice usually of an animal. Countless works of art, stuccos, paintings, sculptures, silver-plate and engraved gems depict such sacro-idyllic landscapes[132] in which an ideal landscape of sacred trees and small shrines, beside springs or small streams is accompanied by an offering of a kid or a young pig.

Shrines to river gods and goddesses were distributed widely, as they had been in the Greek world. For instance the bull-headed river god Gelas, depicted on coins of Gela[133] is an expression of the power of the River Gelas in spate like a charging bull and this veneration continued into the Roman period[134] and the same imagery was often applied to other rivers. However, by contrast, the presiding nymph of the well-mannered sacred spring at Syracuse was the beautiful Arethusa who was often depicted surrounded by dolphins as Syracuse lies on the coast.[135] River gods were, of course, often portrayed as mature bearded men, sometimes equated with Neptune, who in his turn was often confused with Oceanus, who ruled over the wide Ocean stretching beyond the boundaries of the known world. The River Nile was especially sacred, and was connected with the cult of Osiris. Those drowned in the Nile, like Hadrian's beloved young friend Antinous, who perished in the river in AD 130, were in local Egyptian cult assimilated with the deity.[136] Penny Coombe has reviewed this evidence expertly in this volume with particular relation to Neptune and other gods of rivers from the Nile to the Thames.

Springs, rivers, lakes and bogs were also regarded as liminal places in prehistoric Gaul, as Aaron Irvin demonstrates, and this veneration continued in the Roman period, sometimes taking different forms, as is well demonstrated by the many offerings of Roman date to *Dea Sequana* at the source of the Seine[137] or to a divine pair, Borvo (equated with Apollo on one inscription) and Damona, at Bourbonne-les-Bains.[138] Here Sauer demonstrates that the specific offering of coins was a Roman innovation – as it seems to have been also at Bath (see below). Misic (this volume) provides fascinating insight into the veneration of the nymphs at *Aquae Iasae* (Varaždinske Toplice) in Croatia, based on the rich evidence, epigraphic and material from that sanctuary.

This was just as true in Roman Britain as it was elsewhere,[139] even maintaining the poetic theme in the case of an altar erected beside a stream on the east side of Dere Street near the Roman fort at Risingham, Northumberland that is inscribed, albeit not very expertly, with a two line hexameter verse :

---

[131] Horace, *Odes* III, 13
[132] Ling 1991, 46 and 141-146; Brogli 1996
[133] Kraay/Hirmer 1966, 294-5, pls 55-57 nos 154-167
[134] see Walters 1926, 119-20 no. 1031
[135] Kraay/Hirmer 1966, 287-293 nos.72-134
[136] Lambert 1984
[137] Aldhouse-Green 1999
[138] Sauer 2005
[139] Alcock 1965; Henig1984, 43-48

Somnio praemonitus miles hanc ponere iussit
aram quae Fabio nupta est Nymphis venerandis.

'Forewarned by a dream the soldier bade her who is married to Fabius to set up this altar to the Nymphs who are to be worshipped.'[140]

In the same region, at Carrawburgh, there was the sacred well of the nymph-goddess Coventina[141] and also a separate shrine to the nymphs and the local genius set up by a praefectus of the First Cohort of Batavians.[142] A large altar found some 2 km east of the fortress of *Deva* (Chester) in an area of springs that provided fresh water to the Fortress was dedicated by *Legio XX Valeria Victrix* to the 'Nymphs and Fountains', clearly deities who served the community and deserved the grateful worship of all.[143] In southern Britain a fairly recent discovery has been the finding of a cache of jewellery and votive leaves dedicated to *Dea Senuna*, who was evidently a river goddess,[144] but, of course, the most famous case of such a deity in Britain is provided by Sulis Minerva, who presides over the hot springs at Bath (*Aquae Sulis*).[145] Here, numerous coins and other objects, together with pieces of lead inscribed with petitions to Sulis asking her to recover stolen property and punish the thief or thieves responsible, have been recovered from the reservoir surrounding her sacred spring. In this volume Eleri Cousins discusses these dedications, dismissing the supposition that Bath was a major curative sanctuary but instead centring on the chthonic aspects of Sulis, concluding that 'ritual deposition at the reservoir seems to have been in large part concerned with harnessing and controlling feelings of loss or decay through the act of giving objects, either literally or by proxy, to the goddess' waters'. In another context, writing of the river Tees at Piercebridge, Co. Durham, in Northern Britain, Philippa Walton analyses the evidence for votive deposition in the river, perhaps connected with the veneration of Mars and Mercury. These gods were not generally especially associated with water or with aquatic themes, although, as guide of souls, Mercury certainly counts as a liminal deity between the upper and lower worlds.[146] Even wells, which were dug in the majority of cases for purely practical reasons, in order to provide fresh water, were also potentially loci for the veneration of deities, especially those whose realm was the underworld, into whose domain the well-diggers had trespassed and who thus needed to be propitiated, as James Gerrard, indeed, reminds us in his paper.

Water has always possessed more than a prosaic function, never more so than in the Roman period, and the special character of water as the source of life has been continuous factor in human and non-human society. Apart from the almost universal sanctity of rivers and wells, water was employed in religious contexts for purification rituals and for pouring libations. In Late Antiquity, Christians constructed purpose-made baptisteries, sometimes embellished with mosaics, in all parts of the Roman world, from Dura Europos in Syria to Richborough and probably Bradford on Avon in Britain, for the performance of the unique initiation ritual into the community of believers. Amongst them are famous surviving examples in Naples,

[140] Collingwood and Wright 1965, 404 no. 1228
[141] Allason-Jones and McKay 1985
[142] Tomlin, Wright and Hassall 2009, 308-9 no.3316
[143] Collingwood and Wright 1965, 152-3 no. 460; Henig 2004, 6 no.14
[144] Jackson and Burleigh 2018, 140-142
[145] Cunliffe 1969; Cunliffe 1988
[146] see also Eckardt and Walton 2021

Albegna, Ravenna in Italy with vault mosaics, and Salona in Dalmatia and Sbeitla in Tunisia with mosaics on the floor. There are well preserved baptisteries at Poitiers and Frejus.[147] This ancient rite has, of course, continued with modification to our own day; in Antiquity the deep fonts, like the plunge tanks in Roman baths, were intended for adult immersion; the small medieval and later fonts of our day are designed primarily for the baptism of babies. The mosaic on the floor at the entrance to the Salona baptistry depicts two stags drinking from a *cantharus* accompanied by the first verse of Psalm 42, 'As a deer longs for flowing streams, so my soul longs for you, O God.'[148] Such a *cantharus* fountain was derived, of course, from the *hortus*, the garden setting, and one graces the entrance forecourt of the large and well-furnished Jewish synagogue at Sardis in Asia Minor.[149] Another in Phrygian marble (*pavonazzetto*), with panther handles, surely originally designed in the Antonine period as an ornamental basin for a garden evoking Dionysian luxuriance, was re-used in the Early Christian church at Petra, presumably for hand-washing.[150]

Finally, water was involved in more than one way in funerary rituals, not simply the preparation of the body for burial but for ritual ablutions, and the same set of jug and *trulleum* is frequently found together in furnished tombs such as at the Bartlow Barrows on the Cambridgeshire and Essex border.[151] Subsequent to death and burial, the soul was believed to undertake a journey either ferried by Charon over the River Styx to Hades, the land of shades, or, as the sculptural reliefs on so many tombstones and built tombs boldly suggest very much more optimistically, over the mysterious Ocean to the Blessed Isles, hence the frequent funerary imagery on so many tombs of dolphins and mythical sea creatures, sometimes ridden by Cupid, who here represents the soul of the deceased; the mask of the god Oceanus himself is likewise a frequent feature in funerary art. We might note here Procopius' story about *Thanatos* (Thanet)[152] which of course references Britain, even the part nearest to the European mainland, as being across Ocean. Cupid seated on the back of a dolphin and a striking mask of Oceanus were figured as part of the rich sculptural embellishment of a large built tomb, probably a tower-tomb, at Stanwick, Northamptonshire.[153] An Oceanus or Neptune head from Southwark[154] is probably also funerary. An Oceanus mask provides the central feature of the pediment crowning the second-century tombstone of Bodicacia from the Western Cemetery of Cirencester, Gloucestershire.[155]

In one way the rite of Christian baptism, by which water is the medium through which the person is reborn to new life, simply follows an older line of reasoning implicit in the visual language and spiritual hopes of many Pagan Romans too, although in the case of the Bodicacia tombstone, when it came to be reused as the cover for a Christian grave in the fourth century, the face of Oceanus and the crab-claws on his head were deliberately defaced, regarded presumably as a powerful, malevolent idol. However, on a refined fourth-century mosaic

---

[147] Doig 2008, passim; Ferguson 2009, 819-852, pls 11-24

[148] van der Meer 1967, pl. 25

[149] Fine 1996,74-5, pl. XIII

[150] Herrmann 2001

[151] Harris and Henig 2010, 28-29, fig. 1a and b

[152] Procopius, *de Bello Gothico* I.iv.20

[153] Coombe, Hayward and Henig 2021

[154] Coombe, Grew, Hayward and Henig 2015, 37-38 no.63a

[155] Hayward, Henig and Tomlin 2017

from Frampton in Dorset, a mask of Oceanus, identified by the crab claws on his brows, is boldly figured (Figure 6). Two dolphins seemingly emerge from his mouth while others swim towards him. In panels above is a verse in four lines, two on each side of the mask:

Neptuni vertex reg(i)men
sortiti mobile ventis
scul(p)tum cui c(a)erulea es[t]
delfinis cincta duob[us]

'The head of Neptune allotted the domain stirred by the winds, whose dark-blue figure is flanked by two dolphins...'.[156] It is clear that here Neptune and Oceanus have become interchangeable as deities, perhaps simply for the purpose of metre and composition, although the great Greek sea-god Poseidon might be seen as equivalent to both. A similar composition of Oceanus/Neptune with dolphins may be noted in the apse of a mosaic from Fordington High Street, Dorchester, perhaps there dating as early as the second century.[157] Remarkably, below the frieze on the Frampton mosaic, at a hundred and eighty degrees to it, a Chi-Rho, likewise in mosaic, has been placed on the chord of an apse which figured a *cantharus* as its central motif, probably there to be regarded as a chalice. Here, at least, one might suspect a Christian's comfortable appropriation of the image of Oceanus.

Figure 6. Detail of mosaic from Frampton, Dorset depicting the head of Neptune/Oceanus after S.Lysons, Reliquiae Britannico-Romanae. vol. I,1813. Photo: Heir photo archive, School of Archaeology, Oxford

[156] Frere and Tomlin 1992, 88-89, no. 2448.8; Cosh and Neal 2005, 134-6, mosaic 168.2
[157] Cosh and Neal 2005, 100-102, mosaic 165.13

This splendid collection of papers covers many of the themes touched on in this introductory essay and, indeed, I hope suggests a number of others to future researchers. It is very much a personal selection: I got to know the Romans at school in my teens, reading Tacitus and Suetonius and met Catullus and Lake Garda through reading Gilbert Highet's sensitive *Poets in a Landscape* (1957), which inspired a family holiday at Sirmione. Our school excavation was on what we thought was a villa, but may have been an ancillary building to a water shrine on the rolling hillside behind the great seventeenth and eighteenth century mansion at Moor Park, Hertfordshire. Amongst the Roman monuments I visited were the amazing remains of the temple with its sacred spring and the adjoining baths at Bath, *Aquae Sulis* , central to more than one paper in this volume, as well as the little nymphaeum still fed by a trickle of spring water at Chedworth Roman villa, Gloucestershire. Another family holiday took me to Hadrian's Villa at Tivoli, and to Rome with its aqueducts as well as the port of Ostia. Most of my career, however, has been concerned with the Roman antiquities of Britain and the often overlooked proliferation of images on engraved gems and these interests are thus, to a degree, reflected in my contribution to this volume. For me the Romans have always had a strong connection with art, with literature, especially poetry, with gardens and landscape and always with water. As far as I know this is the first collection of papers especially devoted to the subject of the Romans and water and, as such, it is a very important venture which will surely stimulate further research long into the future.

Bibliography

Adam 1994, J.-P. Adam, *Roman Building. Materials and Techniques* (trans. A. Mathews, B. T. Batsford, London).

Alcock 1965, J. P. Alcock, Celtic Water Cults in Roman Britain, *Archaeological Journal* 122, 1-12.

Aldhouse Green 1999, M. J. Aldhouse Green, *Pilgrims in Stone. Stone images from the Gallo-Roman sanctuary of* Fontes Sequanae (BAR International Series 754, Oxford).

Allason-Jones and McKay 1985, L. Allason-Jones and B. McKay, *Coventina's Well. A shrine on Hadrian's Wall* (Trustees of the Clayton Collection, Chesters Museum).

Amorai-Stark and Hershkovitz 2016, S. Amorai-Stark and M. Hershkovitz, *Ancient gems, finger rings and seal boxes from Caesarea Maritima . The Hendler Collection* (Shay Hendler, Zichron Yaakov).

Arnaud and Keay 2020, P. Arnaud and S. Keay, *Roman Port Societies. The evidence of Inscriptions* (Cambridge for British School at Rome).

Barker, Hayward and Coombe 2021, S. J. Barker, K. Hayward and P. Coombe, Londinium's Landward Wall: Material Acquisition, Supply and Construction, *Britannia* 52, 277-326.

Barrett 1989, A. A. Barrett, Caligula. The Corruption of Power (B. T. Batsford, London).

Blair, Spain, Swift, Taylor and Goodburn 2006, I. Blair, R. Spain, D. Swift, T. Taylor and D. Goodburn, Wells and Bucket-chains. Unforeseen elements of water supply in early Roman London, *Britannia* 37 , 1-52.

Brandon, Hohlfelder, Jackson and Oleson 2014, C. J. Brandon, R. L. Hohlfelder, M. D. Jackson, and J. P. Oleson, *Building for Eternity: The History and Technology of Roman Concrete Engineering in the Sea*, (Oxbow Books, Oxford).

Brodribb, Hands and Walker 2005, A. C. C. Brodribb, A. R. Hands and D. R, Walker, *The Roman villa at Shakenoak Farm, Oxfordshire. Excavations 1960-1976* (BAR British Series 395, Oxford).

Brogli 1996, R. F. Brogli, *Gemmen und Kameen mit ländlichen Kultszenen* (Peter Lang, Bern).

Casey 1994, P. J. Casey, *Carausius and Allectus. The British Usurpers* (B. T. Batsford Ltd.,London).

Chrysostomou and Kefallonitou 2001, P. Chrysostomou and F. Kefallonitou, *Nikopolis* (Ministry of Culture, Athens).

Collingwood and Wright 1965, R. G. Collingwood and R. P. Wright, *The Roman Inscriptions of Britain I. Inscriptions on Stone* (Oxford University Press for the Haverfield Bequest, Oxford).

Coombe, Grew, Hayward and Henig 2015, P.Coombe, F. Grew, K. Hayward and M. Henig, *Corpus Signorum Imperii Romani. Great Britain. Volume I, Fascicule 10. Roman Sculpture from London and the South-East* (British Academy, Oxford).

Coombe, Hayward and Henig 2021, P. Coombe, K. Hayward and M. Henig, The Sculpted and Architectural Stonework from Stanwick Roman Villa, Northamptonshire, *Britannia* 52, 227-275.

Cosh and Neal 2005, S. R. Cosh and D. S. Neal, *Roman Mosaics of Britain.II. South-West Britain* (Illuminata Publishers for the Society of Antiquaries of London).

Crow 1995, J. Crow, *English Heritage book of Housesteads* (B.T.Batsford, English Heritage, London).

Cunliffe 1969, B. Cunliffe, *Roman Bath* (Report of the Research Committee of the Society of Antiquaries of London. XXIV, Oxford).

Cunliffe 1988, B. Cunliffe, *The Temple of Sulis Minerva at Bath. 2. The Finds from the Sacred Spring* (Oxford University Committee for Archaeology; Monograph No.16, Oxford).

Cunliffe 1998, B, Cunliffe, *Fishbourne Roman Palace* (revised edition, Tempus Publishing Ltd, Stroud).

Cunliffe 2001, B. Cunliffe, *The extraordinary voyage of Pytheas the Greek* (Allen Lane, The Penguin Press, London).

Cüppers 1982, H. Cüppers, *Aquae Granni* (Beitrage zur Archäologie von Aachen, Rheinische Ausgrabungen 22, Cologne).

D'Arms 1970, J. H. D'Arms,. *Romans on the Bay of Naples: a social and cultural study of the villas and their owners from 150 BC to AD 400.* (Harvard University Press, Cambridge Mass.).

D'Arms and Kopff 1980, J. H. D'Arms and E. C. Kopff (eds),*Roman Seaborne Commerce* (Memoirs of the American Academy in Rome XXXVI).

Doig 2008, A. Doig, *Liturgy and Architecture from the Early Church to the Middle Ages* (Ashgate Publishing Ltd, Aldershot).

Down and Henig 1988, A. Down and M. Henig, 'A Roman *askos* handle from Fishbourne', *Antiquaries Journal* 68, 308-310.

Dudley 1967, D. R. Dudley, *Urbs Roma. A source book of Classical texts on the City and its monuments selected and translated with a commentary* (Phaidon Press, London).

Dunbabin 1999, K. M. D. Dunbabin, *Mosaics of the Greek and Roman World* (Cambridge University Press, Cambridge).

Eckardt and Walton 2021, H. Eckardt and P. Walton, *Bridge over Troubled Water: the Roman finds from the River Tees at Piercebridge in context* (Britannia Monograph); Open Access version https://doi.org/10.5284/1085344.

Farrar 1998, L. Farrar, *Ancient Roman Gardens* (Sutton Publishing, Stroud).

Ferguson 2009, E. Ferguson, *Baptism in the Early Church. History, Theology, and Liturgy in the first five centuries* (Eerdmans publishing, Grand Rapids, Michigan).

Fine 1996, S. Fine, *Sacred Realm. The emergence of the Synagogue in the Ancient World* (Oxford University Press, Yeshiva University Museum, New York).

Frere and Tomlin 1992, S. S. Frere and R. S. O. Tomlin, *The Roman Inscriptions of Britain II. Instrumentum Domesticum. Fascicule 4.* (Alan Sutton Publishing Ltd, for the Haverfield Bequest, Stroud).

Frere and Tomlin 1995, S. S. Frere and R. S. O. Tomlin, *The Roman Inscriptions of Britain II. Instrumentum Domesticum. Fascicule 8.* (Alan Sutton Publishing Ltd, for the Haverfield Bequest, Stroud).

Frost 1969, H. Frost, *The mortar wreck in Mellieha Bay* (Appletron Press, London for the National Museum of Malta).

Gerrard 2009, J. Gerrard, The Drapers' Gardens Hoard: A preliminary account, *Britannia* 40, 163-183.

Grainger 2021, S. Grainger, *The Story of Garum: fermented fish sauce and salted fish in the ancient world*, Routledge, London.

Harris and Henig 2010, A. Harris and M. Henig, Hand-washing and Foot-washing, sacred and secular, in Late Antiquity and the early Medieval period, M. Henig and N. Ramsay (eds), *Intersections: The archaeology and history of Christianity in England, 400-1200. Papers in honour of Martin Biddle and Birthe Kjølbye-Biddle* (Archaeopress, Oxford), 25-38.

Harris 1972, H. A. Harris, *Sport in Greece and Rome* (Thames and Hudson, London).

Hayward, Henig and Tomlin 2017, K. M. J. Hayward, M. Henig and R. S. O. Tomlin. The Tombstone, in N. Holbrook, J. Wright, E. R. McSloy and J. Geber. *Cirencester Excavations VII. The Western Cemetery of Roman Cirencester. Excavations at the former Bridges Garage, Tetbury Road, Cirencester, 2011-2015* (Cotswold Archaeology, Cirencester), 76-83.

Henig 1984, M. Henig, *Religion in Roman Britain* (B. T. Batsford, London).

Henig 1997, M. Henig, The sculpture, in P. Harding and C. Lewis, Archaeological excavations at Tockenham, 1994, *Wiltshire Archaeological and Natural History Magazine* 90, 35, fig. 5.

Henig 2004, M. Henig, *Corpus Signorum Imperii Romani. Great Britain. Volume I, Fascicule 9. Roman Sculpture from the North West Midlands* (British Academy, Oxford).

Henig 2007, M. Henig, *A Corpus of Roman Engraved Gemstones from British Sites* (3rd edn, BAR British Series 8, Oxford).

Henig 2010/2011, M. Henig, Souvenir or Votive? The Ilam pan, *ARA. The Bulletin of the Association for Roman Archaeology* 20, 13-15.

Henig 2012, M. Henig, The gemstones, in B. Philp, *The Discovery and Excavation of the Roman Shore-Fort at Dover, Kent* (Kent Archaeological Rescue Unit, Monograph 11. Dover), 124-130.

Henig 2015, M. Henig, Oceanus and the British Fleet, *ARA News* 34, September 2015, 6-7.

Henig 2017/2018, M. Henig, Roman Life in the New Testament, *ARA. The Bulletin of the Association for Roman Archaeology* 24, 47-54.

Henig and Ross 1998, M. Henig and A. Ross, A Roman intaglio depicting a warship from the foreshore at King's Reach, Winchester Wharf, Southwark, *Britannia* 29, 325-327, pl. XXIVB.

Herrmann 2001, J. J. Herrmann Jr. Crater with Panther Handles, in Z.T. Fiema, C. Kanellopoulos, T. Waliszewski and R. Schick, *The Petra Church* (American Center of Oriental Research, Amman), 335-339.

Higginbotham 1997, J. A. Higginbotham, *Piscinae: Artificial Fishponds in Roman Italy* (University of North Carolina Press, Chapel Hill).

Highet 1957, G.Highet, *Poets in a landscape* (Hamish Hamilton, London).

Hobbs 2016, R,Hobbs, *The Mildenhall Treasure: Late Roman Silver Plate from East Anglia* (British Museum Research Publication 200, London).

Hobson, Molesworth and Trusler 2009, B, Hobson, H. Molesworth and K. Trusler. *Pompeii, Latrines and Down Pipes: a general discussion and photographic record of toilet facilities in Pompeii.* (BAR International Series 2041, Oxford).

Irby 2021, G. L. Irby, *Using and Conquering the Watery World in Greco-Roman Antiquity* (Bloomsbury Academic, London).

Jackson 1988, R. Jackson, *Doctors and diseases in the Roman Empire* (British Museum, London).

Jackson and Burleigh 2018, R. Jackson and G. Burleigh, *Dea Senuna:Treasure, Cult and Ritual at Ashwell, Hertfordshire* (British Museum Research Publication 194, London).

Johns 2010, C. Johns, *The Hoxne Late Roman Treasure. Gold jewellery and silver plate* (British Museum Press, London).

Jones 2002, M. J. Jones, *Roman Lincoln. Conquest, Colony and Capital* (Tempus Publishing, Stroud).

Kapossy 1969, B. Kapossy, *Brunenfiguren der hellenistischen und römischen Zeit* (Zurich).

Keay 1988, S. J. Keay, *Roman Spain* (British Museum Publications Ltd., London).

Keay 2013, S. Keay (ed), *Rome, Portus and the Mediterranean*, British School at Rome, London).

King 1990, A. King, *Roman Gaul and Germany* (British Museum Publications Ltd., London).

Kooijmans, Stuart, Bogaers and Burger 1971, L. P. L. Kooijmans, P. Stuart, J. E. Bogaers and J. A. T. Burger, *Deae Nehalenniae. Gids bij de tentoonstelling. Nehalennia de zeeuwse godin. Zeeland in de Romeinse tijd, Romeinse monumenten uit de Oosterschelde* (Middelburg, Koinklijk Zeeuwich Genootschap der Wetenschappen and Leiden, Rijksmuseum van Oudheden).

Kraay and Hirmer 1966, C. M. Kraay and M. Hirmer, *Greek Coins* (Thames and Hudson, London).

Kunnappilly 2018, A.G. Kunnappilly, The trade of the port of Muziris in ancient times, *International Journal of Maritime History* 30, 519-525.

Lambert 1984, R. Lambert, *Beloved and God. The story of Hadrian and Antinous* (London).

Ling 1991, R. Ling, *Roman Painting* (Cambridge University Press, Cambridge).

Lyttelton 1974, M. Lyttelton, *Baroque Architecture in Classical Antiquity* Thames and Hudson, London).

Macdonald and Pinto 1995, W. L. Macdonald and J. A. Pinto, *Hadrian's Villa and its Legacy* (Yale University Press).

Marsden 1967, P. R. V. Marsden, *A ship of the Roman Period from Blackfriars, in the City of London* (Guildhall Museum, London).

Marsden 1994, P. [R. V.] Marsden, *Ships of the Port of London. First to eleventh centuries A. D.* (English Heritage Archaeological Report 3, Swindon).

Marzano 2013, A. Marzano, *Harvesting the Sea: The exploitation of Marine resources in the Roman Mediterranean* (Oxford University Press, Oxford).

Marzano 2018, A. Marzano, Fish and fishing in the Roman world, *Journal of Maritime Archaeology* 13, 437-447.

McKay 1975, A. G. McKay, *Houses, Villas and Palaces in the Roman World* (Thames and Hudson, London).

Miller 1969, J. I. Miller, The Spice Trade of the Roman Empire 29 B.C.-A.D. 641 (Clarendon Press, Oxford).

Mundell Mango 1994, M. Mundell Mango, *The Sevso Treasure. Part One.* (Journal of Roman Archaeology Supplementary Series 12, Ann Arbor, MI).

Mason 2003, D. J. P. Mason, *Roman Britain and the Roman Navy* (Tempus Publishing, Stroud).

Mathew 2017, K. S. Mathew (ed.), *Imperial Rome, Indian Ocean Regions and Muziris. New Perspectives on Maritime Trade* (Routledge, London).

Mattingly 1960, H. Mattingly, *Roman coins from the earliest times to the fall of the Western Empire* (second edition, Methuen and Co., London).

Meiggs 1973, R. Meiggs, *Roman Ostia* (2nd edition, Oxford University Press, Oxford).

Milne 1985, G. Milne, *The Port of Roman London* (B. T. Batsford Ltd, London).

Nayling and McGrail 2004, N. Nayling and S. McGrail, The Barland's Farm Romano-Celtic Boat (CBA Research Report 138, York).

Neverov 1976, O. Neverov, *Antique intaglios in the Hermitage collection* (Aurora Art Publishers, Leningrad).

Opper 2021, T. Opper, *Nero. The man behind the myth* (British Museum, London).

Painter 1999, K. S. Painter, The Water Newton Silver. Votive or Liturgical?, *Journal of the British Archaeological Association* 152, 1-23.

Pferdehirt 1995, B. Pferdehirt, *Das museum für antike schiffahrt. Ein forschungsbereich des Römisch-Germanischen Zentralmuseums* (Römisch-Germanischen Zentralmuseums, Mainz).

Prag 2014, J. Prag, Sicily and the Punic Wars, in exhibition catalogue, *Sicily and the Sea* (Allard Pierson Museum, Amsterdam), 83-86.

Rice 2016, C. Rice, Mercantile specialization and trading communities : economic strategies in Roman maritime trade, in A. Wilson and M. Flohr, *Urban Craftsmen and Traders in the Roman World* (Oxford University Press, Oxford), 97-114.

Rivet 1988, A. L. F. Rivet, *Gallia Narbonensis. Southern France in Roman times* (B. T. Batsford Ltd., London).

Rivet and Smith 1979, A. L. F. Rivet and C. Smith, *The place-names of Roman Britain* (B. T. Batsford, London).

Roberts 2019, P. Roberts, *Last supper in Pompeii* (Ashmolean Museum, Oxford 2019).

Rudling 1998, D. Rudling, The development of Roman villas in Sussex, *Sussex Archaeological Collections* 136, 41-65.

Sauer 2005, E. Sauer, *Coins, cult and cultural identity: Augustan coins, hot springs and the early Roman baths at Bourbonne-les-Bains* (Leicester Archaeology Monograph No.10, Leicester).

Serban 2009, M. Serban, Trajan's Bridge over the Danube, *The International Journal of Nautical Archaeology*, 38 (2), 331–342.

Starr 1960, C. G.Starr, *The Roman Imperial Navy 31BC-AD324* (2nd edition. Cambridge University Press, Cambridge).

Tomlin 2018, R. S. O. Tomlin, *Britannia Romana. Roman Inscriptions and Roman Britain* (Oxbow Books, Oxford).

Tomlin, Wright and Hassall 2009, R. S. O. Tomlin, R. P. Wright and M. W. C. Hassall, *The Roman Inscriptions of Britain III. Inscriptions on Stone found or notified between 1 January 1955 and 31 December 2006* (Oxbow Books for the Haverfield Bequest, Oxford).

Ugolini 2020, F. Ugolini, *Visualizing harbours in the Classical world. Iconography and Representation around the Mediterranean* (Bloomsbury Academic, London).

Upex 2008, S. G. Upex, *The Romans in the East of England. Settlement and Landscape in the Lower Nene Valley* (Tempus, Stroud).

Van der Meer 1967, F. van der Meer, *Early Christian Art* (Faber and Faber, London).

Wacher 1995, J.Wacher, *The towns of Roman Britain* (2nd edition, B. T. Batsford, London).

Wachsmann 1990, S. Wachsmann (ed.),The Excavations of an Ancient Boat in the Sea of the Galilee (Lake Kinneret) *'Atiqot* 19, 1-138.

Walsh 2017, M. Walsh, *Pudding Pan. A Roman shipwreck and its cargo in Context* (British Museum, London).

Walters 1926, H. B. Walters, *Catalogue of the Engraved Gems and Cameos , Greek, Etruscan and Roman in the British Museum* (British Museum, London).

Webster 1969, G. Webster, *The Roman Imperial Army of the First and Second Centuries A. D.* (Adam and Charles Black, London).

Webster and Chadderton 2002, G. Webster edited by J. Chadderton, *The Legionary Fortress at Wroxeter. Excavations by Graham Webster, 1955-85* (English Heritage Archaeological Report 19, London).

White 1984, K. D. White, *Greek and Roman Technology* (Thames and Hudson, London).

Wightman 1970, E. M. Wightman, *Roman Trier and the Treveri* (Rupert Hart-Davis, London).

Wilson 2014, R. J. A, Wilson, Roman Sicily and the sea, in exhibition catalogue, *Sicily and the Sea* (Allard Pierson Museum, Amsterdam), 107-111.

Woolf 2003, G. Woolf, Seeing Apollo in Roman Gaul and Germany, in S. Scott and J. Webster, *Roman Imperialism and Provincial Art* (Cambridge University Press, Cambridge), 139-152.

Zienkiewicz 1986, J. D. Zienkiewicz, *The Legionary Fortress Baths at Caerleon. I. The Buildings.* (CADW and National Museum of Wales, Cardiff).

Author Biographies

Jenny Amphaeris read *Literae Humaniores* at St Hilda's College, University of Oxford, 2004-2008. This works presents a co-authored updated version of one of her undergraduate dissertations. After a brief hiatus from academia, including work as a professional researcher and translator, she is now undertaking an interdisciplinary PhD between linguistics and biological sciences funded by Bangor University's College of Arts, Humanities, and Business. This involves reassessing definitions of language and constructing a new theoretical framework for the phenomenon to integrate the communication of non-humans. Jenny has recently published an invited article for *Animal Watch*, issue 106, and a co-authored paper for the *Proceedings of the Annual Meeting of the Cognitive Science Society* 2021, Volume 43, as well as an article in Lingua 272, *Overlap not Gap: Understanding the Relationship between Animal Communication and Language with Prototype Theory*. However, Jenny maintains her interest in Classics, particularly the culture, historical perspective on language, and the challenge set by ancient sages to think beyond the limits of current understanding.

Jenny Amphaeris, MA Oxon, MA, AFHEA, Bangor University, Wales, LL57 2DG

j.amphaeris@bangor.ac.uk

Penny Coombe is currently an intern at the Getty Research Institute in Los Angeles. Her research, which was the subject of her DPhil, focuses particularly on sculpture and cultural connections across the Roman north-west provinces. Her most significant contribution to date has been as co-author of the catalogue of *Roman Sculpture from London and the South-East* (2015, OUP, with Martin Henig, Kevin Hayward and Francis Grew), but she has also co-authored several papers in the journal *Britannia* examining a bronze hoard from Gloucestershire, the construction of Roman London's city walls, and finds of sculptural stone reused at Stanwick Roman villa, Northamptonshire. She has taught Roman art and archaeology at the University of Sheffield, Royal Holloway University of London, and in the course of her DPhil at the University of Oxford. Penny has also worked at the Museum of London, the Ashmolean Museum, and the London Archaeological Archive.

https://oxford.academia.edu/PennyCoombe

Eleri Cousins is a Lecturer in Roman History at Lancaster University. Her research focuses on the role played by ritual and religion (broadly defined!) in the construction of provincial society and identity in the Roman Empire, in particular in Britain, Gaul, and Germany, and she is especially interested in the connections between ritual and landscape in the Roman world. Her previous work focused on the Roman sanctuary at Bath and her first book, *The Sanctuary at Bath in the Roman Empire*, was published by Cambridge University Press in 2020. Her current research projects include the dynamics of religion and society on Hadrian's Wall and the religious landscapes of the Roman-period Alps.

e.cousins@lancaster.ac.uk.

Mark Driessen graduated at Wageningen University (tropical forestry and agriculture) and worked for many years in Africa and South America. After returning to the Netherlands he started working as a field archaeologist and studied Provincial Roman Archaeology at the University of Amsterdam, where he also obtained his PhD on the topography, settlement continuity and monumentality of Roman Nijmegen (NL). He excavated and worked on the Roman harbour site of Voorburg-Arentsburg (Forum Hadriani-NL). Since 2011 he is Assistant Professor in Provincial Roman Archaeology at Leiden University and director of the Udhruh Archaeological Project: a joint-venture with his Jordanian colleague dr. Fawzi Abudanah. In ancient times, the steppe in the hinterland of Petra (Jordan) was transformed into a green oasis. One of the main aims of this project is to shed insights in the agro-hydrological systems and societal processes resulting in this transformation. This will be accomplished by practicing an interdisciplinary research approach, in collaboration with the local communities. Mark's fields of research relate to antique harbours, antique water management and agriculture, Roman logistics and trade, the Roman army, landscape archaeology and community based programming.

m.j.driessen@arch.leidenuniv.nl

Hella Eckardt is Professor of Roman Archaeology, University of Reading. Where she teaches provincial Roman archaeology and material culture studies. Her research focuses on theoretical approaches to the material culture of the north-western provinces and she is particularly interested in the relationship between the consumption of Roman objects and the expression of social and cultural identity.

h.eckardt@reading.ac.uk

James Gerrard is a Senior Lecturer in Roman Archaeology and Associate Dean of Education at Newcastle University. Before joining Newcastle, he was a post-doctoral researcher at Cambridge University and worked in the commercial sector for Pre-Construct Archaeology Ltd. He trained as a Roman pottery specialist, but is an expert on the Fall of the Western Roman Empire and early medieval Britain. His books include *Debating Late Antiquity in Britain* (with Rob Collins; 2004) and *The Ruin of Roman Britain* (2013).

james.gerrard@newcastle.ac.uk